Communicating Well

A Fundamental Toolkit

Second Edition

Brecken Chinn
Robert C. MacDougall
John Barrett
Sharon Sinnott
Ruth Spillberg
Marcy Holbrook
Vicki Nelson
Anjana Mudambi
Dorria DiManno

cognella® | ACADEMIC PUBLISHING

Bassim Hamadeh, CEO and Publisher
Kassie Graves, Director of Acquisitions and Sales
Jamie Giganti, Senior Managing Editor
Jess Estrella, Senior Graphic Designer
John Remington, Senior Field Acquisitions Editor
Natalie Lakosil, Licensing Manager
Kaela Martin, Associate Editor
Christian Berk, Associate Production Editor

Cover image copyright © Depositphotos/strejman.
        copyright © Depositphotos/Den.Barbulat.
        copyright © Depositphotos/Yuriy_Vlasenko.

Printed in the United States of America

ISBN: 978-1-5165-0504-3 (pbk) / 978-1-5165-0505-0 (pf)

Contents

Chapter Ten

Public Speaking

Appendices

Glossary

Author Biographies

Acknowledgments

Many people helped to see this second edition of *Communicating Well* to publication. First and foremost we must thank Kaela Martin at Cognella for her extraordinary patience in fielding questions and granting numerous deadline extensions so that we could get those many final edits and content additions into place. Thanks also to Jamie Giganti at Cognella for her sage advice during those early meetings and discussions. Professors Kristen Noone and Bill Shanahan offered valuable edits and comments, which significantly enhanced this new edition. Finally, we must thank our students in *Comm 1010* who pointed out various content errors and typos in the first edition. The many upgrades to this second edition would not have been possible without their close reading and attention to detail. May those good habits continue!

Chapter One
The Communication Process

At the core of our human experience is the desire to love and be loved, to receive and be received, and to share our lives with others around us in ways that are authentic, meaningful, and satisfying. From the moment we are born and utter our first cry, we learn how to express our needs in order to have them met, to gain comfort, security, growth, and belonging. Later, we learn to think about and respond to the needs of others around us. We become connected in ways that form us into mutually-dependent communities—families, teams, tribes, cliques, clans, circles, and other collectives. Like other mammals, we are equipped with sophisticated sense organs and the ability to "make meaning" from the information we receive from the world around us. As humans, we are able to use language along with our basic senses to not only share meaning in the present moment, but to communicate across vast distances of space and time. What does it mean to "communicate well"?

The word **communication** comes from the Latin verb *communicare*, meaning "to share or impart," which stems from the Latin adjective *communis*, which means "common or shared locally." Thus, the root of the word communication implies "communing," or coming together around **shared meaning**. This shared meaning allows us to meet our basic needs (such as food, clothing, and shelter) in the present, and to coordinate action and plan for the future. It also lets us create new meanings and actually transform the world around us, not only the structures we inhabit, but how we relate to each other and live together. How has communication created and continued to shape the world?

While it may seem easy enough to identify communication when we see or experience it, there are subtle nuances that are important to how we study what it means to communicate well. Communication clearly includes speaking or making sounds verbally, as well as using symbols in writing or other visual format to convey meaning. To that end, we must also consider the vast range

Figure 1.1 A "simple" Conversation

of nonverbal modes and forms of communication, from body language to eye contact to tone of voice, as well as other subtle ways of sending messages, such as timing, intention, and silence. For the purposes of our study, we will define *communication* as **"the dynamic contextual process, conscious or unconscious, of using symbols to share meaning with others."**

We all know how good it feels when someone understands us—when someone "gets" our inner, intended meaning. We all strive for that kind of connection and understanding yet the evidence we see in the world around us suggests that we all too often fall short of this ideal. Consider all the unnecessary conflicts, the misunderstandings, the wars, the crimes, the isolations—all the times when people just don't "get it." What would it take to live in a state of pure, open communication in which we could work, play, and contribute our unique gifts to the world in sustainably satisfying ways? If communicating well and "communing" with others in a state of clear understanding is something we all want, why do we so often go way off track?

Modeling the Communication Process

One reason we often fall short of communicating well is because we don't step away and try to understand the larger framework, or **model**, of our communication. Modeling is a good way to get a sense of how something or some process is structured. And, to be sure, communication is a process not a thing. Modelling the process of communication means representing that process in a simple form that illustrates how all the parts fit and work together. What pieces, or variables, should we include? What leads to or affects what? What form or shape do we use to represent the process—a square, a circle, a line? Just as developing a leadership flow chart can help an organization function by helping people know how decisions are made and problems are solved, how we choose to model the communication process can be highly consequential. Here's why:

The field of communication as a formal academic field of study finds its roots in the early part of the 20th century. In the context of that socio-historical moment,

communication technologies such as radio and telephones were starting to become everyday items. People gathered around to listen to media reports about World Wars I and II, which severely impacted not only world politics, but also local economies. Many families had loved ones drafted to serve in the wars overseas, and the only way to get news of the war was through the radio or newsreels shown in the cinema at the beginning of movies. Political leaders like Franklin Delano Roosevelt and Winston Churchill rallied Allied nations on one side of the worldwide political divide, while leaders of the Axis nations rallied their own. Communication at the time was thought to be **linear**—travelling directly (through media) from political leaders into the ears of their people.

Adolf Hitler was one of the first leaders in the world to use the modern tools of mass communication to astounding political effect. Using sophisticated means of persuasion through the mass media, Hitler used a kind of propaganda technique that has come to be called "spiral of silence" (Noelle-Neumann, 1974) to gain tremendous political support for genocide. The more the Nazis could make it seem like people supported their party's platform, the more people felt they had to do so, or risk isolation, or worse, incarceration, or even death. People can act in crazy and even self-destructive ways when we are in groups and fear isolation. Can you think of any other, more common and less severe examples?

Given the highly charged political climate of

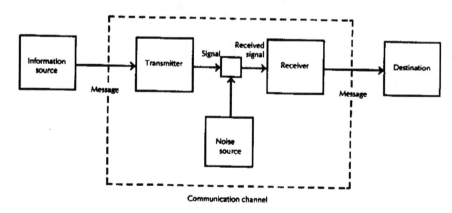

Figure 1.2 The Linear Model of Communication

World War II governments grew increasingly and understandably concerned about the potential effects of mass communication, and invested significant time, money, and resources into concentrated, systematic research to study media effects. Social scientists examined how mass communication influences people; a first step was to develop models to ground this study in the social scientific philosophies of the time. Claude Shannon, a mathematician at Bell Labs, put forward a model of the communication process as he understood it from his work with radio telegraphy. Transmitting messages wirelessly (and through the wire) were important technologies being developed and used in the early part of the 20th century, particularly in World Wars I and II, and they informed how people thought of communication generally. The model (1948), which came to be called the "Linear Model of Communication," Is depicted in figure 1.2

What do you notice about the direction of the arrows, about the big "pieces" of the model? It seems a simple enough process—getting a message through a communication channel to its destination—but of course that annoying thing called "noise" enters the model, such that not all of the meaning gets through as intended. Think about how we might hear static during a phone conversation, or the drone of an air conditioner, or the distracting sounds of a sporting event being watched at too high a volume in an adjacent room. No one likes noise when they are trying to receive or get a message across. Figure 1.3 depicts noise infiltrating the communication process during a modern, highly mediated attempt at multitasking.

Figure 1.3 Some common manifestations of Noise

Today, the model of communication we use (DeVito, 1986) is based loosely on the old Linear Model, but you'll notice some important differences that reflect advancements in how we have come to understand the communication process through the 20th century: Figure 1.4 depicts the transactional model of communication.

What differences do you notice between the two models? What parts of the model have changed, and which have stayed the same? What do these changes mean in

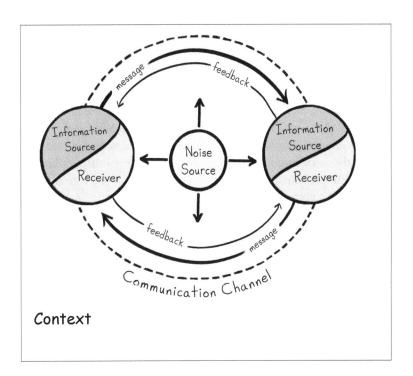

Figure 1.4 The Transactional Model of Communication

terms of how we understand the communication process? Do you think other changes may still be needed to model the communication process more accurately? If so what changes would you argue for?

One major concept to pay attention to is that each participant in the communication process is considered a **"sender-receiver"**—both sending and receiving messages simultaneously. Gone are the days of conceiving of communication as simply "delivering" a message. Old models of communication focused on effectively getting the word out, disseminating or propagating messages (think "propaganda") from sender to receiver. If the receiver received the message, the communication was considered to be "effective," regardless of how *well* the message was received, or what meaning the receiver made of it. Eventually, in working with the Linear Model of Communication, scholars began to draw a **feedback loop** from receiver back to sender so that the sender could know if the message was indeed getting through. Of course, there's more to receiving feedback from a communication partner than simply finding out whether or not they received our message. What our partner does and says impacts our communication in the same moment we are engaged in it. Human communication is not a ping pong match ... far from it.

Another important advancement in our modeling of the communication process that is not evident in the model itself is how we consider the concept of **"noise,"** anything that stands in the way of full, effective sharing of meaning. The original Linear Model basically meant noise to be actual sound interference, such

as static. Today, we recognize that the "noise" that comes between our sharing meaningfully can be physiological, psychological, or something external. Noise is anything that gets in the way of our "being here now" (Ram Dass, 1971). Thus, we need to understand three main types of noise that all interfere with the communication process—one in the environment, one inside the individual communicator, and one inside the message itself:

External noise: interference that everyone in the environment experiences, such as traffic passing, ventilation noise, uncomfortable conditions, even major news that everyone is experiencing (such as a natural disaster or a significant loss) that affects how they perceive current conditions.

Internal noise: a distraction experienced in one's own mind, which can be caused by distractions from inner worries, physical states such as hunger or fatigue, or prejudices that impact someone's ability to be open to send and receive messages freely.

Semantic noise: an impediment to understanding that is built into the actual message, the words themselves, such as it being spoken in another language, or dialect containing jargon that is not understood, or causing offense to the degree that one cannot "hear" anything else.

Communicating well, then, means reducing the impact of "noise" so that meaning can be transmitted, received and shared as fully as possible. For communication to truly flow and be powerful, it needs to go both ways. The more mindful we can be of the noise within ourselves, within our environment, and within the means we use to communicate,

the more effective we can be at truly sharing meaning.

To use a comparison, also known as a metaphor, think of an electric socket. Many people are surprised to find out that electricity doesn't actually just flow "out" of the socket, or from one place to another. What we do when we allow electricity to flow is to create a circuit—a complete loop through which the "juice" or power can flow or circulate. Likewise in communication, "plugging in"—truly paying attention to and responding to the "other"—allows much more meaning to flow than if we just send out messages like cannonballs over a wall. Our power as communicators lies in our ability to create open feedback loops with as little "resistance" as possible in the overall system.

Communicating well relies on creating and maintaining two-way feedback loops that are as open and unimpeded as possible. Thus, to boil down the most fundamental rule of effective communication, it would be genuine **reciprocity,** or full sharing of openness, respect, and commitment to understanding—knowing and caring for the "other" as much as oneself. If you are the one communicating, knowing yourself and "what makes you tick" is crucial to communicating as freely and effectively as possible. Likewise, understanding everything you can about those you are communicating with—whether it be a close friend or a stadium full of screaming fans—knowing as much as you can about what is really going on for your audience, inside and out, will enable you to communicate with them as effectively as possible.

Notice that our model of communication relies on **channels**, or means of transferring messages, that are bounded by **context**—the meaning environment in which communication takes place. Think of the different meanings that could be implied by sending an important message verbally, or by written letter, or by private text message, or by public news forum, etc. The appropriateness of the channel to the message we are sending is determined by the context of our roles, our environment, and the world around us. Think of the different ways you could convey love to someone--telling them face to face, sending them a card in the mail, texting them a heart, etc. How messages, channels, and contexts interact is subject to the process of **social construction**, how we determine what things "mean" through social interaction.

With all of these confounding variables, communicating well can be a tall order—so many different skills are required, yet with practice and openness, we can get to a state where our communication flows naturally, almost effortlessly. Each communication situation is utterly unique, which requires us to engage a skill called **strategic flexibility.** This means to possess a broad repertoire of tools or skills to draw upon, and to know when to use which tool, or to vary the skills we use as we respond to the feedback we receive, and to the needs of various situations. The goal of this course is to add to and enhance your tool kit by expanding your repertoire of communication skills as much as possible, and to set the stage for you to gain ever-increasing levels of strategic flexibility that allow you to enjoy communicating

openly and easily in any situation that may arise.

Levels of Communication

The most basic form of communication is what goes on inside your own head and heart—the stream of constant self-talk that we call **intrapersonal communication**. If you tune into your mind at any given moment, you'll hear a string of commentary that forms the basis of your self-concept, your perception, your thoughts, your attitudes, and ultimately the behaviors that form your entire life. While we'll discover that a good portion of the content of our own mind can be colored and inflected by the thoughts of others near and far, for now, let's consider the intuitive experience of introspection, or intrapersonal communication. There are many forms of intrapersonal communication—from mindless mental chatter, to concentrated attention, to thoughtful analysis. The point is, understanding and being able to skillfully guide the communication we do inside our own heads is crucial to "knowing ourselves" and being great communicators.

The next level of communication is what we do with another person, an engagement we call **interpersonal communication**. Whether chatting with a friend, participating in a job interview, or having a heart-to-heart talk

with a family member, what we consider interpersonal communication is usually situated between exactly two people, a configuration we call a **dyad**. This focus on only one other person at a time gives us the opportunity to concentrate our entire attention on really "knowing the other" in a particularly meaningful way. Some of our life's most vulnerable experiences occur within interpersonal relationships—friendship, romance, partnership—and how these interactions play out can either bring us great pleasure and synergy, or tremendous confusion, disorientation and pain. In this course, we'll focus on gaining tools to make our interpersonal relationships as satisfying as possible.

As soon as we move beyond interacting with just one other person, we enter the realm of **small group communication**. Indeed, it can be argued that as soon as you have three or more people engaged in communication, you have "politics." You need to constantly make choices about the direction and focus of your attention and the nature of your interaction. Communication scholars tend to count groups from 3 to 13 as "small groups," and

Figure 1.5 An early venue built for Public Communication

we will spend time considering configurations and role behaviors within small group interactions, depending on the needs that draw your group together. Like other creatures in nature, we can gain tremendous benefit from coordinating our action with others and operating in groups. Yet groups can also be challenging as we attempt to coordinate our needs and skills, which can lead to "butting heads" or developing dysfunctional group processes like "groupthink." We'll focus on how to mindfully engage in group interactions with an understanding of roles and responsibilities that can lead to synergy and satisfaction.

Beyond small group interaction, when we present ourselves to a larger forum, we engage in **public communication**, which often takes the form of speechmaking or presentations. Many departments of Communication have their historical roots in this area, as it has been a central job of educational institutions for many centuries to help students articulate themselves well, and to understand the forms and functions of **rhetoric**, or "the available means of persuasion." Although speakers have been communicating with publics since the origins of human society, in the West the formal study of rhetoric began in ancient Greece with Aristotle, who worked with his students, to develop an understanding of how speakers shape civic life through public discourse. Athens' and Rome's geographic locations, with miles of coastline amidst the culturally bustling Mediterranean region, allowed them to be among the first cities to develop the most important communication technology of the time—coliseum architecture that

allowed an entire crowd to hear a single speaker. Coliseums were able to bring together large crowds to witness major events and speeches simultaneously, which made revolutionary advancements possible in civic discourse that ultimately led to the foundations of participatory democracy. No wonder speechmaking and persuasion became such an important field of study at that time. Aristotle's exposition of the impact of ethos (credibility), logos (argumentation), and pathos (emotion) continues to be just as important to speechmakers today as during ancient Greco-Roman times. In this course, we will examine and practice all the hallmarks of effective public communication, a toolkit still crucial to one's effectiveness in civic and professional life.

Understanding, in turn, the broad realm of intercultural communication can significantly improve our civic and professional lives as well. A careful and nuanced awareness of cultural differences (big and small) also adds depth, sophistication, and sensitivity to our interpersonal and intrapersonal communication practices. To be sure, **intercultural communication** competence betters one's ability to 'know thyself.' But perhaps most importantly, gaining competence in the intercultural realm holds the promise of building a more just and peaceful world.

Finally, we must not neglect the vital importance of **mediated communication**, particularly in this modern age when so much of the way we work, trade, shop, meet, and entertain ourselves revolves around technological devices that bring us together. Mediated communication is different from public communication in that public communication takes place when presenter and audience are

typically in the same physical space and time. For example, think of the difference in the experience of watching a speaker live in a public venue, then stepping out into the foyer and watching the same event through a televised screen. What is different about these two experiences? Whereas in the public communication setting, you are able to witness the **gestalt**—the entire context of communication, including the environment and various kinds of mediated communication settings, what you perceive is framed and contextualized by the particular technological medium or form, and the producers who created the content. When watching a speech on TV, for example, we are not only experiencing the speech, we are also experiencing the camera angles, the results of careful editing, the attendant commentary, and the general packaging agreed upon by a host of producers and other industry professionals.

Mediated communication can be tremendously broad—for example, in the form of television, radio, or film—or it can be very narrow and even personal, as in texting, online chat, or telephone. The reason why we study mediated communication as an area all its own is because the device itself, and how we use it, becomes an important and often highly consequential part of the entire communication process. Can you think of some ways any particular medium you choose to communicate with and through potentially alters the nature of your communication with others? With yourself?

We need to develop tools in **information literacy** and **media ecolog**y in order to understand how the distillation of our meaning into mediated bits impacts the messages we send and the very fabric of how we relate to each other. Mediated communication can take place through modes that are either **synchronous** (taking place at the same time) or **asynchronous** (taking place at different times), and this consideration of time matters significantly to the overall meaning of the communication. We will consider all of the various mediated modes we use to communicate—phone, mail, email, text, video, audio, books, print, etc.—and how the channel itself impacts the meaning we make from the communication and how we use the information contained therein.

Figure 1.6 A problem of Punctuation

Fundamental Axioms of Communication

As we venture into the various levels of communication study and analysis there are a few axioms, or fundamental principles, to keep in mind. The axioms define and illustrate several very basic notions that underpin our ability to communicate well. These axioms were put forward by Paul Watzlawick, Janet Beavin, and Don Jackson in their classic 1967 book, *Pragmatics of Human Communication: A Study of Interaction Patterns, Pathologies, and Paradoxes*. These axioms are still foundational to how we study communication today, perhaps because each is so thought-provoking, and continue to hold great explanatory value:

1. **You cannot not communicate.** Everything we do, verbally or nonverbally, consciously or unconsciously, communicates some message. Even sitting in absolute silence, we are communicating to others through our positioning, our gaze, and whether this behavior is normal for us or not. If we are asleep, we are communicating that we are asleep, and even after we have passed on, the legacy of the things we have done, or not done, still communicates to the world in some way. Even if we don't intend to forget someone's birthday, our forgetfulness may still be taken as a slight. This Axiom has always been an excellent one to debate. For instance, do you feel that messages have to be intentional to count as "communication"? What parameters and aspects of human behavior do you personally feel should be included in the study of communication? Do you agree with Watlzawick, Beavin, and Jackson that we indeed "cannot *not* communicate"?

2. **Every interaction has both a content and a relational dimension.** In studying communication, we look at both the content of what is said or explicitly stated as well as how the interaction is "taken" by other people in the context of a relationship. Even a simple phrase like "Come here" can come across as affiliation, as a command, as a "come-on", as helpfulness, or as an insult, depending on how we say it. This "how" of the way things are taken by others is defined and re-defined constantly in relationships as our interaction patterns play out over time. Communication scholars examine both content and relational dimensions of communication, recognizing that the "meaning" of both are matters of convention. That is to say, they are socio-culturally constructed. Our history, our culture, along with various social expectations, and our particular social positioning all come together to define what things "mean," both at the content and relational levels. And these factors are all **dynamic**, meaning that they change

and are redefined all the time by how we interact.

The **content dimension** (the "what," or explicit information we are communicating) is sent through words spoken and written, whereas the **relationship dimension** (how we relate to each other) is often contained more in the nonverbal stream. For instance, if someone yells "Come here" at you in an angry way, the information content (the message that person wants you to approach them) is conveyed verbally, while the relational behavior that you may consider threatening or insulting is conveyed nonverbally, through tone of voice, facial expression, body language, etc. However, what if someone says "Come here" in a soft, sexy tone of voice? The entire meaning of the words in this phrase has just changed. Vocal tone is an important aspect of message meaning. As we'll learn, nonverbals often constitute the bulk of meaning in interactions and are thus crucial to communicating well.

3. **Every interaction is defined by how it is punctuated.** Although communication is happening continuously, the meaning we make of particular interactions or incidents depends very much on when we consider the interaction "begins" and "ends." What is the history of the interaction? What do we feel precedes or causes a response? Perhaps someone felt slighted by you in the past, and treats you badly now as a result. You may have forgotten the past slight and feel that the person is being unreasonably hostile. Or

perhaps the person is triggered by some situation between your families or some cultural history that you may not even be consciously aware at that moment. How people view the meaning of what happens often depends very much on how far back we go, or where we put the proverbial "commas" and "periods" in our stream of interaction. Think of a scenario where a parent is watching streaming television on a computer while a small child screams. The parent may be watching to escape the child's screaming, and the child may be screaming because they feel ignored by the parent. However, it is misguided to think about this interaction scenario from the perspective of one or the other individual involved. Indeed, this dyad is the most basic communication system, so we have to think about this systemically in order to understand what's going on. While most of this often occurs below the level of conscious awareness, the meaning a participant "assigns" to these behaviors depends on what they sense in terms of what preceded or caused what. In other words, the meaning of the event for the parties involved depends, in large measure, on how each punctuates or assigns a beginning and end to the interaction.

Symbolic Interaction and Culture

The main context that significantly influences what our communication "means" is a social construction called "**culture.**"

Culture implies a grouping based on some similarity, from a culture of bacteria in a petri dish to an entire civilization. Culture is created around the collective habits, practices, and subsequent beliefs and norms that help a particular grouping of people make sense of their place in the world. Yet it is important not to be too simplistic here—people often conflate (mix up) "culture" for "country," as in "American culture" or "Japanese culture." Or they confuse "culture" with "race," as in "Asian culture" or "Black culture" or "ethnicity," as in some attribution of genetic or biological origin. Yet if we really look at the boundaries of our identity, it would be hard to find a set of norms or beliefs shared by all people of one particular geographic area or genetic line. How we come to actually share "culture" with other people is a more complex social process than simply being grouped together by region or ethnicity. Many of us carry multiple (not different) national or ethnic identities within us. We travel, we watch TV, we interact with people around the world easily now. So, we need to work with a much clearer definition of culture.

For our purposes, we will define **culture** at its most basic level as "**shared meaning that is communicated to others.**" Humans define what things "mean" through a process called **symbolic interaction**, a perspective described in the work of George Herbert Mead (1934) and his student Herbert Blumer (1937) through the following process:

- The meaning of things is formed through social interaction.

- Humans act toward things on the basis of the meanings they assign to those things.

- Meanings are shared and modified through an interpretative process.

In other words, **symbols** (which could be objects, behaviors, colors, words, etc.) take on their "meaning" when humans agree on what they "mean" and use them socially according to communicated patterns. Humans appear to be fairly unique in that we use symbols indirectly, abstractly, and often in quite arbitrary ways to convey meaning beyond the thing itself, like a heart shape to indicate love, a handshake to indicate greeting, or animal mascots to represent schools or political parties. Humans make meaning from many dimensions of experience, such as color, shape, size, texture, smell, or sound. Some symbols are things we choose, like clothing or accessories, but other things we don't choose, like our skin or hair color, can also carry social meaning that goes beyond any meaning we ourselves may choose to ascribe.

One way that symbols carry particular meaning is when they are compared or contrasted with each other. For example, traditionally-defined "masculinity" and "femininity" are **relational symbols**, in that both are socially defined in ways that carry little meaning without comparison to the other. What kind of meaning do we attach to traits like body shape and size, length and location of hair, vocal pitch, choices of clothing and accessories, and various mannerisms? Why is it that we tend to see some people at the gym working out to become smaller than average, and others working out to become larger than average? Humans commonly work to adopt certain traits that carry positive social significance among the population they value most and invite the kind of interactions they want. We may gain social, political, or economic power when we possess particular traits or behaviors—an advantage we call **social capital,** a kind of social currency that gives us power to get what we want. What we often don't realize, however, is that the traits that comprise our social capital are themselves socially constructed through communication, and tend to change over time.

The degree to which we choose (or are forced to accept) a symbol to define us is how we negotiate our **identity**. For example, think of how we use school or team colors. These colors can be described as quasi- arbitrary, in that they don't necessarily "mean" anything in and of themselves; it's all about the social meaning we collectively assigned to them. Once colors or other symbols (like mascots or logos) are settled upon, they come to represent a school or a team through being used on clothing or paraphernalia, we interact around these colors in the process of **identity negotiation**. Imagine seeing someone in a different city wearing school or team colors that you recognize. You have a few choices as to how to respond to the symbol:

1. **Identification**: acknowledging that the symbol represents your identity (say, you went to the same school or cheer for the same team).

2. **Knowledge**: acknowledging that you know what the symbol represents, without identifying with it.

3. **Ignorance or neutrality**: not acknowledging the symbol or its meaning at all.

4. **Dissociation**: separating yourself from the symbol, perhaps by choosing an alternate one.

5. **Scorn**: separating yourself from the symbol in a very explicit way through negative communication or even violence.

For example, many who have had exposure to western religions may choose to **identify** with a Cross as a symbol of Christianity or a Star of David as a symbol of Judaism by wearing or displaying them. Others may have **knowledge** of these symbols, and if they were to see a Christmas tree or a Menorah in the window of a home in December, may associate that household's affiliation with Christian or Jewish practices. Whether or not one chooses to identify personally with a symbol by adopting it or using it in culturally agreed-upon ways, we have knowledge of **normative** (generally agreed-upon) meanings around the symbol and can agree with others about what the symbol represents. Some may **ignore** or be **neutral** toward the symbol, either because they are unfamiliar with it or choose not to acknowledge it as a meaningful symbol at that time. Still others may choose to dissociate themselves from the symbol by displaying an alternate one, or even express scorn in the form of criticism, insults, or violence. How we interact around symbols comes to determine what they "mean" to us, both individually and as a society.

At what point can we say that a communicative pattern (or recurring pattern of symbol-use) becomes a culture? For our purposes, we will define the most basic level of **cultural formation** as when the two individuals agree on the "meaning" of a symbol and communicate that meaning to at least one other. Those who view the symbol can then choose a path of identification, knowledge, neutrality, dissociation, or scorn. We can say that a "culture" forms around meanings that people basically agree upon, the "meaning" of which they have now communicated to others. When the pattern is defined as having some sort of social meaning that can be communicated, we have the basis of cultural formation. The question now is whether the meaning will spread among others, and perhaps be modified through further social interaction.

The process of **cultural transformation** occurs when meanings are challenged or contested. People may choose to adopt another symbol to represent a meaning, or another meaning to represent a symbol. For example, think of what the following "mean" to you, and how these meanings may have changed over time: wearing a wig, wearing earrings, or having a tattoo. As the cultural transformation process plays out, those who identify with particular meanings can be said to reach a **critical mass** when their use of the symbol gathers enough recognition so as to achieve a desired result. Once a symbol has **contested meaning**, or a meaning that is being challenged or re-negotiated, the meaning-making process will be impacted by several factors among those that participate:

1. the numbers of people at the identity and knowledge levels

2. the social status of people at the identity and knowledge levels

3. the use of the symbols in mainstream media

4. the "official" use of the symbols by institutions that hold power in a society

5. the use of the symbols over time

Cultural transformation is a dynamic process that can change the "meaning" of symbols gradually or quickly, and often quite radically, depending on the level of involvement people have with the symbol and the power of the communication they use in the process. Can you think of some recent examples of symbols that have undergone either gradual or radical change?

Our Task

The reader should be starting to get the sense that communicating well is about much more than just giving great speeches. To communicate well, we need to become aware of the entire communication process—our internal thoughts and emotions, how we communicate verbally and nonverbally, how we interact in pairs, in groups, in public, and through mediated forms both cultural and technological. Along the way, we need to consider how the symbols we use to express meaning come to carry those meanings, and how we can be involved in forming and transforming the cultural groupings we inhabit. In doing so, we will need to develop and deploy a range of communication tools (fundamental concepts and behaviors), so that we can use

strategic flexibility as we contribute to shaping our identities, our lives, and our wider worlds.

As the 19th century British author Charles Reade suggested,

"Watch your thoughts, for they become words.

Watch your words, for they become actions.

Watch your actions, for they become habits.

Watch your habits, for they become your character.

Watch your character, for it becomes your destiny."

References

Blumer, H. (1937). Social psychology. In E. P. Schmidt (Ed.), *Man and society* Englewood, NJ: Prentice-Hall.

DeVito, J. A. (1986). *The communication handbook: A dictionary.* New York: Harper & Row.

Mead, G. H. (1934). C. W. Morris (Ed.), *Mind, self, and society.* Chicago: University of Chicago.

Noelle-Neumann, E. (1974). The spiral of silence: A theory of public opinion. *Journal of Communication* 24: 43–51.

Ram Dass. (1971). *Be here now.* San Cristobal, NM: Lama Foundation.

Watlzawick, P., Beavin, J., & Jackson, D. (1967). *Pragmatics of human communication: A study of interaction patterns, paradoxes, and pathologies.* New York: Norton.

Weaver, W. (1948). A mathematical theory of communication. *Bell Labs Technical Journal* 27: 379–423, 623–656.

Chapter Two
Perception of Self and Other

Knowing Self

As media ecologist Susan Langer suggests, the ways we perceive ourselves, others, and the world around us are not entirely up to us. Our modes of **perception**—sight, hearing, taste, smell, touch—have been developed from millions of years of evolution. Our senses are bombarded with countless streams of sense data all the time, and as we grow, we face the necessity of learning which stimuli we most need to pay attention to in order to get through our lives successfully. For instance, noticing a lovely sunset can be inspiring and worthwhile, unless a vehicle is hurtling toward us at the moment, in which case we learn we need to shift our attention quickly to move out of its way. We learn to make sense of which information around us is most worth attending to, and then we pass many of these patterns of perception on to our offspring and those with whom we interact closely to ensure the survival of our species. Many of our perceptual patterns are encoded into our genetic code, and continue to change as our environment changes. How do you suspect human perception may evolve (or potentially devolve) as we move into the future?

When we study perception we are interested in how organisms detect or sense the world around them. In other words, perception is about ways of knowing. It concerns the various ways we detect and decode meaning, find significance in things, and interact with our world. More specifically, perception is the process of selectively paying attention to information and assigning meaning to it according to our needs, interests and expectations. This not only concerns our own expectations but also, and sometimes to a significant degree, the expectations of others. In short, the way we perceive is intimately related to our multi-faceted and multi-layered awareness of what we call "self."

Our Physical Self

Human perception is, in large measure, developed and maintained through social interaction. We experience various stimuli—colors, shapes, sounds, smells, etc.—and assign "meaning" to them in the form of words, feelings, attitudes, and behaviors. For example, we see a white liquid that smells like milk being poured into a cup and decide whether or not to drink it based on our past experience with that substance. This perceptual process is ongoing, and occurs at both conscious and preconscious levels. We see, hear and smell whatever comes near us

Figure 2.1 One consequence of our biological Perceptual Structure.

horned owl, lynx, or even domestic cat, which changes our perception of a nightscape significantly. How might this shift in perception affect how we perceive and function at night? In what other areas might a shift in perception cause us to act in an entirely different way?

As with vision, our ability to hear varies considerably between individuals and deviates wildly from other creatures with whom we share the planet. Our human ears, when functioning properly, can detect sounds in the 20-20000 Hz (or oscillations per second) frequency range. Surprisingly, perhaps, this misses many of the sounds around us, from the ultrasonic calls of bats to the deep infrasonic earth vibrations that may cause perceptive animals and birds to flee from oncoming natural disasters. Although we may be surrounded with many sounds competing for our attention, those sounds we choose to attend to—like a favorite song or a friend's voice—are frequencies that develop "meaning" to us through lived experience. Our senses of taste, smell, and touch likewise also vary greatly under different circumstances, and can be altered (made more acute or dulled) by experience, by our environment, and by substances or conditions to which we are exposed. When might you be most attuned to the sound of water, for example, or

the smell of burning wood? When might a touch feel pleasurable, and when might the very same touch feel uncomfortable or even violent?

Our Social and Symbolic Selves

As we can see, the modes of perception we take for granted are the product of ongoing processes of physical, technological, and environmental conditioning. However, we will discover that it is the human ability to learn language, to self-reflect, and engage in various forms of introspection that make us particularly fascinating (and complicated!) objects of analysis. In order to understand the nature and function of introspection (sometimes also referred to as intrapersonal communication or self-talk), we need to delve into a few of the more "social" details of the perceptual process.

In two of his most important works, including *The Presentation of Self in Everyday Life* (1959) and *Interaction Ritual* (1967), American sociologist Erving Goffman suggests that human interaction is a kind of ongoing public performance. It may seem odd to suggest that we put on different **"faces"** (**personae**, or **outward appearances**) like we might put on different shoes, or hats, or clothes, to get different tasks accomplished, yet we all essentially do just this without even noticing it. Very few people act in the same manner across different social situations. Why? Because social situations are, by definition, composed of other people and their shifting reactions. The way others respond to us can

whether we choose to or not, but the meanings we assigned to those stimuli are formed through ongoing feedback. Some societies find it bizarre and disgusting for adults to drink cows' milk, for example, whereas in other communities this is perfectly normal.

In terms of what we perceive through our eyes, the human visual system typically detects light throughout the "visible spectrum," between 390 and 750 nanometers. This gives us access to a mere fraction of the light emanating from the sun. Unlike humans, many birds, bees, and most insects can see into the ultraviolet range. And while humans can see quite well compared to an opossum, we have relatively poor night vision when compared to any predatory bird, many other mammals, and most reptiles. However, for not much money, an individual can purchase a pair of infrared night vision goggles that almost give us the visual acuity of a rattlesnake, make us feel very good, or very bad, so the presence of others in our lives has a lot to do with how we perceive ourselves and the world around us.

The process of **socialization** teaches us which perceptions and feelings to act upon, in what ways, and in what circumstances. Imagine a stubborn toddler who is not yet aware of the social significance of bad behavior, who yells loudly and without restraint at the store, at a concert hall, at a place of worship, or at Grandma's house. To be sure, teens and adults do this, too—we've all witnessed instances of people (perhaps even ourselves) "acting up," or behaving inappropriately, in various situations. But you might also notice that these behaviors don't get us treated well by others for very long. Humans create and enforce expectations of what it means to be "civilized." Why might that be? What does it mean to be a "mature social agent," or to play the role of an "adult" in our society? Why do we create particular rules of behavior, and socialize each other into living them?

The Story of Anne

To get at how this all works, we might consider the behavior of a person who acts very differently, but also very appropriately, in a wide variety of social settings. Take the case of "Anne." Anne is a college student going through a particularly busy semester. She gets up early every morning to have breakfast with two suitemates before attending her morning classes. On Mondays, Anne also volunteers as a big sister over an extended lunch hour. Then, as with every Monday, she heads across town to her internship at a public relations firm until 5:00 pm. After that, she typically meets up with her boyfriend for dinner at his place around 6:30 pm. Finally, Anne finishes off her busy Mondays as a bartender at a trendy restaurant downtown.

If you were a fly on the wall following Anne through her day, you would probably notice significant alterations in the way she goes about her business in each situation. Chances are, the Anne around the breakfast table with her good friends would be carrying on quite informally —casting sharp if affectionate verbal barbs, interrupting one friend and bluntly finishing sentences for another, employing a host of colorful expletives and quips to get her point across in describing a coworker or a slacking team-mate working on a course project. Anne could often look and sound a bit rough-around-the-edges during those talking breakfasts. Indeed, you might notice that this is not quite the same Anne who sat in the second row during class, nor the "Big Sister" during lunch, nor the Anne negotiating her way through work at the PR firm, or an intimate dinner with her boyfriend, or the witty bartender after hours. After seeing Anne move through the many facets of a typical workday, one might even begin to wonder: "Who is the real Anne?" But, when we get down to it, that might not be a sensible question. Is there such a thing as one particular "real" version of ourselves? How do we define what is real?

Ways of Knowing

There are three basic ways of "knowing" or, more specifically, perceiving the world around us: **objective**, **subjective**, and **intersubjective**. Knowing something **objectively** means using an externally crafted measurement to define it. For example, to say it is "hot" outside, we can use a temperature scale—which could be Fahrenheit, Celsius, Kelvin, or some other societally-agreed-upon scale of measurement. Of course the numbers in the scale only "mean" something to us insofar as we are accustomed to applying the scale to our lived experience—recognizing the degree mark at which we would put on a coat or a pair of sandals, for instance. If you say to someone within the sphere of reference of a certain scale that 100 degrees Celsius is "hot" because water boils at that temperature, across locales and situations, this measure can be understood objectively, outside of one's individual frame of reference. To understand something being "hot" **subjectively**, though, we look inside the lived experience and perceptual structure of a single organism. At 60 degrees Fahrenheit, a person accustomed to colder climates might open a window, declaring the weather to be "hot." Another person from a hotter climate might close the window because it feels "cold." No person's perception is more "accurate" than the other in terms of what is "hot." However, if we can achieve **intersubjective** agreement—a sense shared by two or more people that something is so—then we can agree to coordinate our behavior (setting the thermostat of a shared dwelling, for instance, or open or close the windows) and live together comfortably.

Self as Object

"The self, as that which can be an object of itself, is essentially a social structure, and it arises in social experience."

—George Herbert Mead

Psychologist Kenneth Gergen, in his book *The Saturated Self* (1991) describes modern human identity in particular, as a "pastiche of personalities" wherein "the test of competence is not so much the integrity of the whole, but the correct representation appearing at the right time, in the right context" (Gergen, 1991). Let's return to Anne again to help us unpack Gergen's somewhat counter-intuitive claim. In the morning, assuming proper sleep and diet, Anne is the goofy, sharp-tongued, and sometimes brooding best friend. Around noon she is the responsible and serious but friendly mentor. If Anne does not fulfill the correct role in the appropriate place at the right time, then the very fabric of interaction in those social spaces may begin to unravel. Without being two-faced or dishonest then, Anne must (with varying degrees of conscious attention) put different personae into play throughout her day. Do you detect some affinities with Anne in this regard? As we move beyond adolescence, this is just a natural part of growing up, a

central component of the process of socialization, through which we learn to function appropriately within our social environments. Of course, as mentioned briefly at the beginning of the chapter, there is a more subjective sense of self we can all detect as well.

Returning to how we define this complex notion of "self," we revisit George Herbert Mead who, in *Mind Self and Society* (1934) outlined the components of his theory of selfhood, which centers on two concepts: the "I" and the "Me" (Figure 2.2). According to Mead, the **"I"** part of ourselves is rooted in our natural reflexes and instincts, our spontaneous self that acts as an active **subject**. The **"Me"** part of ourselves, however, is instead the **object**—that which is perceived, judged, monitored, controlled, rationalized. This subject-object dichotomy is, of course, part of an analytical model, but it highlights the fact that we negotiate our identity at all times between two "selves," that which we feel from inside, and that which we perceive is receiving us on the outside. As small children,

all we are aware of is our internal lived experience. However, during our process of development, we gain an ability to view our **"self as object,"** turning a projected lens on ourselves based on how we understand or expect others to view us. Of course this lens is a product of a **self-concept,** which is formed through our reactions to **reflected appraisals**, comments made by people in our environment about our worth. Our self-concept is also formed from **social comparisons**, our own internal view of how we measure up to others in terms of socially-valued characteristics. Our **looking-glass self** is that "me" we *think* we see reflected in the gaze of others.

A graphic representation of Mead's Symbolic Interactionism as it relates to understanding the "self":

Although a "looking glass" is an old-fashioned term for a mirror, the modern notion of a "looking-glass self" is more relevant than ever in our 21st century world of mediated communication and social networking. As we create online profiles and avatars

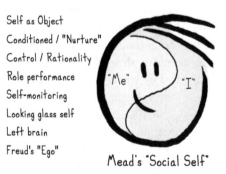

Self as Object
Conditioned / "Nurture"
Control / Rationality
Role performance
Self-monitoring
Looking glass self
Left brain
Freud's "Ego"

Self as Subject
Unconditioned / "Nature"
Spontaneous
Creative, intuitive
Embodied experience
Connected, holistic
Right brain
Freud's "Id"

Mead's "Social Self"

Figure 2.2. A graphic representation of Mead's Symbolic Interactionism as it relates to understanding the "self."

that present us to others as we wish to have ourselves seen, we notice how we can both literally and figuratively "step outside of ourselves" in order to view our ongoing relations with the world. This apparently simple act really is one of the most sophisticated perceptual skills found in nature. It characterizes the manner in which we are both self-reflective and self-reflexive beings. We develop a responsive self-concept and this illustrates how we are at once subjective and objective beings. As we develop our strategic flexibility, we become aware of how we can use both subjective and objective modes of perception to create intersubjective reality, in which meaning is shared in important ways with others.

Knowing Other, Knowing Self

"I am not what I think I am, and I am not what you think I am. I am what I think you think I am."

—R. Bierstedt

Indeed, our way of knowing both self and others is socially constructed, and subject to change. The old nursery expression, "Sticks and stones will break my bones, but names will never hurt me" sometimes just doesn't ring true, because if we pay attention to reflected appraisals, the words and actions of others toward us, it's clear that our awareness of the names spoken and stories told by others can certainly affect the way we think and feel about ourselves … for better or worse. Our being

aware of and, in effect, trying to take on the perspective (or "**perceptual role**") of significant others with whom we interact is a crucial part of how we negotiate our multifaceted identities and shifting roles in the world. Just as a diamond has many facets, individual people can also appear very different from different angles—sometimes shining, sometimes clear, sometimes cloudy, deep and brooding, sometimes dull, sometimes sharp. It's the angle we take, the way we perceive, that determines not only how we are viewed, but more fundamentally, how we view ourselves, and thus what we project to others.

The Self-Fulfilling Prophecy

A **self-fulfilling prophecy** takes place when expectations create our actual lived reality (Figure 2.3). Sometimes this phenomenon is called the **Pygmalion effect** after the Greek myth of the sculptor, Pygmalion, who fell in love with Galatea, a statue of a woman that he himself had sculpted. This effect recognizes the power of our thoughts in shaping our feelings toward the outer world, which

literally create our responses and behaviors, and therefore our outcomes. Depending on the nature of the relationships we maintain, we are always enmeshed somehow in the "prophecies" (i.e. opinions, predictions, hopes, and expectations) of others. This might include other individuals, institutions, cultures, etc. The sociological phenomenon of self-fulfilling prophecy has been described in literature since the ancient world, but was codified and described in detail in the 20th century by sociologist Robert K. Merton. In his book, *Social Theory and Social Structure* (1968), Merton illustrates the concept of self-fulfilling prophecy by describing how when a person falsely believes that his or her marriage will fail, the fears of such failure actually cause the marriage to fail. Think about it for a moment … How can negative expectations contribute to the dissolution of an otherwise healthy relationship?

To illustrate how this might work, let's take the example of a baseball coach considering the prospects of a couple of closely matched rookies during the first practice of the season. Before any substantive relationships have developed, we would need

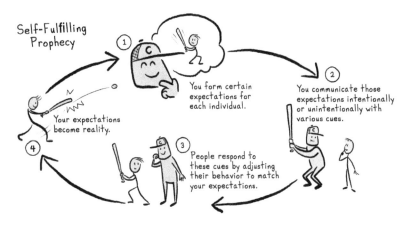

Figure 2.3 One example of a Self-Fulfilling Prophecy in the making

to consider the kind of day each ball player was having, perhaps even what they ate for breakfast that morning. Indeed, with any number of additional variables at play, one individual might appear more skilled than the other.

In any case, we can imagine a coach watching two young players in earnest. Inevitably, the coach begins to form certain expectations about the capacities and possibilities, presumably, inherent to each player (hitting, fielding skills, sportsmanship, etc). Whatever details might be true about the different players at that time, the coach will often, and quite inevitably, begin to communicate his expectations intentionally and/or unintentionally by way of various cues (verbal, gestural, paralinguistic, and other subtle factors). The ball players, being self-aware and self-reflexive beings, will often and quite predictably begin to respond to these cues by adjusting their behavior to match the coach's expectations (positive or negative).

The player who detects positive feedback will feel encouraged and tend to flourish. The one who detects something else will, in the vast majority of cases, not do as well (Martens, 2004). Although a simple example of how self-fulfilling prophecies might unfold, this scenario provides a basis for appreciating the way people can be helped—or hindered—by the physical, linguistic, and symbolic (i.e., communicative) activity of others.

Frames of Reference

Elaborating further on how human perception works, we can borrow some perspective from the ancient study of **rhetoric**, which

we've learned is "the available means of persuasion." A rhetorical view nicely illustrates what is implied by a frame of reference (i.e., "personal" perspective), which is important to clarify in order to communicate effectively. Because communication means communing and sharing meaning, being able to consciously reflect on your own perception of something is the first step to helping others see what you see. Indeed, all communication is persuasion to some degree, as we persuade others, even unconsciously, to see and react to the world the way it appears to us.

The Greek philosopher Aristotle, and his teachers Plato and Socrates before him, felt that the process of effective communication is, as rhetorical scholar J.F.M. Hunter (1974) puts it, a "rational strategy of moral persuasion." This means that effective persuasion can be achieved by way of enlightenment and engagement, as opposed to various forms of mystification, manipulation, verbal trickery, or coercion. Under this view, persuasion is about changing others' perspectives in such a way that they "come to see" something they were unable or unwilling see before. Persuasion, then, really is about changing conceptions, perceptions, and frames of reference. Of course, changing baseline reference frames (or how we compare what we *perceive* with what we *know*) first requires a change in perceptions (or ways of seeing). More than this, it's about assembling thoughts and ideas in new and interesting (literally, interest-generating) ways that, in turn, lead to new ways of knowing, seeing, and being.

We'll consider the art of rhetoric and persuasion in more depth in the Public Speaking

chapter of this book. For now, it should suffice to point out that a genuinely persuasive person prompts the people around her/him (i.e., audience members) to say: "you know, I never thought much about that idea, but now that you've put it in this way, it just makes a lot of sense to me." Good communicators, in other words, shift both subjective and objective realities.

Frame of reference refers to the perspective through which people see the world. Or consider how many people are standing on opposite sides of a north-south street, and a car travels southward on the street, to one person the car is moving toward the left and to the other person, the car is moving toward the right. Effective communication means helping people see the view from our side of the street.

For example, many people believe (or at least seem to hold the opinion) that where automobile safety is concerned, bigger and heavier means better. Extending this admittedly conventional logic, the VW Beetle, the BMW Mini, or little "smart cars" must be less safe than a 17-foot, three-ton sport utility vehicle (SUV)? The problem with such an assessment is that it ignores many safety advances made over the last several decades. Innovative structural design, composite space frames, and airbag placements have tipped the scale to such a degree that "bigger=better" does not necessarily apply anymore. In other words, our culture's frame of reference is changing. We're apt to notice things we did not notice before—like inconsistencies and incomplete explanations, unstated assumptions,

Figure 2.4 Depiction of Plato's Cave.

or missing premises—and this unfolding awareness has clear impact on our values, behaviors, and spending decisions.

At the very least, this discussion may prompt something that some psychologists and cognitive researchers like to call a perceptual **gestalt shift**. A gestalt describes a fundamental change in perception or awareness or conception of the world. It comes about by way of new information. Whether that's a collection of new facts or a new or slightly different angle of view, a gestalt shift occurs when your way of seeing and/or thinking about something has changed. And it usually changes in a way that cannot be undone. Your world, your reality shifts. You are changed in one small but not insignificant way. Big or small change, the world is different somehow because you are different.

In ancient Greek work, *The Republic*, the philosopher Plato described an allegory of a cave in which people have been chained for their entire lives, with their entire view limited to the shadows they see projected on the wall from the fire behind them. If the people were to stand up and see the actual reality of the cave, and realize that all they had seen all their lives were merely flat shadows against the wall, they would indeed experience a gestalt shift from one "reality" to a fuller reality of their environment. Throughout our lives, we may have many such shifts in perception, some subtle and others dramatic, which allow us to see the world around us in very different ways.

Continuing with the SUV example, we have flipped the **figure/ground relationship** between big and small motor vehicles. This happens when something noticed in the forefront of one individual's awareness is barely perceptible for someone else, or when our perceptual frame changes over time. For example, think of how acorns hanging on a tree might look to you, and to a squirrel. To you, acorns are likely not something your attention zooms in to focus on, whereas for a squirrel, acorns are likely to be in the forefront of awareness. Likewise, someone casually passing through a building might not notice a few pieces of litter. However, the eyes of experienced maintenance staff members might find their eyes zooming in on every speck of trash. When one is looking for something, it becomes **figure**; when one has no particular interest, it simply fades into **ground**.

Toward the end of the 20th century in the United States, the SUV was the ground. Indeed, these larger vehicles comprised the background of our highways and byways. They were everywhere—and because of this, we tended not to notice them at a conscious level. Today, however, we are seeing fewer of those larger vehicles on the road. And because of this, we begin to notice them more consciously in the stream of other vehicles speeding along. Rising fuel costs, along with other notions of efficiency and practicality, and up-to-date safety assessments have altered the scene. As we move further along into the future, smaller and more efficient vehicles should continue to become more common. In the process, they will begin to form the (back)ground of experience, as they SUV becomes less common and the figure of our experience in this regard. The SUV will become the figure because it will become more salient in our consciousness. To reiterate, what is most noticeable to us at any given time becomes the "figure," just as what is less noticeable fades into "ground." Like the music in a shopping center, or the hum of a fan or refrigerator at home, anything that is not salient at the moment becomes "ground," the background of experience.

Examples illustrating the perceptual flipping of figure and ground abound. Throughout the 18th and 19th centuries, tanned skin in people of European descent was frowned upon by the landed gentry. If your skin was browned, it was perceived that you must be a laborer who toils in the sun. As any "right-thinking" citizen knew, laborers and landowners do not mix! However, by the last quarter of the 20th century, dark tans become markers for wealth and leisure for people fitting the "Caucasian" designation in mainstream America. By 1980, very white skin became, in effect, frowned upon. The meaning of the perceptual marker (skin hue) for a certain segment of the population had flipped position. Over time and for various reasons, the markers can flip back. By the end of the 20th century, the deep tan had gone out of vogue. New awareness concerning the dangers of skin cancer and other ailments associated with prolonged exposure to the sun prompted a turning away from the beach and the tanning booth. "Spray on" tans, "tanning pills," and other commercial efforts to buck the trend continue to the present, but most people don't tend to associate skin hue with socio-economic status in the same way they once did. Time, as part of the communicative context, brings changes to our personal and collective perceptions in this way.

Or consider how geographical location operates as part of the communicative context: late at night in many of our inner cities, we find streets filled with the piercing sounds of sirens, racing emergency vehicles, train whistles, and car alarms. That cacophony can be the basis, or ground, for a restful sleep. Indeed, it is not uncommon for people who live in or near urban centers to report being awakened when there is a lull in these background sounds of the city. For them it is the "sounds of silence" that prompts a poor night's sleep, with some

people reporting too much quiet that night. Surprisingly, perhaps, for these folks it is the "sounds of silence" that prompt a poor night's sleep, with many reporting it was "too quiet last night." For others living on the outskirts of town or in the suburbs, the sound of trains, taxicab horns, car alarms, and sirens often predictably wakes them up. One person's ground is another person's figure, all depending on our context of "normalcy."

What makes people and things what they are (what fills them with meaning) also has a lot to do with what (or who) they are not. While there are certainly some subtleties and shades of gray to be considered in this kind of analysis, the tension and interplay between what is and what is not salient is the basis of the figure/ground relation.

For example, take this popular version of a famous ambiguous picture (Fig. 2.5). The "old lady/young lady" image is often employed to demonstrate the visual version of the figure/ground gestalt shift. No matter what you see first, and no matter how much difficulty you may initially experience in trying to see the alternative image, once you have come to see things the other way, a kind of "mental switch" is flipped forever. For the vast majority of people, it is exceedingly difficult to go back to their old way of seeing the image. From there on, most people tend to report seeing both figures simultaneously. SUVs or Minis, tanned or blanched skin, sirens or silence, old women or young ones, in each of these cases we see how the notion of

an objective reality that stands outside of subjective experience begins to lose credence. This is the nature of the figure/ground relation underlying human perception.

Perceptual Filters

Clearly, we are unable to process all the sense data that surrounds us. We develop ways of tuning out much of the information we don't value, like all the acorns on that tree, or how many compact cars are waiting at the intersection, and tuning into the things that matter to us most—the voices and opinions of people we know and respect, information that helps us in some way, etc. Human perception is mediated in significant ways by a unique mix of perceptual filters that helps define who each of us are as individuals. (Figure 2.5). Any notion of an objective reality "out there" that someone might consider real and

Figure 2.5 What do you see?

William Ely Hill / Public Domain.

true is inevitably colored by our assigned and acquired values, interests, needs, and goals. The difference between something being assigned or acquired depends on whether those attributes or tendencies were given to us by birth or learned, either consciously or unconsciously, through experience. This applies to the way we perceive people, things and ideas. Our unique realities are additionally created and maintained by our language (or languages), the many cultural systems we inhabit, and the media systems we participate in and are exposed to.

Our **cognitive system** is our total perceptual structure through which we gather information, make meaning from it, and integrate it into our overall **worldview**. This complex system is the unique lens through which we view the world. Interestingly, our cognitive systems tend to build upon themselves in ways that support the patterns of information that have come through our system in the past. As this system develops, there are several ways the stimuli and information that helps constitute it is filtered and formed. How does our view of the world become skewed over time when we only expose ourselves two experiences or viewpoints that confirm our pre-existing world view?

Selective exposure is our tendency to expose ourselves most often to information and opinions that we like. As media scholar Joseph Klapper noted in the 1960s, people tend to avoid media and information that does not confirm or uphold their existing beliefs. Theoretically, this is considered to be because we feel cognitive dissonance (Festinger, 1957), or a sense of mental discomfort, when the information in our mind does not add up neatly. To avoid this feeling, we expose ourselves most to news and opinions that match our worldview. Can you think of ways that you or those you know seek out or avoid particular channels of information? For example, in the cultural realm, selective exposure shows up when people avoid interacting with people across cultural boundaries. They may feel uncomfortable with other languages or dislike being exposed to unfamiliar odors, styles of dress, or different habits of interaction: touching or not touching, speaking in different ways, or maintaining or avoiding eye contact differently than they do. People who dislike or fear the presence of foreigners or people with unfamiliar behaviors (**xenophobia**) are likely not to step outside of their comfort zone, and their worldview, and communication skills will be limited as a result. In the political realm (dominated these days by media), people often limit themselves to channels, stations, websites, gatherings, and other outlets that uphold their preferred political ideas or worldview. How might

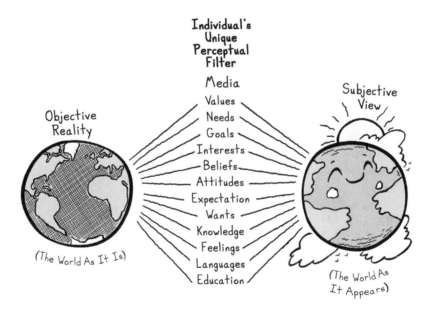

Figure 2.6 Some Common Perceptual Filters

our view of the world be skewed over time by only exposing ourselves to experiences or viewpoints that confirm our preexisting worldview?

Even when one is "exposed" to a diversity of viewpoints, **selective attention** comes into play when we only pay attention to messages that interest us. If you are driving along the interstate with a full belly you're probably not paying attention to or even noticing a series of signs for various eateries at an upcoming rest area. On the other hand, if you haven't eaten in the last 10 hours, it's likely that those signs are the first things you'll notice and focus upon as they quickly approach. But while physical hunger is also a state that alters our ability to attend, many other facets of experience can affect and even direct our ability to perceive. For example, if we hunger in a different way for that long lost love, we might see the beloved's face in our "mind's eye," or in a cloud formation, or maybe even in a pile of rocks at the edge of the garden. Indeed, our felt needs and wants also have much to do with the way we see and perceive the world around us.

Once we have been exposed to and paid attention to a particular message, **selective perception** or **selective interpretation** is applied in the sense we make of it. The aspects of the message we pay the most attention to, the way we interpret the meaning, any media potentially involved in its representation, and how we integrate the message into our overall worldview all go into forming our selective perception of the experience. For example, perhaps a loved one tells us, "I love you." We can hear the sentence, but perhaps we interpret

it contextually as something the person says "all the time" (and is thus less meaningful), or it was said "less genuinely" than usual, or was said "only to get something." Like a curved mirror in a fun house, the sometimes rough, rocky, twisted, or distorted terrain inside us can take a message and turn it into something entirely different than was perhaps intended. Our perception of ourselves, our perception of the "other," and our perception of the context sometimes converge in mysterious ways to potentially trigger all kinds of alternative interpretations.

Finally, our cognitive system often exhibits the all too convenient ability to engage in **selective retention**, when we intentionally or unintentionally forget information that we do not wish to retain. Forgetting to do a particularly onerous chore or assignment, losing track of information that doesn't confirm a cherished belief, or repressing painful or unwanted memories are all ways the stimuli and information that passes through our perceptual apparatus doesn't find a firm or permanent place in our memory. Many times, deep introspection, emotional work, or even dreams can conjure difficult thoughts or experiences from the past that we may have forgotten or repressed, reminding us that even though something falls outside of our conscious awareness, our minds are better recorders of experience than we may realize. Our overall attitude on life makes a significant difference in terms of what information we choose to attend to and retain. One person may trip and fall in the morning and obsess about

the experience for weeks, thinking "what a clumsy idiot I am," whereas another may laugh it off and forget about it quickly. How does our self-concept impact the way we perceive and remember negative or positive experiences?

The Map is Not the Territory

In a very real sense, perceptual filters help us make our way through the world—sometimes for better, sometimes for worse. Noticing how the perceptual filters of ourselves and others function can be a very useful tool for understanding the "hidden terrain" that we don't see on the surface. If you think of your inner world as a constantly-shifting territory of peaks, valleys, smooth road, potholes, and everything in between, it becomes clear that the process of truly seeking to understand ourselves and others can be an ever-deepening adventure. Whether we view these inner explorations as fascinating or dangerous reveals much about our attitude toward life itself.

Polish-American philosopher Alfred Korzybski coined the phrase, **"the map is not the territory."** This adage means that our mental representations of the world are completely inadequate to represent the world itself, that there is a fundamental separation between perception and reality. Think of an actual map for a moment—are you thinking of a topographical map, a street map, a political map, a map of local businesses? Any map we could render would be, of necessity, incomplete and have to leave out many important details about the area being mapped. The only complete map is the place itself.

The way we map an area, as we've learned, relies entirely on what is important to us in the moment, and thus our map may turn out to be completely different from the way someone else would map the very same place, event, or process..

Korzybski is best-known for his theory of general semantics (the study of meaning), in which he argued that our knowledge of the world is limited most significantly by the human nervous system. But he quickly added that the general structure of language takes a close second in its ability to shape human perception, thought, and action. Korzybski maintained that people do not have direct knowledge or awareness of reality. Instead, we have access to perceptions sensed by our bodily organs, from which "meaning is made" through our set of beliefs formed, in turn, through interaction with others. What we react to is not actually the world "out there," but the map we have created of it in our mind. It is through the process of Symbolic Interaction that we define and re-define what things "mean" through communication with others—all of us working, of course, with what can often be very different maps.

Determining our Own Map

"Whether you think you can, or whether you think you can't, you're right."

—Henry Ford

As we've discussed, maps can be very useful in helping you get where you want to go. But where are you going? Welcome to the most fundamental, and often the most challenging, aspect of becoming an effective communicator. Being "effective" means getting results that you desire, but what do you truly desire? If you don't make up your mind, there are plenty of others in the world who would be all too happy to decide for you. And, as we know, that doesn't always go well for all concerned.

Think for a moment about building a sand castle. There are different kinds of goals we might have: one person might want to try getting their castle to a particular height (an **objective** standard), another person might want to build the most interesting castle on the beach (a **subjective** goal, for sure). Yet another may not particularly care what the castle comes out like, as long as they can enjoy the sand and sun and a day laughing with friends (**intersubjective** experience). Ultimately, all our "sand castles" (accomplishments and experiences) will eventually fade into the background of human history, right? The question we need to ask ourselves now, as we set off on a journey of connecting ourselves with others through communication is, what do I really hope to achieve when I communicate, and why? You might want to achieve a particular grade (an objective measure), a particular type of inner satisfaction (a subjective sense), or a feeling of connectedness with others (an intersubjective experience). Before you begin a communication encounter, whether a speech or a challenging discussion with a friend, it helps to know what you are setting out to achieve in order to know if you did "well" at it.

Who gets to determine what goes "well" in a communication encounter? Really think about it for a moment—what does it mean to "communicate well?" Who decides? Since communicating means communing, and since communing means sharing experience and meaning with others, the answer is that *everyone* involved in the interaction has a part in deciding what went well. We are all senders and receivers simultaneously. And not only are we sending messages around *outside* of ourselves, we are also sending messages around *inside* of ourselves. The sense we make of that inner dialogue will determine what standards we set for success, and how we are doing at getting there.

This is where "the map is not the territory" comes in. Although it may seem we are making slow or no progress on one map, shifting the map to another perspective can make a world of difference. If one looks from above at an ant walking around, the little creature may seem to be zigzagging all over the place. But if we can get to the ant's viewpoint, we may notice tiny peaks and valleys in the ground that it is following or avoiding—the ant's path may be much more logical than we think. Or say we see someone walking, but not on any established roads, completely "off the map" (if we are using a street map, that is). They miss all the attractions, the fast food joints, the malls. But perhaps the person's goal is to climb to the highest point in the county—they are using a topographical map to chart their progress. In that case, avoiding the roads is an intelligent choice, and the person is making the swiftest journey possible to the highest peak. Only a person who knows his or her goal would chart an off-the-map course, and only someone who understands that person and their goal would be able to appreciate their choice. This is what it means to communicate well—to know your goal and pursue a path toward it, and to communicate this to others in such a way that they can aid your path, or at least stay out of the way.

Reaching Goals

The problem in reaching our goals is that it is we ourselves that most often get in our own way. All of us have deep grooves and potholes in our **self-concept** that we fall into as we try to make progress—the little habits, weaknesses, addictions, and vulnerabilities that make us uniquely challenged in coping with our environment. Remember all those reflected appraisals and social comparisons, stored consciously or even subconsciously in our minds over time? We are usually our own worst critics, and the information that tends to make it most easily through our perceptual filters is often negative about ourselves. We take the fears, insecurities, and limitations we've encountered and use them to build our own fences around our vulnerabilities.

This means that we are the ones who hold the tools to take down the fences we build. We are the only ones who know the fullness of our inner territory; we are the ones who best know the reasons for what we do. This means that communicating well begins with our **intrapersonal communication**, through which we can consciously examine and re-write our inner stories in ways that more accurately project what we want to others.

Think of someone who walks around projecting the negative belief, "I'm such an idiot." Perhaps this belief was programmed by negative appraisals at some point, or perhaps just through the person's own social comparison with others. If the person can "shift the map" and realize that, actually, a lot of what he or she does is very smart and purposeful, they can shift this inner belief to, "I'm pretty sharp" or "I learn from my experiences." Consciously adopting a more positive perspective and reconditioning oneself to legitimately accept that can often project an entirely new persona to others. And more significantly, what sorts of behaviors and perceptions might undergo changes as a result?

The field of communication continues to be informed by other fields, particularly psychology and sociology, since communication is the bridge between the two fields in studying how our inner world interacts with our social world, and vice versa. One area of psychology-communication praxis (the applied blending of theory and practice) that can provide a helpful frame is **Neuro-Linguistic Programming (NLP)**, which grew out of the work of John Grinder and Richard Bandler at the University of Santa Cruz in the early 1970s. NLP is based on the fundamental notion that the body and mind form an inseparable whole. Although the human sensory apparatus (our eyes, ears, mouth, nose, skin, etc.) is the most basic vehicle through which we form impressions or representations of the world around us, in large measure, our values and beliefs together function as a powerful filter for the sense data we actually take in. For example,

An artist, a lumberjack, and a botanist taking a stroll through the woods will have very different experiences and notice very different things. If you go through the world looking for excellence, you will find excellence. If you go through the world looking for problems, you will find problems. Or, as the Arabic saying puts it, "What a piece of bread looks like depends on whether you are hungry or not." Very narrow beliefs, interests, and perceptions will make the world impoverished, predictable, and dull. The very same world can be rich and exciting. The difference lies not in the world, but in the filters through which we perceive it. (O'Connor and Seymour, 1990, p. 4).

The practice of NLP suggests that we examine a few of our basic filtering strategies, or "behavioral frames," to examine which beliefs serve us well, and which inhibit our ability to get what we really want. These five frames help us to stay in a more empowered state of mind, which fuels us both inwardly and outwardly in moving in the direction we desire.

The first frame is consciously **focusing on outcomes rather than problems**. Many of us spend considerable time focusing on what we don't like about ourselves and our lives, analyzing in detail what is wrong with us. This "blame frame" programs these beliefs further into the mind and leaves us feeling worse and less empowered to actually find solutions. What we focus on expands.

The second frame to shift is to **ask "how" rather than "why" questions**. "Why" questions lead to justifications, defensiveness, and more programming of the same inhibiting scenarios into the mind. "How" questions, on the other hand, help us better understand the structure of a problem, which is far more useful in helping us figure out how to solve it. Instead of asking oneself, "Why me?" when something bad happens, try asking, "How can I best respond when something like this happens?"

The third frame we can adopt to stay in an empowered frame of mind is to **see feedback rather than failure**. If you choose to punctuate your life's journey with a comma, rather than a period, after an unwanted outcome and keep moving, the so-called failure becomes a very useful piece of feedback for redirecting your efforts toward what you want. From this frame of reference there is no such thing as failure, only information that can fuel us on our way. As the British statesman Winston Churchill famously said, "If you're going through hell, keep going."

The fourth frame is to **focus on possibilities instead of necessities**. Rather than getting mired down in a battle over something ultimately less important, keep an eye on the larger view and see beyond the barrier. Strive to see choices rather than constraints. For example, if you have a particular challenge, see it as a resource for growth. If you've been through a painful struggle, think of how much empathy and assistance you could give others going through the same (or a similar) struggle.

Finally, it helps to **adopt an attitude of curiosity and fascination** rather than making

assumptions. A young child learns quickly by simply being curious and experimenting, with no worries about looking silly over asking questions. Seeing differences in people and difficult situations with an eye of curiosity can help us retain the perspective we need to learn what we want to know. Just as a child would notice, "Oh, that falls when I push it off the table," we can notice, "Oh, he/she gets cranky when I bring up that topic." This attitude allows us to ask good questions of ourselves and others, rather than retreating into a defensive space.

To reach our goals, the first step is realizing that change is something we will experience throughout the course of our lives (think of how you've already changed since, say, elementary school). Deciding to be mindful about how we wish to change and then being positive as we work toward our goals is the only way to achieve the kind of real growth we desire. Once we realize the power of our thoughts and inner dialogue to literally shape our lives, we can consciously use **affirmations** to lay the groundwork for the life we want to live. These should be positive and stated in the present (i.e. "I think I am gaining a little confidence each day"), because carefully deployed words can literally re-program the "map" in our minds. Thinking something like "I wish I were more confident" conveys a sense of lack and separateness from our goal that we then re-create as a pattern. Focusing on a mental image of the desired outcome, *as if it were already so*, literally **primes** (prepares the way for) our entire system to act in ways that support our goals, but to

prepare ourselves to notice and receive those desired outcomes as they happen.

Recognizing that we can choose to shift our perception, even about ourselves, in ways that serve our highest goals is a crucial stepping-stone on our journey toward what we really want in life. Likewise, recognizing that no two people see the world in precisely the same way is critical to our ability to communicate effectively, to get along in the world, and to sustain high-quality relationships with others and with ourselves.

We are the subject and object of any sentence we write about ourselves, which gives us a powerful position to create the maps we want to follow. Seeing ourselves positively and manifesting our goals through the affirmations we choose allows us to be the director of that film called "self" that we project out into the world.

References

Festinger, L. (1957). *A theory of cognitive dissonance*. Stanford, CA: Stanford University Press.

Klapper, J.T. (1960). *The effects of mass communication*. New York: Free Press.

Merton, T. K. (1968). *Social theory and social structure*. New York: Free Press.

O'Connor, J. & Seymour, J. (1990). *Introducing NLP: Psychological skills for understanding and influencing people*. London: Thorsons.

Chapter Three
Verbal Communication

Words as Symbols

Words are some of the important tools we use to express ourselves. We have things that we want to say, that we want to communicate to others, and words are a primary way we accomplish that. The words are not *what* we have to say; they are what we use to describe what we have to say. They are culturally agreed-upon symbols a code we use to convey to others what we are thinking. The words we choose and the way we arrange them are critical to expressing ourselves well, to be able to accurately communicate with each other what is important to us. Words are a crucial element in communication. So, what is a word?

A **word** is a symbol that stands for something we can or have experienced. We are surrounded by things: a table, a pen, a house, other people. In addition to these physical objects, we have feelings: happiness, anger, boredom. We are also aware of concepts, ideas: bravery, laziness, generosity. In order to indicate to each other that we are thinking about any of these things or ideas, we need some symbolic way to represent them. When you see or hear "pen," an image comes into your mind, but the letters p-e-n are not themselves the pen. They are merely shapes on a page or screen, or sounds in the air. They are symbols that we have agreed mean the usually slim, traditionally straight thing, containing ink, with which we write. This agreement with each other about what p-e-n means is what makes pen a word, and that concept is the basis of language.

If telepathy were as common in the real world as it is in science fiction, there would be no need for language. You would think of what you mean by pen, and everyone would instantly understand it

Figure 3.1 What is a pen?

in exactly the same way, but that isn't the way it works in reality. In order for you to convey something to another person, you must put it into language. You must use the symbols or sounds that everyone agrees represent the object, idea, or action you want to describe or express. Of course it must be a language that you share with someone. If you want to talk to an English speaker about where you live, you might refer to your house. But, h-o-u-s-e may very well mean nothing to a French or Chinese speaker. The French person would say m-a-i-s-o-n and the Chinese person would write 房子. People all over the world share the same basic understanding of the concept of house, but each language has a different arrangement of shapes on a page or sounds in the air to express that concept. Each linguistic community attempts, in its own way, to assign a mutually understandable set of symbols or sounds to each object, idea, or sensation so that one person can express to another what he or she is thinking.

Communication requires the participation of at least two parties, two sender-receivers. In order to communicate, one must connect with another person either by speaking or by writing (whether on paper, or by texting, or in some other way). The process does not really begin until information is received. If you encounter someone on the street and begin to ask for directions and the person you are addressing happens not to speak your language, that person won't understand you. You would be speaking perfectly clearly, but you would not be communicating, because your speech would make no sense to your listener, an example of semantic noise where

the meaning cannot be conveyed. If you put a note into a bottle and toss it into the sea, you have written some words but you have not communicated anything until someone finds the note and reads it. Thus, the reception process is vital, and it is worth remembering that the communication is not always what the sender intended, but it is always what the receiver perceives—whatever your receiver understands from you is what has been communicated, whether that was what you meant or not.

For example, say you tell a friend to meet you tomorrow at ten. You mean ten in the evening, but you were not specific; your friend shows up at ten in the morning. Your friend heard ten in the morning, perhaps because she is more of a morning person or for some other reason particular to her. Ten in the morning is the time that was communicated to her, even though you, the sender, did not intend that. Try to remind yourself that everyone is misunderstood some of the time. Don't assume that because what you want to say is clear in your mind, that it is necessarily clear in your words.

Even if two people are speaking the same language and making an effort to be clear, words can convey very different impressions, depending on the context. An extra-large milkshake might well be described as a big drink; an aircraft carrier is a big ship. Each of these standing alone could be called "big," but put the milkshake on the pier next to a berthed aircraft carrier and the big milkshake becomes almost unimaginably tiny. The way we see the milkshake has been changed by moving it to a new place, thus changing its relative comparison. We have

changed the physical context in which we see the milkshake, and in so doing have changed the way we perceive it. In order to communicate effectively, we need to do our best to use words to let others in on the pictures in our minds.

Language in Context

Changing the verbal context in which we use a word works in the same way. Words don't stand alone. The other words surrounding them in sentences and paragraphs may alter the sense we get from a word, adding shades of meaning to the dictionary definition or sometimes helping us to understand which meaning of a word is intended.

Take the word *fast*. When you read it just now, you probably thought of the concept of speed, something quick or rapid, but the word has many different meanings. The *Merriam-Webster Online Dictionary* lists eight meanings for the word "fast." The first meaning listed is "firmly fixed, tightly shut, adhering firmly," so when people say that something is stuck fast, they usually mean that it is stuck firmly or tightly, nothing to do with time or speed. Now suppose that a careless driver wanders off the road and immediately gets stuck in some mud. Someone standing nearby might say that, "He got stuck fast." Does she mean that he got stuck firmly or (since it happened immediately) that he got stuck quickly? We need some more **context** to be sure. If our observer says "He got stuck fast. He's going to need a tow to get out of there," she probably means stuck firmly. But, if she says, "He got stuck fast. He probably didn't

Figure 3.2 He got stuck fast.

have any time to react." She might mean stuck in a hurry. You cannot be sure about which sense of fast is intended by looking at just the one word.

Context can also change our sense of the word in other ways. If you are watching a friend who is an athlete competing in a race and see that she is running fast, that is a good thing. If you get a new watch as a birthday present and notice that it is running fast, that is a bad thing. In the two contexts, running fast represents contradictory evaluations, one positive, one negative. Runners are supposed to run fast; watches are not. The context dictates whether the same set of words means a good quality or a poor one.

Denotative and Connotative Meaning

Almost all words have two levels of meaning, their **denotation**, the dictionary definition, and their **connotation**, which gives us all of the impressions, emotions and sensations that have attached themselves to the word. Contained in the connotation are the subtle differences that allow us to express fine distinctions between similar words, letting us choose just the right word, out of all these similar words, to more precisely express what we mean. The differences between denotation and connotation can be large or small, often depending on the kind of word in question.

Concrete words, such as *pencil*, do not usually carry with them a connotation very different from the dictionary denotation. More **abstract** words, however, have often developed shades of meaning that can convey very different impressions. The words *frugal, thrifty, cheap*, and *economical* have a similar denotation—an unwillingness to spend a lot of money. In most dictionaries, there will be comparatively little difference in their definitions. There is, however, a considerable difference in connotation. To most people, being thrifty indicates cleverness about money, the ability to get a good deal, to make the most of one's money. Being thrifty is usually considered a good thing. To be cheap, on the other hand, usually connotes being bad with money, being unwilling to spend when it would be wise to do so,

"too cheap to grab a good deal." In both cases, the person being described is not spending a lot of money; the denotation is roughly the same, but the connotation is very different.

Word choice refers to your strategic use of words and involves more than denotation and connotation. Also important is the difference between **accuracy** and **precision**. If you see an elephant today, you might say that you saw a "gray thing." You would be accurate—what you saw was a thing that was gray. But you would hardly be precise. A battleship is a gray thing; so is a storm cloud, or a mouse. A good writer does not settle for just being accurate. A good writer strives to be precise, to explain, as clearly as possible, in terms the recipient will understand.

Hayakawa's Ladder of Abstraction

The noted educator, S. I. Hayakawa, in his book *Language in Thought and Action* (1939) explored the concept of a "Ladder of Abstraction." Suppose someone says he or she is "wealthy." What comes to mind—a big house, fancy car, jewels, or something else? If the person were to go on and mention that their wealth is tied up in "livestock"—are you now imagining a big ranch, tractors, huge fields? No, it turns out the person declares the wealth is specifically of the bovine variety, related to cows. Are you imagining a scene with cowboys riding the range after big herds now? Actually, it turns out that the person, a farmer, feels "wealthy" because he owns

Figure 3.3 Hayakawa's Ladder of Abstraction

one cow, a particularly fine one named Bessie. In the region where this farmer lives, other farms may have some chickens or even a goat, but no one except the very wealthy could possibly afford to keep a cow. Are you imagining a very different scene now?

As you can see, meaning is entirely bound in context. You cannot assume that others listening to you can see the image in your mind, especially when you communicate across cultures. This is why Hayakawa points out that it is crucial to strive for **specificity** in our communication—choosing concrete words over abstract words. "Wealth" is an abstract concept because it is entirely relative and context-bound. "Bessie," on the other hand, is rather concrete—one particular cow with that name. As soon as the farmer describes Bessie and his pride in having a cow when others do not, recipients have a much clearer image in their mind of what the farmer really means, and more effective communication is possible.

On Hayakawa's Ladder of Abstraction, the most specific term, Bessie, is on the first rung of the ladder. As we go up the ladder, each rung presents a word that includes Bessie but also, increasingly, more and more items as the scope of the terminology widens. At the first rung or level of abstraction, we are talking about a particular cow. The second level includes many other cows; the third adds a range of other animals: horses, chickens, goats, to name a few. All of this livestock can be found on a farm, but so can silos and tractors and barns and fields. Assets like these can be considered forms of "wealth" if used to enhance the quality of life of those in ownership of them. Hayakawa's ladder is a helpful metaphor to remind us to "come down to earth" as we climb down the rungs into greater levels of specificity that can be more vivid, engendering much clearer mental images.

For example, what do you think of when you hear someone say that he "has issues" with someone else? We know that, as commonly used, it means that there is some sort of problem between people, but what kind of problem? Does the first person dislike the second, fear him, envy him, or something else altogether? We don't know, because the term "issues" is far enough up the ladder that it covers many different possibilities. If we are consciously trying to protect our friend's privacy, then we might well choose a word that is somewhat abstract, but if we are trying to make the situation clear to a third party, then we need a more specific word. "Mark thinks Tom is rude when their friends are around" is much clearer than "Mark has issues with Tom."

Of course, there are times when we all speak or write on a more abstract level, for example, "Each person should try to do good in the world." It would be foolish to attempt to list every single way in which a person could do a good deed for another. The simple proposition that each person should strive for good is perfectly clear in the sentence and, in this case, limiting the scope of good to a list of choices would defeat the intent of the writer. Each rung of the ladder has a purpose and each rung is appropriate for certain usages, but it is generally a good practice, when in doubt, to be more specific rather than less. Remember where we started at the beginning of the chapter; the words are the vehicle we use to convey ideas from one to another. No matter how clear the idea might be in your head, if the words you use to express that idea are vague or too abstract, then your listener or reader will likely get an incomplete, or worse, inaccurate picture of what you are trying to say. Hayakawa's ladder reminds us to be very specific and to create mental images with our words in order to communicate well.

Language and Perception

The words we have access to in our language may actually affect the way we see the world around us. Likewise, the environment we inhabit can have a profound impact on the language that we use. For example, Khalid, walking in a forest, sees trees. Ellen, a botanist, a biologist who studies plants, sees elms and maples and oaks and firs and white birches, gray birches, and red birches and hundreds of other types of plant life. Ellen is aware of a difference between this tree and that one that Khalid is not. Since they are all just "trees" to him, all he sees are trees. To some extent, the actual differences between the various trees are lost to Khalid and are obvious to Ellen. To some extent, this is an issue of **jargon**—the specialized language that we learn related to our profession, field of study, or life environment. However, to some extent these differences in language may actually represent differences in our perception, and ultimately our cognition, or how we think about things. Of course, these different ways of seeing and perceiving can matter quite a bit as we communicate and strive to share meaning with others.

This phenomenon of **linguistic relativity**—the idea that our thoughts and actions are influenced by the language we speak—has come to be called the **Sapir-Whorf Hypothesis (or Whorfianism)**. Two prominent linguists Edward Sapir and Benjamin Lee Whorf pointed out ways in which our cognition is impacted by our language, both the vocabulary and the grammar we use, and vice versa.

It's a two-way street—the environment around us impacts our language, and the language we are taught impacts what we perceive about the environment around us. One famous example is that the indigenous (native) people of the snowy northern Arctic regions, have an unusually complex vocabulary around the concept of snow. Having many words to describe snow in a snowy environment would be adaptive, because it could be helpful to know if snow is falling fast or slow, if it is powdery or crusted over with ice, etc. Humans develop vocabulary

and grammatical structures to describe the important realities in our environment, and in turn the process of learning this vocabulary and grammar causes us to see the world in particular ways.

In the case of Khalid and Ellen, the Sapir-Whorf hypothesis would describe a person just seeing "trees" in a naïve way as actually perceiving a forest differently from the person who understands the important variations between the various trees. The words and concepts we are trained to use **prime**, or prepare, our minds to see the world according to the categories and connections drawn by our language. Ellen, armed with a complex vocabulary that helps her characterize types of trees, may have a very different view from Khalid on whether a forest is "healthy" or "mature" because she can perceive differences and patterns that Khalid, seeing only "trees," may not perceive.

To use a grammatical example, the Spanish language has two different words for you: "tú" and "usted," which are used with different verb tenses. Thus, speakers of Spanish are, by virtue of their language, trained to notice differences in context and status every time they use the word "you." English, by contrast, has no such distinction. Even more complex, languages like Japanese and Korean have hierarchical relationships built throughout their entire grammatical structure—there are politer ways of conjugating verbs that you must use when speaking to someone older or of higher status, for instance. Thus, speakers of these languages are trained to perceive differences in age and status more readily than people who speak languages without such grammar. Can you imagine how using different verbs with different kinds of

people might affect our perception of others?

Going even further, scholars of **cognitive linguistics** like George Lakoff point out that the **metaphors** we use in describing subjects deeply impact, even subconsciously, the way we approach those subjects. For example, Lakoff and Johnson, in *Metaphors We Live By* (1980) point out that the words we use to describe arguments are in terms of struggle or battle:

- She *won* the argument.

- Your claims are *indefensible*.

- He *shot down* all my arguments.

- Her criticisms were *right on target*.

- If you use that *strategy*, he'll *wipe you out*.

Lakoff wonders how our interactions might be different if we were to view argument without the warlike metaphor, perhaps instead as a transaction or even as a dance. Might we be able to better envision cooperative or equal outcomes? Does the cognitive priming that an argument is something to "win" make us more likely to get our egos involved in ways that can become destructive? How do metaphorical wordings like "score a date" or "get to first base" make you think of dating interactions? How do the words often used in traditional wedding ceremonies, such as "give away the bride" or "I now pronounce you man and wife" (as opposed to "husband and wife") set us up, even subconsciously, to view these relationships?

The words and metaphors we use to describe things prime our minds to view the world in particular ways. When communicating verbally, orally or on paper, in private conversations or public speeches, it pays to consider how the words we choose may frame interactions and set up images and conceptual structures in other people's minds. The Sapir-Whorf Hypothesis reminds us that communicating well sometimes means using our words to reframe existing concepts in people's minds, helping them see things in a new way. Once Ellen the botanist teaches Khalid new vocabulary to see the difference between a birch, an elm, and a maple, he can now see trees in more the way she sees them and they are more able to "commune" in their experience of the forest.

Words and "Isms"

Because words frame our attention, the way we characterize people in verbal communication can go a long way toward how we view society—what is normal or different, what is desirable or forbidden, and into which categories we place people. **Social organizing principles** are the rules, spoken or unspoken, that we use to determine which characteristics are relevant in fitting people into groupings. We often sort people by race, gender, and age, for example, but don't often group people in terms of their allergies, blood type, or birth order, although these can matter just as much in certain ways. Of course, it is crucial to understand social history as we make sense of the words and categories we hear and use, because the groupings we buy into can have serious consequences, such as **discrimination** or even violence. Using labels or derogatory language can **stigmatize**, applying negative

associations, or **marginalize**, confining certain categories of people to the lower or outer edges of society. Language is received viscerally—in our ears, eyes, and bodies—as well as cognitively, and can even impact fundamental physiological processes that lead to health or disease. According to neurologist Dr. Vinod Deshmukh, "One of the most stressful sources of trauma reactions in the human brain is words, or the memory of words."

Language has been the lifeblood of both human limitation and advancement throughout time. Can you think of any words that trigger strong reactions in you? If you can find no reactions that come up, contemplate whether you may inhabit a privileged social position that feels relatively safe, respected, and free. Some consider a concern over respectful language to be merely "PC," or "**politically correct**," a trivializing term often used to mock language that takes the rights and dignity of others seriously. However, consider for a moment the power of words to literally shape our social reality. Language engenders associations in our minds, and once forged, these associations are often difficult to undo. Comments such as "That's so gay" or "that's so retarded" may not even be referencing particular people or communities, but just using these terms as insults at all fosters negative mental associations that damage people's perception of themselves and others. Using loaded language carelessly can cause very deep pain for those affected, and often, the sender will not even realize the damage caused by the supposedly "harmless" remark.

Discriminatory language fosters or reinforces attitudes that marginalize or stigmatize people based on social categories, such as **racism** (based on race or ethnicity), **sexism** (based on biological sex), **ageism** (based on age), **ableism** (based on physical or cognitive ability), **homophobia** (based on sexual preference or gender presentation), etc. Perhaps you are aware of other ways we use language to label others in limiting ways. Once you have witnessed the negative impact of discriminatory speech, you will see clearly that dismissing concerns as merely "PC" trivializes how important our language is to shaping the social world we inhabit.

One subtle way that we use language to define what is "normal" in a society is **spotlighting**—making mention of a person's background or social category in such a way that makes it seem relevant. Consider the following examples:

> *The two candidates are David Kwang, a successful businessman, and Phylis Hoffman, a former teacher and mother of three.*

Why does the writer think that it is significant that the female candidate is a parent? Does Mr. Kwang have children? The fact that only Ms. Hoffman's parenthood is mentioned here reinforces the notion that women's familial status is relevant to their political candidacy in a way different than for men. If the two candidates above are running for a position on the School Committee, the question of parenthood may be relevant, as it could be reasonable to want to know if they will have children in the school system. If they are running for the zoning commission, however,

When you are in a position to use language that makes mention of social difference, you may want to check whether there is a **style guide** available, prepared by members of that community to provide clarity about preferred linguistic conventions. For example, the National Center on Disability and Journalism (ncdj.org) has a helpful style guide for anyone speaking or writing about people with disabilities:

"When describing an individual, do not reference his or her disability unless it is clearly pertinent to a story. If it is pertinent, it is best to use language that refers to the person first and the disability second. For example: "The writer, who has a disability" as opposed to "The disabled writer." Disability and people who have disabilities are not monolithic. Avoid referring to "the disabled" in the same way that you would avoid referring to "the Asians," "the Jews," or "the African-Americans." Instead, consider using such terms as "the disability community," or "the disability activist." Also consider avoiding the following terms:

- **Afflicted with** (also see "stricken with," "suffers from," "victim of"): These terms carry the assumption that a person with a disability is suffering or living a reduced quality of life. Not every person with a disability "suffers," is a "victim" or is "stricken." It is preferable to use neutral language when describing a person who has a disability, simply stating the facts about the nature of the disability. For example, "He has muscular dystrophy."

- **Birth defect:** Avoid the term "defect" or "defective" when describing a disability because it indicates that the person is somehow incomplete or sub-par. It is preferable to use terms that simply state the facts about the nature of the disability when appropriate, such as: "congenital disability," "born with a disability," or "disability since birth."

- **Handicap, handicapped:** These words should be avoided in describing a person but are appropriate when citing laws, regulations, places or things, such as "handicapped parking."

- **Invalid:** Avoid using this word to describe a person with a disability. It implies that a person has no abilities and no sense of self, whereas this is rarely the case for the vast majority of persons with disabilities.

- **Special, or having Special needs:** Avoid using these terms when describing a person with a disability or the programs designed to serve them, with the exception of government references or formal names of organizations and programs. It is more accurate to use the term "specific," "specific accommodation" or "disability," depending on the context.

- **Wheelchair-bound:** Unless mentioning a wheelchair is essential to the story, leave it out. Avoid using "confined to a wheelchair" or "wheelchair-bound" as it implies a judgment. Similarly, avoid phrases such as "wheelchair-rider" and "vertically challenged." Non-users often associate wheelchairs with illness and aging and regard them with fear. Keep in mind that a wheelchair can be a source of freedom and independence and that people who use wheelchairs might otherwise be confined to their home or their bed. It is preferable to use "person who uses a wheelchair" or "wheelchair user."

Figure 3.4 Is there an "ism" in the offing here?

parenthood is likely irrelevant. In either case, if it is notable for one candidate, it is worth mentioning about the other.

The spry seventy-eight year old still walks a mile to the coffee shop every day.

The writer may be attempting to offer praise by using the word "spry," but the implication is that most people of that age are *not* spry. By treating this person as an exception, the writer implies that others of a similar age are not physically able. If the seventy-eight year old is running marathons as the only member of his age category, the accomplishment may be exceptional and his age worth noting. Otherwise, we are led to assume that walking to a coffee shop is an **anomaly**, or different from the norm, for someone of this age.

Every guy wants to marry a girl who reminds him of his mother.

Not every guy wants to marry a girl. Not everyone is heterosexual. Not everyone wants to get married. Whenever you are tempted to use the word "every" or some similar **generalizing** term, be careful that your statement truly includes *every* one.

The lady doctor finished the operation in record time.

Would the writer have said, "*The man doctor finished the operation in record time*"? Why would the doctor's gender have any bearing here? Like "male nurse" or "lady firefighter," spotlighting a person's gender in the context of their professional work makes gender seem relevant when it need not be.

In certain cases, however, distinctions might be appropriate, as in:

Ms. Borgson was the first female scholar ever admitted to the library of the cloistered monastery in its 700-year history.

In this instance, overcoming a 700-year tradition of banning women underpins the significance of this landmark moment.

In general, the best rule of thumb is to treat everyone with dignity and equality and to use common sense. The **"Golden Rule,"** treating others as you'd want to be treated, is certainly a crucial component of communicating well. When in doubt about the best words to use, it can be helpful to do research or to ask. Just as you may inquire of someone, "How do you prefer to be called?," it can be very reasonable to ask people about what particular words and labels mean to them. The person you casually call "African-American" may actually be Caribbean; the person you term "Native American" may prefer to be called "American Indian." Remembering that communication is a multi-dimensional experience, not just a one-way street, having conversations about what these complex symbols we know as words really "mean" to us can be extremely fruitful.

Figurative Language

Whether speaking or writing, your language should be vivid, lively, and descriptive. Remembering Hayakawa's Ladder of Abstraction, the better you can evoke specific mental images in people's minds, the more clear and memorable your speech will be. There are many effective ways to use **figurative language**, rhetorical devices that achieve special effects by using language in particular ways. Here are just a few:

- **Simile**: comparing one thing to another using "like" or "as." "She ran like lightning!" is much more interesting than, "She ran very fast."

- **Metaphor**: whereas a simile compares one thing to another, a metaphor transforms one thing into another, as in " Mike is a rock on the offensive line." A rock is solid, immovable—a strong image for an offensive lineman. The metaphor tends to be a more forceful tool than the simile.

- **Personification**: applying human attributes or thoughts to animals, plants, or inanimate objects. "My dog keeps telling me she wants to go outside" or "The mountains cried out in protest of the devastation" would be examples.

- **Hyperbole**: exaggerating to heighten emphasis or impact, as in "Ben is the cruelest person in the whole wide world." The speaker may not have actually polled everyone on the planet to determine who is cruelest, but the speaker's feelings of disgust for Ben's cruelty are made quite clear.

- **Understatement**: deliberately making a situation seem less serious or severe. Saying, "It would be a bummer if your head got cut off" to warn someone about a low doorway may be a humorous way to downplay the threat. Do not confuse understatement with **euphemism**, substituting a more socially-acceptable term for something awkward or difficult. Saying someone "passed away" is a euphemism, not an understatement.

- **Paradox**: a statement that appears to contradict itself. "No one goes to that restaurant because it's too crowded" or Oscar Wilde's quip, "I can resist anything except temptation" are interesting because of the perspective-shifting clarity they offer. An **oxymoron** is a particularly compressed version of a paradox, such as "jumbo shrimp," "random order," or "definite maybe."

When using figurative language, be careful to avoid **clichés**. A cliché is an overused expression. Saying that a runner went like lightning or that an offensive lineman is a rock are both clichés; you may have heard them and read them a thousand times, which lessens their impact. Be inventive. Make your writing your own; don't just recycle other peoples' images.

Sound Devices

Language has different purposes and we use different linguistic structures for these different purposes. The words that we use for one purpose are often not very useful for another. This is especially true in terms of the difference between writing something meant to be read and constructing something meant to be spoken. Have you ever looked online to find out the lyrics of some song you liked? Chances are that you found the lyrics on the page far less powerful than when you heard them as part of the song. Of course, the music is missing, but something else is missing—the sound of the words in your ear. Take a look at the first stanza of Edgar Allan Poe's, *The Bells*:

> *Hear the sledges with the bells-*
> *Silver bells!*
> *What a world of merriment*
> *their melody foretells!*
> *How they tinkle, tinkle, tinkle,*
> *In the icy air of night!*
> *While the stars that oversprinkle*
> *All the heavens, seem to twinkle*
> *With a crystalline delight;*
> *Keeping time, time, time,*
> *In a sort of Runic rhyme,*
> *To the tintinnabulation that so*
> *musically wells*
> *From the bells, bells, bells, bells,*
> *Bells, bells, bells-*
> *From the jingling and the tinkling of the bells.*

Read the poem both in your mind and aloud. Is the experience of hearing the words different from seeing them on the page? Poe chose the words above for how they *sound*, not how they *look*. If you were writing a paper for astronomy class, you would probably not say that the stars

Figure 3.5 Mike 'The Rock'

"oversprinkle" all the heavens. "Oversprinkle" is a word that Poe invented because he needed that sound to rhyme with tinkle and twinkle. You understand what he means when you read the poem, but you need to hear it in your ear to know why he had to have that sound. Being creative with rhyme and meter (rhythm or cadence of the language), Poe uses linguistic rhythm to great effect.

Along with rhyme and meter, there several specific linguistic devices that deal particularly with the way things sound, such as:

- **Onomatopoeia**: An onomatopoeic word is a word that sounds like what it means: plunk, bash, squish, vroom, buzz. When you hear or see "*squish,*" you can almost feel something being squished at that moment. Onomatopoeic words are useful on the page or spoken aloud, but can be particularly effective in spoken communication.

- **Alliteration**: repeating the same initial sound in at least two words, as in "slithered through seething slime." The repeated S sound conveys a certain feeling when repeated, particularly in association with a snake.

- **Assonance**: repeating the same vowel sound in multiple words, as in "lying blithely on their sides."

- **Consonance**: repeating the same consonant sound within multiple words, as in "the murmuring river purred as it poured over rocks and rills."

- **Repetition**: There are many ways to repeat words or phrases that add emphasis or structure to your speech. Martin Luther King Jr.'s famous "I Have a Dream" speech provides a perfect example of how repeating the same phrase at the beginning of each point can not only cue listeners to the structure of your argument, but add energy and emphasis as well.

"And this will be the day—this will be the day when all of God's children will be able to sing with new meaning:

My country 'tis of thee, sweet land of liberty, of thee I sing. Land where my fathers died, land of the Pilgrim's pride, From every mountainside, let freedom ring!

And if America is to be a great nation, this must become true.

And so let freedom ring from the prodigious hilltops of New Hampshire.

Let freedom ring from the mighty mountains of New York.

Let freedom ring from the heightening Alleghenies of Pennsylvania.

Let freedom ring from the snow-capped Rockies of Colorado.

Let freedom ring from the curvaceous slopes of California.

But not only that:

Let freedom ring from Stone Mountain of Georgia.

Let freedom ring from Lookout Mountain of Tennessee.

Let freedom ring from every hill and molehill of Mississippi.

From every mountainside, let freedom ring.

And when this happens, when we allow freedom ring, when we let it ring from every village and every hamlet, from every state and every city, we will be able to speed up that day when all of God's children, black men and white men, Jews and Gentiles, Protestants and Catholics, will be able to join hands and sing in the words of the old Negro spiritual:

Free at last! Free at last! Thank God Almighty, we are free at last!"

(The Rev. Dr. Martin Luther King, Jr., "I Have a Dream" speech, delivered August 28th, 1963 at the Lincoln Memorial, Washington DC.)

When you are composing words to be said or sung, think about how the words sound, not just what they mean. Say them aloud to yourself. Understand that your audience will not only see or hear the words, but also experience them throughout their bodies as vibration that will carry its own impact. Realizing that your words convey meaning on multiple levels—from the socially-constructed history of their usage to the way the sound resonates in the present moment—can be useful in ensuring that your speech has the maximum impact.

Targeting Your Audience

Remember that the fundamental rule of all effective communication is to know your source and to know your audience. Think about the person or persons for whom your writing is intended, your **target audience**. Most of us do this unconsciously—we speak differently with our friends than we do around a teacher or an employer; our writing in a paper for a class is much more formal than a text to a family member or friend. Get to know as much as you can about your target audience. What kinds of words and sentence structures will be effective in communicating to that person or that group of people? What are *they* interested in?

For example, when writing to a prospective employer about a job, ask yourself what the employer wants. She wants to know that her company will get their money's worth for the salary that they will pay you. Many people will write in about how much they want the job, how it would be good for the *applicant* to get this position, but the applicant who can convince the employer that hiring him is good for the *company* is going to the head of the line. Crafting your writing to strike home with your target will greatly increase its effectiveness.

Every time you start to write, ask yourself to whom you are writing. What is that person interested in? What is important to him or her? What does that group have in common? What is significant to them collectively? Your words will be much more effective if focused on your reader. Applying **strategic flexibility** is crucial to appropriately selecting different skills and devices for different situations.

Words matter. Each word you choose matters and the way that you arrange them together matters even more. The most elegant and sophisticated thought in your head is useless if you are not able to communicate it effectively. Clear writing or speaking begins with clear thinking. What is it that you want to get across? Take the time before you begin to write to make sure that you have a clear sense of exactly what you want to say. Then ask yourself, what are the best words to truly convey your meaning?

References

Carroll, J. B. (1956.) *Language, thought, and reality: Selected writings of Benjamin Lee Whorf.* Published jointly by Technology Press of MIT, John Wiley and Sons, Inc., Chapman and Hall, Ltd.

Deshmukh, V.D., & Meyer, J.S. (1978). *Noninvasive measurement of regional cerebral blood flow in man.* New York: SP Medical & Scientific Books.

Hayakawa, S.I. (1939). *Language in thought and action.* Expanded edition, 1978. San Diego: Harcourt Brace Jovanovich. (Originally published as *Language in Action.*)

Lakoff, G., & Johnson, M. (1980). *Metaphors we live by.* Chicago: University of Chicago Press.

Chapter Four
Nonverbal Communication

"What you do speaks so loudly that I cannot hear what you say."

—Ralph Waldo Emerson

Words can be powerfully efficient symbols for communication, but think about it—the vast majority of our experience of the world takes place nonverbally. Through sight, sound, smell, taste, feeling, and other forms of perception, we are constantly receiving and sending far more messages than words could ever convey. "A picture is worth a thousand words," the old adage goes, and if you include the whole realm of sense experience, it is clear that nonverbal communication is often the greatest untapped dimension in learning to communicate well. Reviewing our Axioms of Communication, you'll remember that the nonverbal channel is referred to as "analog" because it carries meaning perpetually, and nonverbal behavior can communicate both content and relational meaning. Reflect on the last time you did some people-watching at a local mall, festival, or party—how many layers of meaning were being sent nonverbally?

When you were researching colleges, chances are you first looked at them online. You saw the beautiful pictures of the campus and the smiling students having fun. These images may have been the first impression you had of the college. When you visited the campus, did those images come alive? When you watch a sporting event on television, do you have the same experience as attending the event? Chances are, your college visit was a much different experience from your online college tour, and your attendance at a sports stadium was different from watching on television, because you were able to encounter many aspects of nonverbal communication that go beyond visual images. On television and online, you missed the smell, the noise, the music, and the overall energy of being somewhere in person. In this chapter, we will examine the many functions and mechanisms of nonverbal communication from which we make meaning on a nearly constant basis.

Nonverbal communication is communication other than written or spoken language that creates meaning (Beebe, Beebe, & Ivy, 2007). Nonverbal communication is often believed to be more credible than verbal communication, perhaps because it is a primary source for conveying and identifying emotions. If someone says, "I love you" with gentle, open eyes, this conveys a mighty different message than saying it through clenched teeth, no? Can you think of other ways that nonverbal behavior can communicate alternate meanings to what is being said verbally?

According to Albert Mehrabian (1972), up to 93% of the emotional meaning of our messages comes

Figure 4.1 A Verbal/Non-Verbal 'Disconnect'

across nonverbally, with as little as 7% of our emotional meaning communicated through explicit verbal channels. Nonverbal communication has several functions that add meaning to our verbal communication. They are: to substitute, to complement or contradict, to repeat, to regulate, or to adapt meaning from the verbal stream of communication. Many nonverbals have meanings that are culturally bound, whereas others are universal. For example, a smile sends a positive message no matter where you travel around the world. All of us consciously and subconsciously use these functions in our daily interactions, especially when expressing emotions. During a conversation with friends, you may intentionally give direct eye contact and a serious facial expression to a specific friend. This may be *substituting* verbal communication to let your friend know that you want them to stop talking about a topic or to signal you want to leave. Your friend assigns some kind of meaning to your nonverbal and may ask, "Are you okay?" Your response may be to say "I'm fine!" in a tone that doesn't match what they are seeing as an emotion. The way you answer and the body language you display may

complement or *contradict* the words, "I'm fine!"

Another function of nonverbal behavior is to *repeat* our intended meaning. For example, your friend may sense from your body language and vocal tone that you are 'not okay' and may say, "let's go to another place" and wave a hand to come forward. The hand waving is repeating the same meaning as the verbal message. If you are with a group of friends, it may be difficult to leave without causing extra attention. In this instance, your body language will help to *regulate* your conversation. You may start to decrease your eye contact with friends and may start to stand up or start to turn away from the conversation. In this instance, you are *regulating* your message as you are disengaging and moving on.

Finally, we often use *adaptors* as a function of nonverbal communication. Your friend may have noticed by your body language that you are impatient or upset by the way you tap a pen, bite your nails, or fidget in your seat. These are ways we are *adapting* to particular situations. All of these nonverbal functions are used as part of our overall communication, and although we often use them without even noticing, becoming more aware of how we use and interpret nonverbal behaviors can be an important part of improving our effectiveness as communicators.

We will examine eight categories of nonverbal communication: *appearance/artifacts*, *kinesics* (body language, which includes facial expressions), *proxemics* (the study of space and territory), *haptics*

(the study of touch), *chronemics* (the study of how we use time), *paralanguage* (the study of vocal elements), *environment* (the study of our surroundings), and *olfactics* (the study of smell). Although we will learn about each independently, keep in mind it is the simultaneous exchange and overlap of many of the categories that contribute to conveying our overall nonverbal messages.

Appearance and Artifacts

Your appearance comprises the many visual elements through which you present yourself. Appearance is a contributing factor of someone's first impression of you. Remember the old adage, "You never have a second chance to make a first impression." We use our appearance to express who we are, and oftentimes, groups of people may be labeled by their appearance, which can lead to stereotyping. Managing our appearance to convey specific messages is referred to as **impression management**.

Your appearance may include the clothing and shoes you wear and the way you have your hair cut and/or colored. Appearance can convey a whole host of images and give us clues as to people's ethnicity, religion, or profession. What do you think of when you see someone in a military uniform, a business suit, a burqa, or hospital scrubs? What kinds of assumptions do you make? Regardless of our profession, the clothing or other accessories we select will undoubtedly project an image. Some choose body art and piercings, and although the meaning of tattoos or body art has changed over the last several decades, many businesses have rules or guidelines regarding the location and types of tattoos allowed in the workplace. Over time, the meaning we assign to various fashions or elements of appearance can shift dramatically—think of the powdered wigs and frilly clothing popular in the 18th century, or the various fashions that have come and gone just in the past 100 years. Consider how the social meaning of hair—body hair, long or short hair, facial hair—can also carry powerful cultural messages. What do you think causes the social meaning we attach to appearance to shift over time?

Artifacts are objects that convey messages about us—anything from accessories like watches, bags, eyeglasses, or earrings, to possessions like cars or property. When getting ready to go to a job interview or preparing to attend a party, how do you decide what you want to look like? Do you prepare in the same way for both events? What are some factors that play into your decisions? All of these areas contribute to the overall 'impression' you are trying to convey

Figure 4.2 Artifactual Communication

to others about yourself. Consider also how we use virtual "artifacts" to give meaning to our online presence via social networking profiles, avatars, etc. Artifacts can be tangible objects, images, or even abstract designs that we use to express our identity and convey messages to others about our values. Notice the artifacts you and your friends use. Like the music in a shopping center, or the hum of a fan or refrigerator at home, they can become the "ground" of experience, the backdrop that we become accustomed to and barely notice. But if you make artifacts the "figure" for a moment and analyze their meaning, what do the artifacts you see around you "mean" in how you perceive others? Driving an expensive car or wearing an expensive watch may convey a sense of accomplishment or it may convey a message of greed. The meaning we make from artifacts in our social world is something we are taught by our environment and the process of social construction around us.

Kinesics

Kinesics refers to the interpretation of body language or movement. Stemming from the root word "kinetic," or relating to motion, the study of kinesics examines body posture, gestures, facial expressions, and the overall way we use our bodies to convey meaning. For instance, your body posture in a classroom conveys a steady stream of messages to your professor and those around you. By sitting up, leaning forward, and providing

head nods, you are conveying that you are paying attention and processing the content of the class. If you are sitting in the back row, leaning back on a chair, with your head looking down, you may be sending the message that you are bored, uninterested, or that you are attending to something other than the class.

Posture and **stance** can also play an important role in displaying our attitude and our confidence. When you are about to give a speech, walking to the podium confidently will convey a message that you are prepared and ready. This will add to the acceptance and believability of your message. If you walk to the podium timidly with your head down and act as if you don't care about your speech, it will convey a message that you didn't prepare, you are about to waste the class's time, and students may be less likely to accept or like your presentation.

Hand gestures are also very important. Think about how gestures are used when we discussed the functions of nonverbal communication. We use our hands and arms to send messages that *substitute, complement/contradict, repeat, regulate* and *adapt* our messages. Although you may be sending certain messages by your body language, they may not be interpreted as you intend. Body language may convey powerful messages, so be aware that what you consider to be obvious may come across very differently to someone socialized differently. When travelling to different countries, be sure to have a general understanding of non-verbal gestures within various cultural contexts.

Facial expressions are a particularly important aspect of kinesics, in that they are one of the most trusted indicators of our internal state, and the only aspect of nonverbal behavior that can reliably be interpreted the same way across cultures. Experts in the field of facial expressions, such as psychologist Paul Ekman (2009), have found that emotions such as sadness, anger, disgust, contempt, fear, surprise, and happiness have proved to be emotions that we are born with innately, and thus can be identified across cultures, even among those who are blind and have no way of learning facial expressions visually. We may, however, depending on our conditioning, learn to "mask" or try to hide our emotions by controlling what shows up on our faces. For example, if you are trying to politely smile to show you are interested in a conversation, experts who study "micro-expressions" could tell whether it is a fake smile or a genuine smile just by looking at the symmetry of the different areas of your face. Experts such as law enforcement officials who are trained in studying facial expressions may be able to identify 'trigger' movements by watching the way someone uses their eye contact, moves an eyebrow, or moves the muscles around the mouth; deviations may lead to further investigation or questioning.

Chronemics

Chronemics is the study of how we use time to communicate. Particularly today, with synchronous communication more than ever, like the music in a shopping center, or the hum of a fan or refrigerator at home,

they become the background of experience. The way we use time can convey powerful nonverbal meaning. Think of how it feels when someone gets back to you right away after you leave an important message. When you are watching a public program, can you tell by the order of presenters and the amount of time allotted to them, which are considered to be the most important? Monitoring our own chronemics can give us a deeper understanding of our internal values and processes. Are you someone who is always early for classes and events, or do you run late, regularly keeping people waiting? Are you more productive in the mornings or at night? The use of time is also culturally bound. In Western culture, you may be familiar with the term "fashionably late," which means that being a half hour or more late for a social event, may be acceptable or even desirable. However, in other countries, being a half hour late may still be two hours too early! In Western culture, being on time reflects a great deal about a person. Being early to an interview and to business meetings is generally considered professional and can add to one's credibility, as can using time efficiently during meetings and phone conversations.

The modes of synchronous communication available today have added another component to the use of time—immediacy. By texting a friend, we may be expecting an 'immediate' response that allows for very quick answers to questions or responses to conversations. A 'slow' response time may, intentionally or unintentionally, send a nonverbal message to the sender about our lack of

care. When we do not receive an immediate response, we may get impatient because we assume that the recipient is ignoring our messages. Some people may then get impulsive and feel the need to constantly send more text messages until they get an immediate response, as the societal expectation of texting is 'quick response.' Conversely, email, which may be referred to as the new 'snail mail' has a different acceptance level of timed response. A professor will generally respond to a student within 24 hours of receiving an email. This duration of time is accepted as reasonable given the channel of communication, and the context of communication between the sender and recipient. Understanding and managing time effectively can be valuable tools, both personally and professionally.

Proxemics

Proxemics refers to how we use and inhabit the space around us. Think about how we use space and how we 'mark our territory.' When you go to the college dining hall or when you go to your class, you probably sit in the same location that, over time, can be considered 'your territory'. If you are in the library and you want to reserve a table, you place a backpack or some other object to 'save your place.' Others viewing this will most likely not sit in that spot. These are unspoken rules of nonverbal communication and how they can convey messages to others. The next time you are in the library, sit at a table with other people. Watch their reaction. Oftentimes they will be perplexed why you were sitting there, feeling

Figure 4.3 Too close for comfort

that 'you invaded their space.' Try changing your seat every time you come to class—this can also help you to meet new people. Remember the axiom, "You cannot *not* communicate." Your nonverbals regarding your use of personal and public space are constantly sending messages.

Edwin Hall (1966), in his book *The Hidden Dimension,* describes four layers of space that we inhabit. First, **intimate space** is usually the space about 18 inches around your body, particularly your upper body. This is, of course, the space where touch is most likely to happen—touch that could be pleasurable, painful, or even dangerous. Thus, we typically reserve this space for people we trust, like close friends, family members, or people with whom we're open to deep personal interaction. Intentionally entering this space without permission, especially in the workplace, is usually unacceptable and can lead to discomfort and possibly some level of sanction. However, there are times where it is not possible to avoid being in intimate range with others, such as riding on a crowded train or being on a full elevator. In these cases, we tend to increase the "sense" of interpersonal distance by positioning our bodies indirectly and possibly avoiding eye contact.

The next layer of space around us is our **personal space**, which is between 18 inches and around four feet, or about an arm's length away. This is generally accepted space among friends and coworkers that allows for personal contact without 'invading' intimate space. One's personal space is actually rather subjective, in that there is wide variation in the range of personal space we need, based on our personal and cultural upbringing. Some people are comfortable in very close proximity with others, even strangers, whereas other people, particularly those who have ever been subject to emotional or physical violation, may feel the need for a wider, firmer ring of personal space. Communicating well means being clear about your own preferred level of personal space, and also being able to notice and respect that of others.

The third level of space is **social space**. This is generally 4 to 12 feet around you, and is usually the accepted space between people at work or at social functions, our "social territory" at which voices can be heard comfortably without entering personal space. When we enter this 12-foot range of someone, whether at a gathering or on the street, it is typically polite to greet them in some way, even with simple eye contact. Think of how it feels to pass someone you know in a hallway within this range—if there is no greeting, visual or otherwise, one or both parties may feel ignored or slighted. Learning how to engage people appropriately at social distance, whether with a glance, a smile, or a well-placed comment, can be a hallmark of people considered friendly. Like the music in a shopping center, or the hum of a fan or refrigerator at home, they became the background of experience to be friendly or skillful communicators.

The broadest level of space is **public space,** which is generally everything outside of about 12 feet, or situations in which we are communicating in a "public" way. The dynamics of what feels public can vary widely depending on the space you are in. For example, 12 feet can feel very different in a large space or outdoors, as opposed to in a smaller room or in a home. We can most easily judge public distance as the distance at which you use your **"public voice."** (Try speaking to someone near you, and then to someone farther away, and note the difference in your voice.) Whenever we address a number of people together, particularly in a more formal way, we can be said to be in public space. This difference in voice can be felt on the airwaves, as well—think of the difference between the vocal quality of an announcer using a public, personal, or intimate voice. Which programs or contexts are most suitable for these different modes of communication? Which levels of space tend to be the most naturally comfortable for you, and which tend to stretch your comfort zone?

It is important to recognize that the use of proxemics is not universal. Every culture has different rules for communicating meaning through space and distance. What matters most is to be sensitive to how identity, power, and affiliation are communicated through our use of proxemics. Like other mammals, we tend to view "territory" as power. How is space allocated in a home or office? Who gets the biggest room? Who gets easiest access to doors, windows, and running water? Who is given private space, and who is expected to communicate with whom on a regular basis? How do the spaces and furnishings invite or inhibit different kinds of communication? If you look through a place where people work, you'll usually see many subtle but important messages about how privacy, privilege, and power are allocated. What territory can one consider "their own," and what rights and privileges do they have in that space?

Haptics

Haptics is the study of touch. Touch is an important component of our nonverbal communication that begins from birth and conveys powerful messages about our affiliation and safety. Holding a baby provides comfort and warmth, petting a dog or cat shows affection, greeting someone by shaking hands or offering a hug

Figure 4.4 From High+Low-Contact Cultures?

conveys a welcoming impression. The use of touch is also bound by culture. As you travel around the world, you'll notice that there are **high-contact** or **low-contact cultures** (you'll know the high-contact cultures by the hugging, kissing, hand-holding, or back-slapping). **High-contact cultures** may find it polite to greet others, even strangers, with a hug and kiss(es), while in **low-contact cultures**, this type of greeting may seem invasive. For yourself, think of when the following might be appropriate, and when they might be very inappropriate: a kiss, a punch, a slap on the back, sitting on someone's lap, massaging someone's shoulders. We define and re-define appropriate uses of touch as we interact through the ins and outs of daily life, as we do with all nonverbal behaviors.

Richard Heslin's (1974) five categories of touch help to define the roles of touch in Western culture. The first category is **functional/professional** touch. This type of touch would be having someone cut your hair, greet you with a handshake, or a health care professional touching you to perform a medical exam. The second level is **social/polite** touch. Depending upon the culture, these would be acceptable uses of touching someone to show them through a doorway, or hugging to say hello or goodbye. They are short exchanges and are not intended to convey any intimate meaning. The third category is **friendship/warmth**. Usually this category is used among close friends. It may be

sitting close to friends on a sofa, hugging to provide comfort, or patting someone on the back. The fourth category is **love/intimacy**, which is touch that conveys strong emotion and is part of loving personal or family relationships. The final category is **sexual arousal,** which generally involves people in an intimate relationship and targets sexual areas. The love/intimacy and sexual arousal categories can often overlap. How easy do you find it to communicate with others about what behaviors you find appropriate in these categories?

Like other aspects of nonverbal communication, our sense of touch conveys tremendous amounts of information to us, much of it often unconscious. For example, research at the Massachusetts Institute of Technology has shown that people's negotiating behavior, such as bargaining for a car, can be made "harder" by seating them in hard chairs. Half the participants were seated in hard wooden seats during the bargaining sessions, while the other half were given soft cushioned chairs. Those on hard chairs were less flexible in their negotiations and, without exception, offered less money—on average, $347 less—to purchase the car. The conclusion was that hard surfaces make people "harder" in their negotiations because the physical sensation of hardness triggers concepts of stability, which the unconscious brain translates into a more confident bargaining position (Mercer, 2012).

Although centered around the importance and meaning of human touch in society, the field of haptics is growing in new directions due to advancements in technology—touch screens on mobile devices, tactile experience via virtual reality, remote examinations and surgery through telemedicine, the proliferation of holistic health modalities like massage, chiropractic care, reiki, etc. So much can be communicated through skin-to-skin contact, and now that a large portion of our intimate communication is available through mediated channels, haptics has become a particularly rich field of study, both philosophically and technologically. Can you remember any instances when issues around touch became important for you?

Paralanguage

Paralanguage comprises the many ways we add emphasis or meaning to our language. You may have heard the expression, "It is not what you say, but the way that you say it!" This is a very apt statement as it relates to nonverbally conveying emotions and feelings. The prefix "para-" stems from the Greek prefix for "beside, next to, near, or from," and relates to the even more ancient Sanskrit word for "beyond." Paralanguage refers to those aspects of communication that fall alongside or beyond language to give our utterances a particular packaging or emotional impact. Paralanguage often focuses on the way you use your voice, and in this context can also be referred to as **vocalics**. However, in this age of text-based mediated communication that often lacks these vocal elements, we can still add paralanguage back into our messages through **emoticons** (little faces we add into our text using punctuation marks), **acronyms** such as "LOL" (laughing

out loud), or using capitalization, color, or alternate fonts to indicate emphasis. Paralanguage is an area of nonverbal communication that may often be taken for granted, but with understanding and practice, it can be an important part of a communication repertoire that can serve us extremely well in personal and professional relationships.

Voice, like music, has a number of facets that make it powerful: tone, rate, volume, pace, emphasis, articulation, and pitch (Bell & Smith, 2004, p. 39). When you listen to music, pay attention to each of these elements, one by one. You will notice that different notes are very quick and others are drawn out; sometimes the melody will go very loud and fast and at other times, it will slow down and get softer. Think of these things when you use your voice in conversation and when giving presentations. There are many aspects of paralanguage that you can develop and expand greatly. By recording your voice, you can take an inventory of how you use your voice and can learn to incorporate the following areas of paralanguage.

Your **tone** of voice has to do with the overall quality of meaning you communicate through the sound of your voice. It could have to do with the accent, lilt, or meaning infused in your words. This depends very much on context, which determines how your voice is subjectively perceived by listeners who interpret meaning from your tone.

The **rate** or **pace** of your speech is how fast or slowly you utter your message. Sometimes, people will speak very rapidly when they are nervous. Be aware and be in control of the speed of

your speech. Try to vary the rate. If you are saying something exciting and engaging, then your voice should speed up. Conversely, if you are making specific important points, then you could punctuate each word very deliberately and incorporate pauses (or **strategic silence**) to enhance the impact. Controlling and implementing pauses will slow down your delivery, and will also allow you to breathe and will diminish any vocalized pauses or **vocal fillers** like "um's" and "ah's." The rate of your speech can also keep your audience engaged because you are demonstrating your commitment to every word that you say, which in turn will add to the commitment from your audience. If you give a presentation and just try to fly through it, to "get it over with," your audience will have the same impression and may not take your message seriously. Rate is one of the easiest areas of paralanguage that you can practice and control.

Volume is the loudness or softness of your voice, like the volume dial on a stereo. It can be linked with rate to make very expressive and engaging conversation. Your normal volume should be at a place where your receivers do not have to strain to hear you. When speaking, publicly or privately, you need to be aware of your surroundings and make judgments on your volume level. For example, if you are in a public space (more than twelve feet away from people), you need to increase your volume to be comfortably heard. Your volume can also convey emotion. Screaming and yelling at someone often has an adverse affect on your message (verbal aggression). Keeping your voice calm and collected will add more to the impact of your message and to your credibility.

Emphasis is how you emphasize words. Words should sound like they mean. By raising and lowering your vocal range and adding 'feeling' to your words, vocal expression can have an incredible impact on your message. You can also use **verbal interjections** like "wow," "hey," and "boom" appropriately to add sparkle and interest so that your words don't take on a flat, monotonic quality. For example, when reading a children's book to a young child, you naturally change your voice to represent many of the characters in the book. When giving a presentation, use this story-telling technique to add expression and emphasis to your message. It will convey an energy and emotion that can make an impact on your audience.

Articulation has to do with how crisp or fuzzy our sounds are. Sometimes we want to emphasize. each. word. precisely. Other times we may get more impact by slurring our speech or sounding breathy. If we really want to emphasize a word or sentence, we can insert a **strategic silence**—pausing for a few seconds to let the words really carry through the room and sink in. Try it—audiences exposed to the blah-blah-blah of constant talking tend to perk up and take note (or even start clapping) when a perfectly-timed silence hits the room. As American performer Will Rogers said, "Never miss a good chance to shut up."

Pitch has to do with the vibrational wavelength of sound—how high or low our voice is. Think of the effect of hearing a high-pitched voice and a low-pitched voice. Most humans, when they talk to babies, use a higher-pitched

Figure 4.5 Olfactics: Powerful Signals

voice, which is very adaptive, because babies' smaller eardrums hear higher pitches more easily. Which sounds sweeter, more authoritative, more appealing to you personally? For which contexts do you think a higher or lower pitched voice would be more appropriate? Can you vary your own voice to achieve these effects under different circumstances?

Try experimenting with new and different paralanguage and try increasing your strategic flexibility. **Vocal variety** is a key element to communicating well. Without variety, our speech turns into "white noise," like a refrigerator hum or background noise that we no longer notice. Humans tend to notice contrast and texture, so expanding the "toolkit" of vocal effects you can achieve will set you apart as an outstanding communicator.

Environment

All of our surroundings comprise our **environment**. The colors, textures, smells, lighting, furnishings, sounds, and artifacts that surround us have a powerful impact on how we feel internally, as well as on how we communicate. Think of how you may feel and act differently at a shopping mall, at a library, at a sporting event, at a place of worship, or at a party. What are the environmental elements that cue us as to how we might most appropriately act and communicate in these spaces? What physical surroundings invite different types of communication, and what surroundings inhibit us from communicating? Savvy businesses and organizations know that, to be successful, they must spend as much time and energy on their environment—the space itself, the acoustics, the air quality, the visual surroundings—as the products or services they offer. So too, must we view environment as an important aspect of nonverbal communication and actively engage with selecting and sometimes modifying the spaces in which we communicate.

Likewise, all of us convey messages about ourselves by creating our own personal environments. When you decorate your room, residence hall, or apartment, for example, you create a particular energy for that particular space. You make personal choices on the 'feeling' you want your room to convey by deciding how the furniture is arranged and by choosing specific color combinations, lighting, music or sound, etc. Our identity can be communicated clearly through the décor and furnishings we provide (or don't provide—remember, "You cannot not communicate"). Even aspects of our space that we seem to have no control over (the noise of traffic outside, or the ventilation system, or the neighbors) can impact how we communicate, so it pays to choose and/or modify our physical surroundings mindfully as an important component of our communicative life.

Olfactics

One of the most subtle and overlooked areas of our nonverbal communication is **olfactics**, or the study of smell. In the animal kingdom, smell can be a fundamental component of affiliation and mating, of finding sustenance and protection, and of social patterning in general. Likewise for humans, smell is an important component of our own personal interactions and plays a role in our choices and habits. Because smell is the sense most linked to our memory, even subtle smells can carry many messages and evoke feelings that we may or may not realize.

Think of how smell impacts your communication on a regular basis. What smells are you attracted to, and which do you avoid? Think of the different reactions evoked in you through the smells of hugging your grandparents, your romantic partner, or a new baby. When you are going out socially, do you use perfume or cologne to convey a message? Just the smell and touch of a close friend or relative can provide comfort that leads to greater openness.

Also, consider how businesses and organizations strategically use scent—for example, how real estate agents often bake cookies in a house before showing it to make the space feel more "homey," or how retail stores that sell baby products may scent their store with baby powder to evoke feelings of nurturance. In the Dutch city of Rotterdam, studies were conducted in prisons that showed that people's behavior can be unconsciously modified through odors—pumping an orange blossom scent into prison cells triggered calmness among inmates, who showed demonstrably less aggression, less vandalism, and a drop in the use of sedatives (Mercer, 2012). Conscious or unconscious, scent is powerfully linked to our emotional structure and can influence behavior in significant or substantial ways.

Scent can also be a powerful part of our personal identity, as in the scented body products we choose (do you notice differences by gender?), or the way we fragrance our personal spaces like our homes and cars. We also use scent and taste experiences to punctuate various occasions, seasons, or holidays. What do different scents evoke for you, positively or negatively? Are there any smells that you associate strongly with particular people, places, or occasions? How might these associations impact your behavior, consciously or subconsciously? The bottom line is that effective communicators use all senses—both the obvious and the subtle—to consciously make meaning and interact with our surroundings.

Using Nonverbal Communication

To communicate effectively, we need to hone our sense receptors—to open and pay attention to the messages we receive through our sense organs, including our skin. As our perception of our social and physical environment becomes broader and more attuned, we can find our communicative ability enhanced naturally. Because communication means sharing or communing, the vast majority of this "tuning" into our world is done on subtle, nonverbal levels. A good practice to attune ourselves to our environment is to take even a minute (or more) to focus completely, 100%, on the sense data we are receiving—scan our environment with the open, non-judging curiosity of a baby. Remove our headphones, look away from our screens, and really feel the space around us. A regular practice of this "sensory bath" can be crucial for effective communicators.

With the increased use of mediated communication in personal and business interactions, we become conditioned to tune out many important components of nonverbal communication—the sound, the feel, the scent, the extended view. As we've learned, up to 93% of the most crucial meaning of our communication can be conveyed nonverbally. When we use technology, we may gain immediacy and instant connection or gratification, but we come to pay far less attention to the broader range of sense data about our physical environment that our ancestors found crucial. What impact do you feel this shift plays on the direction of human society, and on your own interactions with the world? How can you as a communicator stay skillfully attuned to the whole spectrum of nonverbal communication?

References

Beebe, S.A., Beebe, S.J., & Ivy, D.K (2007). *Communication principles for a lifetime* (3rd ed.). Boston: Allyn & Bacon.

Bell, A.H., Smith, D.M. (2004). *Interviewing for success.* Upper Saddle River, NJ. Pearson Education, Inc.

Ekman, P. (2009). *Telling lies.* New York: W.W. Norton & Company.

Hall, E. (1966). *The hidden dimension.* Garden City, NY: Doubleday.

Heslin, R. (1974) *Steps toward a taxonomy of touching.* Paper presented at the Western Psychological Association Convention, Chicago, IL.

Mehrabian, A. (1982). *Nonverbal communication.* Chicago: Aldin-Atherton.

Mercer, J. (2012, May). Hidden persuaders. *Ode Magazine,* Retrieved from http://odewire.com/hiddenpersuaders?inf_contact_key=48afa4742c5233540341144b24a18f04d4a2aa9a2eef0ce98c77d439464db261.

Chapter Five
Listening and Interviewing

"Education is the ability to listen to almost anything without losing your temper or your self-confidence."

—Robert Frost

"**C**OME TOWARD MY VOICE..." These four words appeared in thick, bold capital letters on the cover of the Dec. 10, 2001 issue of *US News & World Report*. On Sept. 11, 2001, a few of the people who were suddenly trapped inside the crumbling walls of the Pentagon after it was attacked by terrorists were able follow this direction. As they inched their way towards the sound of the voice, they realized that careful listening was going to be the one and only way they could possibly survive. In situations such as this, effective listening can be a life-or-death skill. Indeed, there is no communication experience in which listening is not crucial.

Listening is defined as: "the process of receiving, constructing meaning from, and responding to spoken and/or nonverbal messages" (International Listening Association, 1994). The International Listening Association was formed to support the study, development and teaching of effective listening throughout the world. When we think of communication, we often focus almost entirely on the sending of messages and forget how crucial good listening is to effective communication. Because we are all simultaneously sender-receivers, keeping ourselves open to be able to receive and process the full range of messages being sent ramps up our ability to communicate appropriately in countless ways. Good listening is truly a hallmark of communicating well, yet we understand and practice so little of this essential skill.

Hearing Matters

Our hearing never stops, even after we go to sleep. Our brain selects signals we need, such as the wake-up tone on an alarm clock, from unwanted noise we don't need, like the sound of an air conditioner turning on and off. Tune into the sounds around you right now—what sounds can you hear around you that you were not actively listening to before turning your attention to them?

The delicate hairs in our inner ears are particularly easy to damage. Once they are damaged, the damage cannot be undone. Loud sounds damage these hairs, creating noise-induced hearing loss (NIHL) or perhaps **tinnitus**, a condition of constant ringing of the ears.

Many portable music players offer volume levels of 120 decibels, which is far more than human ears can handle for long periods of time. Some manufacturers offer sound limiting software. Hearing experts recommend these devices should only be played at 85 dbs. or less. Listening expert Julian Treasure warns that *any time* you hear music leaking out of someone's headphones, this person is doing damage to his or her hearing.

Pete Townsend, lead guitarist for *The Who*, now actively campaigns for raising awareness of the dangers of loud music among young musicians and fans. Townsend blames his hearing loss on years of headphone use during recording rather than on all the concerts he has done. According to Townsend, "Hearing loss is a terrible thing because it cannot be repaired. Music is a calling for life. You can write it when you're deaf, but you can't hear it or perform it" (as cited in Treasure, 2007, p. 58). Since hearing loss is something that cannot be reversed once it happens, it is wise to wear earplugs at concerts and in other noisy environments.

Hearing Versus Listening

Both "receiving" and "hearing" are terms for the first step in the listening process. This first step in the process is the one and only completely passive step, the only part that happens whether we exert effort or not. If what we hear is of interest to us, we then actively focus our attention to receive, construct meaning from what we hear, and respond. Listening requires continued intention, attention, and focus.

People with hearing difficulties must get through the experiences of daily life without the benefit of helpful sounds such

as doorbells or alarm clocks. Bonnie Poitras Tucker, who has been profoundly deaf since the time she was a toddler, explained, "I use my eyes when you use your ears. What you hear, I lip-read" (Tucker, 1995). Yet people who are deaf or hearing-impaired can still "listen" incredibly well, by tuning in with their eyes and other senses to a whole host of information, from people's body language to vibrations in a room. (There are indeed deaf dance parties where people dance to the vibrations of the music.) Listening well is a fully multi-sensory experience, not just something that happens with the ears.

The terms "hearing" and "listening" are often used interchangeably in conversations. Sometimes people use one of the terms but they really are talking about the other. Pay attention to their entire message to understand whether they are talking about hearing, listening, or the deeper step—motivated, active listening. The degree to which we attend and listen to something is more like a volume knob than an on/off switch. Listening comes with many degrees of depth.

Three-Step Model of Listening

Step 1: Hearing. Hearing is the first sense we develop. It happens as early as twelve weeks after conception, when we first hear the steady sound of the beating of our

Figure 5.1 Listening is a Continuum, a 'proportional process'

Copyright © Depositphotos/ molaruso.

mother's heart. We are able to hear the soothing tones of our parent's voices from the moment we take our first breath. If we have normal hearing, we hear the sounds around us whether we want to or not. According to Julian Treasure (2011), "We actually hear with our whole bodies. Ears happen to be our specialists, evolved to hear better than any other part of us, but all of us can hear: bones, tissue, organs—even our eyes hear" (p. 53).

Step 2: Listening. Attention bounces back and forth in this step between passive drifting of competing thoughts and conscious focus on the topic at hand. When we are listening passively, we might be following along with the speaker. Perhaps we are even able to repeat the words just spoken. However, complete understanding does not necessarily happen. Did we hear something different than the speaker said? Did we misinterpret the message? What if the speaker actually sent the wrong message by mistake but we didn't realize this? Any or all of these situations can cause misunderstanding to happen.

Is it easy to listen? Groundbreaking research by

Figure 5.2 Three Steps

Dr. Ralph Nichols as early as the 1940s on the listening skills of 7,000 college students found otherwise. These students listened to lecture material and were then tested on the accuracy of their recall. Their comprehension on listening to lecture information was only 50%. Several later studies by other researchers found actual accuracy of listening to lectures dropped to 25% within just eight hours if no notes were taken.

Note-taking systems such as the **Cornell method**, **outlining**, and **mapping** can boost your ability to accurately remember information. Not only do the notes themselves help to boost your recall later, but the process of note-taking itself, even if you never look at the notes again, can be a powerful tool to help you stay focused and listen carefully as you write and organize the information mentally. This helps you ask good questions when you find there are gaps in your notes. For great tips on improving your ability to listen well and remember information, go to www.listen.org, the website of the International Listening Association.

Step 3: Motivated Listening. Listening actively in an intentional, focused way allows us to get the most we can from the time, energy and effort we spend communicating. To engage in motivated listening, here are a few important tips to follow:

1. **Prepare** ahead of time. Reflect back to last time, if there was one. Get familiar with ideas & terms.

2. **Stay focused** and positive during the actual listening activity.

3. **Breathe** deeply, deliberately, and slowly if the speaker goes too fast or is hard to follow. Take notes as you can.

4. **Remember** that even on a good day, you only focus and pay attention for 5-20 seconds at a time. Recognize when you zone out, daydream, or worry. Catch yourself so you tune back into your job of listening.

5. **Realize** that important ideas are often given by the speaker in the first and last ten minutes of the session. If your mind is elsewhere, you can miss a lot.

6. **Review** and revise notes within eight hours. Summarize the best ideas. This will give you something to look over next time so that your listening can be even more effective.

Motivation Matters

Research by Janusik and Wolvin found that college students spend more than half their communication time listening (O'Hair & Wiemann, 2012). Listening to mediated communication channels (TV, phone, email, music and radio) was the category with the single largest amount of use. The channels of speaking, writing and reading followed, in decreasing order in terms of use. Think of your own patterns of listening—what do you listen to most often, and how actively? What kind of listening motivates you the most?

Personal interests and motivations affect the amount of energy and effort we put into our everyday listening encounters. Stop reading for a moment and think about your own habits as a listener. *Do you listen differently when you want to listen than when you have to listen?* If you are like most people, you probably answer "yes" to this question. Think back to a time when you really listened well and paid attention to every detail because the topic was one you really cared about a lot.

What if you were to put this same energy into an important class or required meeting you have to regularly attend? There are many different levels of energy we can invest, all of which can benefit us greatly to some degree:

1. **prereading** parts of the book or the minutes for the meeting ahead of time

2. **identifying** major terms and ideas

3. carefully and correctly **using key terms** of the particular content area

4. **researching** the issue or **following** important related stories in the news

5. **getting** active in organizations related to the course or meeting

6. **networking** to expand your contacts in areas of interest

Cognitive Ability and the One-Process Brain

The human ability to concentrate is a lot like working with a special computer. This computer only is able to have one window actively open at the forefront of our mind. Whenever something new occurs, the attention shifts to that new stimulus. In other words, the one large window gets taken over by the new thought. The previous thought is still on the desktop, but it has automatically been minimized.

This process happens countless times a day, every day, for everyone. The challenge of the **one-process brain** is that human beings can only focus fully on one thought at a time. Because listening is a process, interruptions can happen at any step along the way. As we've learned, **selective attention** is the sustained focus we give to something we value, such as comments made by a boss or peer that might affect us in some way. Our mind also has the instinct to pay **automatic attention** to anything that suddenly happens around us. For this reason, a car honking will temporarily attract our automatic attention. Selective attention and automatic attention compete with each other countless times throughout the day. Each time this happens, the mind switches from paying attention to one or the other. (Pearson, Nelson, Titsworth & Harlow, 2011).

Memory and Multi-tasking

Early research on listening focused on **short-term memory**, the limited capacity one has for remembering information immediately after perceiving it from hearing, seeing, touching, tasting, smelling or sensing it. The research revealed that our short-term memory is able to hold onto limited (seven, plus or minus two) items or chunks of information for up to half a minute without rehearsal. If the goal is to retain information in the short-term memory until it can be used, strategies such as **repeating things out loud**, **chunking information**, and **noticing logical patterns** can help. Because input and retrieval of information happen quickly, problems can occur if one is interrupted right in the middle of doing something (Brownell, 2013).

Long-term memory has infinite storage capacity, whether at the conscious or unconscious level. Locating information that has been stored in the long-term memory may take time and can require techniques to aid your memory recall. Who were you with? When did this happen? Long-term memory is a process, rather than a particular place in the brain. It functions by developing connections and integrating patterns in stimuli to which we are exposed over time. Memories can consist of the interrelation of many neurons (brain cells) in many locations of the brain. This complexity explains why you may sometimes experience frustration when you are trying to remember answers quickly. Like a computer, a brain may need time to retrieve information.

Modern research on the human brain (Janusik, 2011) shows that effective listening uses the **working memory** system within the brain. Our computer-like minds juggle multiple items simultaneously, but can only focus on one at a time. This memory system is involved whenever we are "trying to understand information, remember it, or use it to solve a problem. Working memory allows us to shift message content from and into long-term memory" (Janusik, as cited in Engleberg & Wynn, 2011, p. 69).

Welcome news or not, modern research such as that cited here seems to reveal that "**multi-tasking**" is a myth. We can only truly pay attention to one complex thing at a time. This is especially so when it comes to efforts at tracking two or more distinct linguistic streams. As much as it may seem as though we are attending to different things simultaneously, at the neural level of the brain, what is actually happening is rapid flipping between attending to one thing and then another. This is why performing any behavior that requires mental attention, such as texting, is such a terrible idea while driving.

Indeed, it seems that the term "pay attention" is not a random coincidence. Like time and money, attention is something that is finite, or limited. We must make choices about what we are going to "pay" our precious attention to, and when. Good decisions in these choices will pave the way for satisfying conversations and better relationships.

Take the Listening Self-Assessment in the appendix.

Schema and Metacognitive Awareness

One of the basic assumptions about how we take in and process information is that the human mind is finite and must make choices about its allocation of mental energy. "A person's ability to process information is limited. Processing messages requires mental resources, and people have only a limited (and perhaps fixed) pool of mental resources"(Lang, 2000). There are two main reasons why all messages may not be received completely thorough processing. First, the message recipient may choose to devote fewer resources to a task because of different priorities or other practical constraints. Second, the message may require more resources than the message recipient has available to give to the task. In either case, the recipient of the message is determining, perhaps quite subconsciously, the level of resources that will be devoted to processing the information at hand. Our brains are limited in the amount of data that can be handled at once, thus tradeoffs must be made in gaining the most benefit for the energy expended. One's mind will, therefore, tend to capitalize on patterns that help us quickly process the information we take in and appropriately tailor behavior to our situation (Turner, 1994). For example, we hear a fire alarm and begin to execute any evacuation procedures that are needed. These mental patterns are called **schemas**.

Schema is a term for the interrelated sets of things that you remember together in a lasting way. Turner (1994) described a schema as a packet of knowledge representing a pattern encountered (or expected) in the world, which can be either provided by another person or learned from experience. When we listen, we automatically experience schemas coming up for us—something that someone says may remind us of a thought or experience we want to share, and soon we are off on a tangent in our mind that distracts us from the current listening at hand. Unfortunately, this mental trip-taking limits our abilities to take in what is being said and integrate it into our active schema, which has potential to make it all the richer. Good listeners are able to let schema become active while listening without allowing the entire mental process to be derailed by inner chatter.

One major schema that we all have to some degree is **metacognitive awareness** of ourselves as learners. Metacognition goes beyond understanding the ways one learns best to include becoming aware of how one is doing something. Sometimes this metacognitive process can be constructive as it highlights *how* we are doing things, which can allow us to improve our efforts. However, metacognition can also become distracting if we are so caught up in our self-consciousness that we get stuck in an old story or schema and become unable to really listen to whatever is being said in the context we are in. When a student in class gets into a mental loop of "Why can't I understand this? I'm so dumb; I've always been dumb," it's easy to see how inner schema can quickly turn into a negative self-fulfilling prophecy.

Expressive and Receptive Language

Expressive language is the ability to use words well, to communicate expressively, when sending messages. Communicators with good expressive language skills are comfortable using a **thesaurus** to find the most vivid, suitable words possible to express experiences and emotions. This expressive use of language creates mental images in listeners' minds, making it easier to pay attention and follow what is being said.

Receptive language is the ability to effectively receive words. You can build your receptive language skills as you prepare for courses and meetings by identifying and looking up words to make sure you fully understand what things mean. You can also conduct a basic "**audience analysis**" by finding out more about the backgrounds and interests of the people involved in whatever situation you'll be in, which can help you understand their vocabulary and literally "speak their language." Taking time to "do your homework" and become familiar with the people and situations you'll be facing can give you a significant edge, both personally and professionally.

Language is one of the primary ways we have to learn from each other. Yet, despite our increasing exposure to media in every corner of our lives, it has been found that both our expressive and receptive vocabularies are shrinking. "The typical American six to fourteen year old of the 1950s had a vocabulary of 25,000 words; by the year 2000, this had shrunk to just 10,000 words" (Spretnak, as cited in Treasure, 2007, p. 91). Bucking this trend means truly paying attention to words and constantly expanding and deepening our understanding and appreciation of the words we choose to communicate meaning.

Semantic Reactions

Turn on any reality show and you will hear words that may produce strong semantic reactions for you in a very short time. **Semantic reactions** are strong positive or negative emotional responses to words. **Green-flag words** like "sale" may make you happy. Advertisers deliberately use them to get you to buy their products. **Red-flag words**, on the other hand, produce negative emotional reactions or semantic noise. It hurts when somebody deliberately puts you down. Learn what words or phrases are red-flag words for you and those with whom you interact. This way, you are prepared to stay balanced when they come at you. Also, try not to use these words on others or yourself.

It is impossible to entirely avoid red-flag language, however. Some students find that words like "quiz," "test," and "presentation" bring up red-flag reactions for them, yet avoiding these words is almost impossible. One way to cope with red-flag words is to imagine you are standing on a balcony, safely looking down at a stage below. Pretend to see yourself down on the stage, hearing the same words, but knowing you are putting distance between you and the emotional or physical reaction. To help you strengthen your defenses against negative people or ideas, deliberately spend more time around positive people and fill your mind consciously with thoughts that serve you

best. Choose to do more of the things you like. Realize that all the sensations you take in—sounds, sights, tastes, smells, feelings—are all food for your inner body and mind. If you are fully nourished and grounded, it's much easier to manage your energy and not become triggered by red flags.

Framing and Reframing

Think for a minute about a photograph or painting you've seen recently. If it is framed, is it framed in dark wood, clear plastic, or ornamented gold? How does this frame affect your perception of the image? Imagine reframing it in a frame of a completely different size, shape and material. The new frame can make the original picture look very different. The same thing is true about actual mental snapshots you have of yourself and others from different times in life.

Think of a person with a very negative self-concept, which we know has been formed through negative reflected appraisals and social comparisons making their way past the person's perceptual filters into their mental schema about themselves. How might the person reframe themselves in a way that could make their frame look very different? Think of a photo of a congested city or an old farmhouse—how might the way it is framed make it look depressing, or make it look artful and cool?

By deliberately reframing old negative pictures, you have a better starting point from which to begin each new experience with others. You can frame an interaction as a burden or as a fascinating window into another person's mind. Keep in mind the old saying that, "You can't step in the same river twice." The

river keeps changing, every moment. You keep changing, too. The other people in your life change, as well. Thus, we never encounter the same situation twice. "We learn and grow by listening to ourselves analytically and listening to others with an open mind, free of pre-judgments" (Diamond, 2007, p. 69).

Flow

Shafir (2003) says the concept of **flow** is used to describe the ability "to attend completely and joyfully to the task at hand" (p. 7). Think of the last time when time absolutely flew by, when you were truly focused and in a state of enjoyment and openness to the present moment. When we function in a state of flow, energy is high. Flow happens once your attention becomes highly focused, such as when you are really "into" doing something. Time seems to disappear, and you lose track of everything except for what you are doing. Buzz terms for this state of flow are: to be *in the moment, present, in the zone, on a roll, wired in, in the groove, on fire, in tune, centered,* or *singularly focused.* This is the state when deep listening happens at its finest.

The concept of "flow" is laid out in research by Hungarian-American scholar Mihaly Csikszentmihalyi (1975). He studied artists who would essentially get so lost in their work that they would disregard their need for food, water and even sleep for periods of time. Historical accounts show that Michelangelo may have painted the ceiling of the Vatican's Sistine Chapel while in a flow state. Martial arts master Bruce Lee also spoke of flow in his book the *Tao of Jeet Kune Do*

(1975). In his book, he compares the state of flow to water: "Be like water ... Empty your mind, be formless. Shapeless, like water. If you put water into a cup, it becomes the cup. You put water into a bottle and it becomes the bottle. You put it in a teapot, it becomes the teapot. Now, water can flow or it can crash. Be water, my friend."

In order to really drop into a space of deep connection and resonance with others, getting into this state of "flow" can be very helpful—it can not only help you to listen and understand better, but it can also make time spent together very enjoyable and even transformative. This is why learning to pay attention to one thing at a time—to truly shut down internal chatter and stay in the present moment—can be one of the most powerful skills we can hone as communicators. Imagine yourself like a satellite dish, completely open, receptive, and focused squarely on the object of your attention.

Certainly you can "listen" with your ears and your eyes, but also notice signals in your body that you receive from others. Most people tend to think of communication solely in terms of overt signals expressed through facial movements, vocal quality, gestures, and body movements. Yet scientific evidence now also shows that a subtle yet influential electromagnetic or "energetic" communication system operates just below our conscious level of awareness. "The smoothness or flow in any social interaction depends to a great extent on the establishment of a spontaneous entrainment or linkage between individuals. When people are engaged in deep conversation, they begin to fall into a subtle dance, synchronizing their movements and postures, vocal pitch, speaking rates, and length of pauses between responses, and, as we are now discovering, important aspects of their physiology can also become linked and entrained" (McCraty, 2004).

Entrainment happens when our biological rhythms come into alignment—our heart rate and pulse, our brain activity, and the subtle workings of our nervous system. This can happen inside of ourselves, when our mind, body, and emotions are in alignment. This state of **psychophysiological coherence** naturally has significant benefits, both physically and emotionally, as well as making us available to communicate more openly with others (McCraty, Atkinson, Tomasino, Bradley, 2009). Think of how effective communication can be when we are truly linked and entrained physiologically and emotionally, both within ourselves, and with others.

Three Listening Positions

Because listening is a complicated process with many twists and turns along the way, Julian Treasure has identified three separate ways to look at the listening process, ways in which we can frame or tune our focus toward the overall meaning most appropriately. These **listening positions** are like dials that we can tune one in one direction or the other to focus on different ends of a spectrum, depending on our needs.

Active-passive spectrum: Active listening involves deliberate attention, focus, reflection, and summarizing. The goal of active listening is to understand someone and make him or her feel heard. To do this, we may nod, say "uh-huh", ask questions, take notes, or summarize our understanding of what the person has said. At the other end of this scale is passive listening, which Treasure describes as "fully conscious listening without any interaction, commentary or evaluation" (p. 68). By "passive," we don't mean uninterested or apathetic, we simply mean quietly receptive. Many people find this kind of restful release when they listen to music or meditate, or just keep the TV or radio on in the background without any active attention.

Critical-empathic spectrum: "Listening for the gold" is the way Treasure talks about critical listening (p. 69). Critical listening

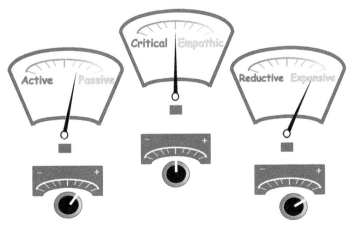

Figure 5.3 Three listening positions to adjust.

involves being on the lookout for the obvious or not-so-obvious value of the available information. When you listen to a political debate, interview someone about a crime or for a news story, or hear a sales pitch, you need to keep critical listening skills engaged to discriminate truth from fiction, dig out valid facts, and come up with an opinion about the worth of what you have heard. On the other side of this scale is empathetic listening, in which the goal is to support the listener's feelings. Empathic listening encourages the speaker to feel safe, open up and share ideas freely. You don't have to evaluate the worth of what is being said or come up with value judgments. Your only role is to show you are in tune with the person's feelings and hold space to let him or her feel heard, valued, and respected.

Reductive-expansive spectrum: Reductive listening is listening for the bottom line. People who are listening this way want the speaker to get to the point as quickly as possible. They get satisfaction from hearing what's needed, finding the solution, fixing the problem, and moving onto the next challenge. This kind of listening can be powerful and results-oriented, but it can also leave the speaker feeling frustrated and unappreciated as a person. Expansive listening is "a journey with no defined destination: The only goal is to enjoy the journey." This kind of experience is "where flow originates and where creative ideas come from," says Treasure (p. 74). Like chatting among friends, this type of listening in brainstorming sessions can create common ground among participants because all ideas are valid and nothing should be tossed out. Listening expansively without an agenda can also promote positive attitude, trust, teambuilding, and good will.

Interviews

An **interview** is a conversation with a purpose. Interviews can help people gain information, solve problems, make decisions, fill job openings, or just explore new territory. The way we prepare for and execute an interview depends on its purpose and structure. There are several different types of interviews, each of which are approached differently:

1. **Informational Interview:** The objective of this kind of less goal-oriented interview is to ask for advice and learn more about a career field, employer, or particular job. Interviewing experts in their field is a way to become more occupationally literate. The knowledge that you gain can make you a sharper and more informed. You can also make good contacts and further develop your network.

2. **Screening or Telephone Interview:** A phone interview is a cost effective way to screen candidates. You should prepare like you would an open book exam. It is recommended that you have in front of you your resume, the job description, information about the company or institution, a list of references, and possibly some prepared answers to challenging questions. The vast majority of communication is non-verbal. Because they can't see your body language, it is critically important to have positive and polished answers with an optimistic, energetic tone. Be sure to ask what the next step is.

3. **Individual Interview:** This is the most common type of interview and often called a "personal interview." It is typically a one-on-one exchange at the organization's offices. In order to best prepare, you will want to know the length of the interview that can usually range from

Figure 5.4 Interviews come in many guises

Listening writer and researcher Michael Purdy (2002) studied 900 college and military students to identify good and bad listening habits. The responses described the following traits of those perceived to be good or poor listeners.

Good listeners:

1. Used eye contact appropriately.
2. Paid attention to words and body language of the speaker.
3. Were patient and didn't interrupt.
4. Used verbal and nonverbal ways to respond.
5. Asked questions in a nonthreatening way.
6. Paraphrased, restated, or summarized what the speaker said.
7. Provided constructive verbal or nonverbal feedback.
8. Worked to understand the speaker's emotions.
9. Showed interest in the speaker as a person.
10. Demonstrated a caring attitude and were willing to listen.
11. Didn't criticize and avoided judging the speaker.
12. Were open-minded.

Figure 5.4 Good listeners

Poor listeners:

1. Were impatient and interrupted the speaker.
2. Didn't look at the speaker...their eyes wandered.
3. Were easily distracted, fidgeted, and did not pay attention to the speaker.
4. Demonstrated no interest in the speaker. They daydreamed or didn't care.
5. Gave very little or no verbal or nonverbal feedback.
6. Changed the subject.
7. Expressed judgment.
8. Were closed-minded.
9. Talked too much.
10. Seemed self-absorbed.
11. Dispensed unwanted advice.
12. Were too busy to listen.

Figure 5.4 Poor listeners

Michael Purdy, from "The Listener Wins." Copyright © 2005 by Monster Worldwide. Read the full article here: http://career-advice.monster.com/in-the-office/workplace-issues/the-listener-wins/article.aspx.

30 to 90 minutes. In shorter interviews, try to be concise and have a high impact with your answers, whereas in longer interviews you will want to go into more depth and be prepared with specific examples to support your generalizations. Make sure your appearance, apparel, and nonverbal behavior are suitable to the situation. As the old saying goes, "You never have a second chance to make a first impression."

4. **Small Group or Committee Interview:** Sometimes, you are asked to meet with several decision-makers at once. This can be an efficient way to interview candidates and allows for different interpretations or perceptions of the same answer. Be sure to make eye contact with everyone, no matter who asked the question. It's important to establish rapport with each member of the interview team. Try to find out the names and job titles of the participants.

5. **The Second or On-Site Interview:** After your first interview, you may be asked back again for a "second date." They like you enough that you made the first round of cuts, but they would like to know more about you before making their final decision. These types of interviews can last either a half or full day, so it is best to check and get an agenda. You may be meeting with representatives from Human Resources, potential supervisors, and/or other office staff. The more you

know about the structure of the process, the less anxious you are going to feel and the better you will perform. This is the last step before an offer is made, so it pays to be alert and enthusiastic.

6. **Behavioral-based Interview:** Behavioral-based interviews allow employers to find out how the interviewee acted in specific employment-related situations. The logic is that past behavior will predict future performance. The best techniques for handling a behavioral interview include preparing for the interview questions you may be asked, discovering as much as you can about the company and the job so you have an idea of what skills the employer is seeking, and being ready to include specific points in the responses you give.

7. **Task or Testing Interview:** This is a problem-solving interview in which you are given some exercises to demonstrate your abilities. A company may ask you to take a short test to evaluate your technical knowledge and skills. Sometimes a presentation to a group is necessary to determine your communication skills. If you are trying out for a team, a performing role, or a trade, you may be asked to "show your stuff." Just relax as much as possible and focus on enjoying the task to hit your best flow.

8. **Stress Interview:** During this rare type of interview, you may be baited with stressful questions or scenarios to see

how you will respond. The objective is to find your weaknesses and test how you hold up to pressure. Tactics such as awkward silences, constant interruptions, and challenging interrogation with antagonistic questions are designed to push your boundaries. Be prepared for these possibilities, and learn to stay open, breathe, and smile.

Question Types and Uses

Whether in interviews or conversations, the way we word questions is important to how the interaction will play out. Like the three listening positions, there are also three types of questioning techniques that can take answers in very different directions. First, how open or closed is the question? Second, is it primary or secondary? Third, is it a neutral or leading question?

Open or Closed: An open question gives you room to answer any way you want, especially if it is asked near the start of an interview. It's best to be prepared for such questions so that you know where to start and the energy of the conversation doesn't fall into nervous silence.

Open questions:

"What should I know about you?"

"Tell me about yourself."

"How are things?"

Closed questions have a particular range of possible responses and are usually answered more concisely.

Closed questions:

"Which days are you available to work?"

"Do you have any allergies?"

"When do you have to leave?"

In interviews, especially employment interviews, answer open questions by bringing in ideas related to the type of work you would be doing. Answer closed questions by using two or three thoughts, not just two or three words. Open them up by giving examples and explanations as appropriate.

Primary or Secondary: Primary questions are questions on new topics. Secondary questions are follow-up questions. All good interviews cover the different aspects of their topics with some primary questions on each topic, and secondary questions on areas of particular importance or interest. It is a good idea to be prepared to ask follow-up questions back to the interviewer. Answers to follow-up questions can make an enormous difference in the important nitty-gritty details of finding a perfect fit.

Primary questions:

"Tell me about your last job."

"What interests you about this position?"

Secondary questions:

"How did you feel about this responsibility?"

"Do you have any examples?"

Neutral or Leading: Neutral questions ask for information, but do not in any way try to influence the answer by the actual words used in the question. Leading questions tend to make certain answers more likely just by the way the question itself is worded.

Neutral question:

"What is your opinion about the economy?"

Leading question:

"We're headed in the wrong direction, aren't we?"

Tips for Effective Interviews

Remember that interviews are like dates—it's important for both parties to find the right fit. If an organization decides to set up an interview with you, this is a sign that your resume contains evidence of the necessary skills for the position. In staying open to your environment and the verbal and nonverbal cues of your interviewer(s), you can tune into the energy of the organization and the individuals with whom you'd be working. Although you should put your best foot forward in preparing your appearance and knowledge before the interview, once the interaction begins, it's best to just be yourself and let the interaction flow naturally rather than trying to force particular points. Stay open and aware—you are interviewing them as well.

Listen carefully to each question. Answer the question you were asked. If you are asked about your experience with something you do not have experience in, answer honestly but positively by giving an example of something with similar challenges that you have done well. Never bad-mouth a former school, employers, or others. Do not ask about salary.

Lots of advice for job interviews exists online these days. The latest information is just a few clicks away. If you are looking for a new job or even thinking about looking in a month or so, online resources, social networking websites and local groups can help you jumpstart your efforts. Even your public library and favorite bookstore can add to your stock of useful information. If you know anyone in relevant fields, by all means do your homework and ask questions. Be sure you listen to the answers.

References

Brownell, J. (2013). *Listening attitudes, principles and skills, 5th ed*. Boston: Pearson.

Diamond, L.E. (2007). *Rule #1: Stop Talking!* Silicon Valley, CA: Listeners Press.

Engleberg, I. N. & Wynn, D.R. (2011). *Think communication*. Boston: Allyn & Bacon.

Hybels, S.& Weaver II, R.L. (2012) *Communicating effectively*, 10th ed. New York: McGraw Hill.

Lang, A. (2000). The limited capacity model of mediated message processing. *Journal of Communication*, 50: 46–70.

Lee, B. (1975). *The tao of jeet kune do*. California: Ohara Publications.

McCraty R. (2004). The energetic heart: Bioelectromagnetic

communication within and between people. In P. J. Rosch & M. S. Markov (Eds.), *Bioelectromagnetic medicine* (pp. 541–562). New York, NY: Marcel Dekker.

McCraty, R., Atkinson, M., Tomasino, D., & Bradley, R. T. (December 2009). The coherent heart: Heart–brain interactions, psychophysiological coherence, and the emergence of system-wide order. Integral Review (5)2, 10–115.

O'Hair, D. & Wiemann, M. (2012). *Real communication, An introduction, second edition.* Boston: Bedford St. Martin's.

Pearson, J.C., Nelson, P.E., Titsworth, S., Harter, L. (2011). *Human communication, 4th ed.,* New York: McGraw Hill.

Shafir, R.Z. (2003). *The Zen of listening.* Wheaton, Il: Quest Books.

Treasure, J. (2011). *Sound business: How to use sound to grow profits and brand value.* Management Books 2000 Ltd. 11–76.

Tucker, B.P. (1995). *The feel of silence.* Philadelphia: Temple University Press.

Turner, R.M. (1994). *Adaptive reasoning for real-world problems: A schema-based approach.* Hillsdale, NJ: Lawrence Erlbaum Associates.

Chapter Six
Interpersonal Communication

Why Relationships?

Humans live in and through relationships. Although interpersonal relations can be some of the most time-consuming, challenging, vulnerable parts of our lives, they can also carry some of life's most important, satisfying, and enriching pleasures—kinship, friendship, collegiality, romance, parenthood, etc.

We are drawn into relationships in countless different ways because communicating deeply with others is how we find mirrors for ourselves and how we grow. We can view each relationship as a **microcosm** (a "world in miniature") of how we show up in our lives generally—our vulnerabilities as well as our strengths. Relationships are like a screen onto which we project our inner world.

The foundation of what we call interpersonal communication is the **dyad**—a pairing of two beings who agree they are somehow in relationship. There are countless types of dyads—acquaintances, friends, partners, siblings, parent-child, teacher-student, employer-employee … and these can morph and change over time.

What characterizes a dyad is that there is some sort of relational energy that holds the pairing together. Like rungs of a ladder, there are many levels of connection that can hold two together. But as soon as a third enters the mix, there emerges a new form of communication, because the relational energy we invest—from our gaze to our time and resources—must now be distributed. Choices must be made. With a dyad, we experience partnership. With a triad or more, we begin to experience politics. So, for the purposes of exploring how we fundamentally manage relational energy through communication, we focus our attention for now on dyads.

We define **relationship** as a connection with meaning. We exist in a complex web of countless relations—we are fundamentally linked to all of life, from bacteria to insects to birds to animals to other humans. Yet, because of circumstances, some of these relationships take on particular meaning to us. We may experience a fleeting connection with the bird that sings outside our window in the morning, yet not give that bird a name or even be able to distinguish it from other birds. However, birds (and cats and dogs and other creatures) can also become significant companions to us.

When we take on a companion animal and give them a name, we enter a relationship that may develop with some level of mutuality and commitment over time. We may come to understand aspects of this creature's behavior and traits, and perhaps take on responsibility for their feeding, grooming, health care, exercise, and even socialization. We celebrate successes (like a dog's new trick), invest resources (like buying toys and treats), and mourn losses (like a hamster passing away). With humans, our relationships are even more multi-faceted and complex. We invest time, we invest resources, we invest emotion. What do we gain?

Social Exchange

We align relationally with others through exchanging what communication scholars call **bids**, or moments of interaction that invite connection. A bid can be "a question, a gesture, a look, a touch—any single expression that says, 'I want to feel connected to you" (Gottman & DeClaire, 2001). Anything we do that invites communication and affiliation makes us a bit vulnerable as we wonder if our opening will be received and reciprocated.

When people receive our bids positively, we trust them and are more likely to repeat and deepen our interactions. When our bids are shut down, we tend to break off communication. Looking around, we may notice dozens or even hundreds or thousands of bids in the course of a day. We make them, and others make

them—which position do you feel is the more powerful, giving or receiving bids for interaction?

Social Exchange Theory (Homans, 1958; Roloff, 1981) proposes that we live our lives and negotiate our relationships based on the "cost" and "reward" we give and receive through our interactions. We expend effort and make ourselves vulnerable; we receive various levels of reward or satisfaction. The basic equation is:

Worth = Rewards – Costs

Social Exchange theorists would say that we value relationships when their "worth" feels positive to us, and we tend to let go of them when it doesn't. When we feel "met" more often than not, we feel satisfaction in the balance of energy we put forward. This is not to say that all relationships have to be "receiving" in the obvious sense, like receiving goods or services.

A parent, for example, may put forth 100% effort for no obvious "gain" from their child, but may be receiving tremendous satisfaction, which counts as a reward. It is this balance that makes us prioritize particular relationships. We need to receive the kind of benefit that works best for us, and this can change throughout our lives and the various roles we inhabit. We might enjoy being active and giving in some relationships, and value being nurtured and cared for in other relationships, or strive for a balance between those two dynamics. These feelings may change over time.

As we've learned from the lens of Symbolic Interactionism, there are two ways to experience ourselves—as both a subject (the "I" self that experiences the world and acts within it) and as an object (the "me" self that is experienced from outside and is acted upon). The course of our human development depends upon both of these experiences—fully inhabiting our own

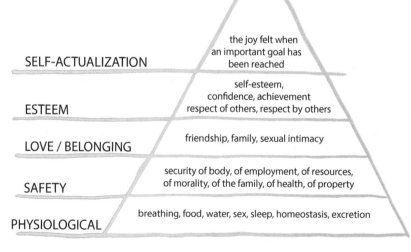

Figure 6.1 Maslow's Hierarchy of Needs

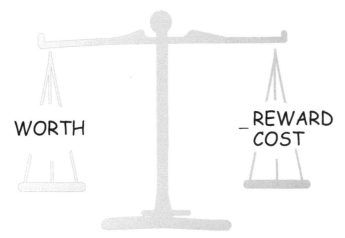

Figure 6.2 Social Exchange Theory.

inner subjective experience of the world, as well as opening to multiple levels of objective reality that we see as existing outside of ourselves.

As we grow from baby to child to youth to adult and beyond, we develop skills to see not only ourselves and others as "objects," but the relationships between us—the intersubjective communicated linkages—as having energy and meaning in themselves. Just as "self" can be an object, "relationship" can be an object, too.

Entering and managing relationships is a fundamental part of our growth and evolution through various levels of awareness. Examining **Maslow's Hierarchy of Needs** (Maslow, 1943), interpersonal relationships help us with each level of our development. At the most basic level, we must procure basic **physiological needs** like food and shelter. From there, we seek to find **safety** through connections to family, tribe, and employment. Once those needs are met, we long to experiencing **love and belonging** through intimacy and community. From there, we seek **esteem** by gaining confidence and respect from others. Finally, we reach a stage of **self-actualization** when we find

our own inner compass in the form of our morality, creativity, problem-solving, and fulfillment.

At every stage of our growth, relationships can provide a valuable mirror to where we are, what we need, and what we can become. Rather than being a stage in themselves, relationships are like an elevator that can carry us all the way from bottom to top of our development. The stages we pass through aren't discrete moments in time, either. We can be very much immersed in self-actualization, and still need to eat and sleep and protect ourselves from hungry bears.

Relationships, like elevators, can transcend all of these stages, moving up and down and up and down and transporting us where

we need to go in the moment. How have various relationships assisted you with your growth, and perhaps changed form over time? For example, do you view your parents differently through the lens of young adulthood than you did as a baby or small child? How might these relationships continue to evolve?

Like communication itself, interpersonal relationships come in countless forms and varieties, and our relations with others are dynamically changing all the time. As such, instead of trying to categorize relationships by type, it may be more useful to describe types of **relational energy** that can move through our relations with others at different times and for different reasons—affection, competition, romance, affiliation, commitment, attraction, reciprocity, admiration … the list could be endless.

Because relational energy is what invests our relationships with meaning, and because that meaning can shift and transform endlessly, we begin our study of interpersonal communication with the recognition that relationships are like clouds—constantly shifting, moving, coming together and apart, sometimes radiant and sometimes stormy, but always

Figure 6.3 Sometimes we 'put on' a Relational Face

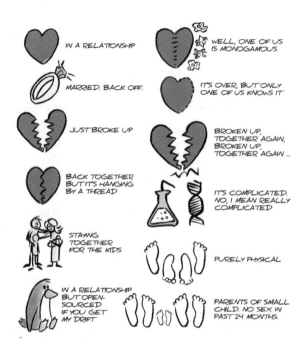

Figure 6.4 Relationship Status

changing. Because humans grow and develop perpetually, it is difficult to hold a relationship in a particular shape or form. All we can do is focus on the relational energy that draws us together and continually negotiate and renegotiate what things *mean* to us.

A relationship itself is a kind of symbol that is perpetually being defined and redefined through social interaction. Think of how many expectations have been socially defined for different types of dyads. How do these change over time?

Often dyadic relationships are privileged and protected in human society, as these are the most common partnerships for mating and raising young. As such, many partnerships have a **public dimension** that becomes a kind of social symbol. This symbol, and how it fits into the society around us, may be very different from the **private dimension** that

is experienced interpersonally between the participants. Because having a partnership can itself can be part of the social exchange equation, often relationships take on a **"face"**—the way things seem on the surface may not be how they are in real life.

Self-Disclosure and Social Penetration

The lifeblood of relationships—the force that keeps them alive, growing, and nourishing—is what we call **self-disclosure**, the act of sharing important information about our inner world to others, either consciously or subconsciously. Self-disclosure is not just sharing factual information, like what we had for breakfast this morning, but more about revealing our thoughts, feelings, preferences, aspirations, failures,

successes, fears, ideas, goals, attitudes, and beliefs.

Self-disclosure is sharing the "juicy" things about ourselves that could potentially make us vulnerable. We are motivated to self-disclose because it creates a sense of **affiliation** between us—a feeling of trust, bonding, and respect. Think about the last conversation you had in which you revealed truly personal information about yourself. How did it feel? What motivated you to share? Do you feel like it was easy for you to self-disclose—why or why not?

Communication scholars Irwin Altman and Dalmas Taylor (1973) put forward a theory of relationships known as **Social Penetration Theory**, which places self-disclosure as the main way that relationships become deeper. Making a comparison to an onion, with surface layers on the outside and deeper layers in the center, this theory points out that we need to go deeper past the initial outside layers before we can know how well we can relate to another person at a deep relational level. Even as we penetrate past the onion's surface and go deeper toward the core, we may find more and more layers of subtlety unfold.

Through self-disclosure, we build **intimacy**, a revealed state of emotional transparency—the word intimacy even sounds like "into me see." Just like the intimate space we discussed in proxemics, intimacy means that someone is so close to us that they could touch us—literally or figuratively—and thus bring us deep comfort, deep pleasure, or even deep harm.

Of course, intimacy doesn't have to be physical to be meaningful, as shown by the many different ways we can connect deeply with others through virtual and mediated channels. Because humans can use words and symbols to express our inner experience, we develop intimacy through a wide variety of ways. Relational information can be conveyed both verbally and nonverbally, and intimacy is built when we experience these "Four R's of Intimacy":

1. **Respect**—for how we show up in the world and an intention to support us, or at least do us no harm. This allows us to feel accepted and appreciated for who and what we are. They respect our time, our boundaries, our various needs and desires, and receive our gifts while forgiving our challenges.

2. **Release**—when someone can accept a wide range of our emotions and keep them private. This shows that we can self-disclose and process things emotionally without being shamed or having our private information shared publicly. Like tea leaves in warm water, we unfold and release our full essence.

3. **Reciprocity**—It feels good when someone demonstrates willingness to match our energy and our level of self-disclosure and trust. We feel "met"—able to give and take without being over-used, abandoned, or unappreciated. We feel trust and balance when we know that others will show up for us in ways that we show up for them.

4. **Resilience**—when we can process challenges together, heal, and move on, relationships grow ever deeper. If

we come through something hard together, even a rift that left us feeling vulnerable and alone, yet we gravitate back together again, we develop an extra layer of faith that, even in tough times, things will work out between us. Nothing brings us closer than knowing that nothing can break us up.

The Johari Window

An interesting way to show how self-disclosure operates in evolving relationships was developed by Joseph Luft and Harry Ingham, who combined their first names into a model called the **Johari Window** (Luft, 1970).

The idea of the Johari Window is that there are two parties involved—you, and the other person. Information can either be known or unknown. The process through which information passes from the unknown to the known is through self-disclosure. Like life-

blood, the flow of self-disclosure is literally what keeps relationships alive and vibrant.

There are four panes to the Johari Window:

a) Open pane: information that is known by both you and by another. This could be basic information like your name and demographics, as well as any facts you are willing to share openly.

b) Hidden pane: information that is known by you, but not by another. This would comprise secrets you keep that you don't want to disclose, like personal information or feelings.

c) Blind pane: information that is known to another, but not to you. This could be facts, mannerisms, or tendencies that you have that you haven't noticed, but are apparent to someone else.

d) Unknown pane: information unknown by both you and others. This area has no possibility of disclosure, because no one knows it yet. This has to do with futures, latent possibilities, genetic or subconscious issues, etc.

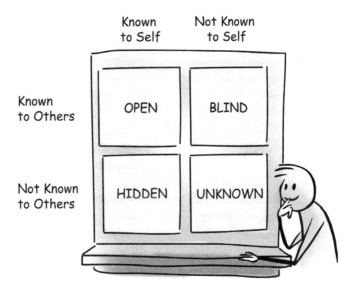

Figure 6.5 Johari Window

The point of the Johari Window is to demonstrate how the size and proportion of the panes—between Open, Hidden, Blind, and Unknown—changes over time during the course of a relationship. In a relationship with healthy self-disclosure, the Open pane will grow larger as information which was previously not discussed from the Blind, Hidden and Unknown areas gets discussed.

Interesting to notice is the proportional size of the Blind and Hidden windows, because this reveals our tendencies and fears most clearly. What do we tend to hide? What information do we avoid sharing with others? Are you the kind of person who would tell someone if their shoe were untied, or they had food on their face? What does our tendency to share or hide certain types of information show about our deepest needs and fears?

Intimacy, "into me see," deepens when the Open pane grows proportionally larger in our relationship. Most of us fear having our faults exposed, being criticized or abandoned, or losing our individuality or dignity. How much are we willing to acknowledge and share these feelings? Because self-disclosure can involve the most vulnerable and personal aspects of ourselves, opening the Hidden and Blind areas of our relationship to communication can be both scary and yet empowering.

Being willing and able to self-disclose in relationships is an aspect of **strategic flexibility**—having a wide range of communication skills available to apply appropriately. These tendencies tend to be impacted by our culture and environment—what kind of sharing is considered "appropriate" in your various cultural spheres? How comfortable are you adjusting to different contexts as you grow?

Stages of Relationship Development

We can view relationships as living things—growing, evolving, changing, transforming. As such, they tend to have identifiable stages through their "life cycle." Understanding these stages can give us a lot of clarity around what is going on in our relationships and the steps we need to take to achieve the outcomes we want.

Communication scholar Mark Knapp developed a theoretical model of how relationships come together and grow apart (Knapp, 1984). The model has ten stages, five for coming together and five for coming apart:

1. **Initiating:** We may pass by many people throughout the course of the day, but communicate with few of them. In the initiating stage, we make a first contact, either by being placed together somehow, or someone extending an initial **bid** to interact. This "first impression" phase can set the tone for whether or not there is mutual interest to continue communicating.

2. **Experimenting:** Once contact has been initiated, we may exchange small talk and/or attempt to set up other opportunities for interaction. We put out bids and watch for reactions to see if we are being received. If so, we may recognize that we both enjoy interacting and set up chances to do it more often.

3. **Intensifying:** In the intensifying stage, people recognize a degree of commitment and start to prioritize developing the relationship. We may turn down other opportunities in order to be together. There starts to be a sense of "we" and commitment to the relationship in some way.

4. **Integrating:** We are now being recognized as a partnership, a pair, or a couple. Others expect us to prioritize our relationship, and other opportunities start falling away. We build our schedules around each other to some degree and spend time exploring what it means to be partnered.

5. **Bonding:** A formal, public commitment takes place, and significant others are invited to witness and hold space for our partnership. Some commitments are worked out, perhaps legally or socially, and others who are important to us are able to support our commitment to sustaining the partnership.

Not all couples are able to remain in this "happily ever after" stage of relationship indefinitely. It is natural for relationships to begin the coming-apart process, and may spiral from there back into coming-together and perhaps back again. There is no one optimal "outcome" for relationships, as each is unique.

These next five stages constitute the dissolution process, but

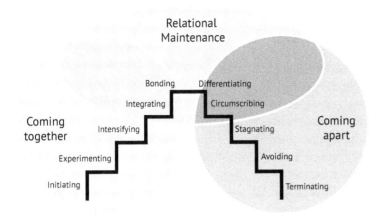

Figure 6.6 Three stages of relationship development.

it is possible to return from one of these stages back into coming together, depending on the intent of the participants:

6. **Differentiating:** Partners start to notice ways that we are different. "You do it this way, and I do it that way." There is still a sense of "we," but we recognize our unique identities, preferences, or attitudes. We "live and let live" and maintain a sense of connection despite the differences.

7. **Circumscribing:** Because there may be some discomfort in trying to find common ground on every issue, partners may decide to "circumscribe" or draw a virtual circle around particular activities or attitudes. We may decide to "agree to disagree" and not involve each other in particular areas of life or decision-making that don't work for the other.

8. **Stagnating:** Like a pond where the water does not move or get any fresh, new oxygen to keep it healthy, a relationship can slowly become the same, predictable old way day after day. There is still a sense of shared space and/or identification with the relationship, yet little fresh energy to keep the "life-blood" of the relationship flowing.

9. **Avoiding:** Once a relationship begins to feel toxic, participants will avoid sharing deeply with each other. Participants may go out of their way to avoid contact time, and investment in the relationship dries up.

10. **Terminating:** When a relationship no longer serves the participants, there may be a formal, public statement of the relationship's ending. This allows freed participants to no longer be identified with the former partner, and offers a chance to reach out to other possible partners in the future.

Considering where our relationships are within this stage framework can help us gain clarity on what we may be doing or not doing to make our relationships closer or more distant, whether consciously or unconsciously.

Like the First Axiom of Communication, "You cannot not communicate," we are always communicating something to our relational partners, either through our attention or inattention. Relationships are always changing and transforming as both partners grow.

The key to keeping relationships vital and close is self-disclosure. Like blood in a body, when the blood slows down, the organism will become cold or even die. Just as we exercise our bodies to enhance our bloodflow and our health, we need to exercise our communication regularly to keep the relationship healthy and nourishing. Even if they're with people we don't see often, if we can jump right into honest and open sharing when we visit, this can still be a sign of a strong relationship. The key is the quality of the communication.

Communication in relationships doesn't mean we always need to be talking, however—sharing touch, working side-by-side, and doing activities together can be just as important. In an **instrumental style** of relational communication, we use actions (such as giving a gift or washing someone's car) to show our care and affiliation. Using an **affective style** of communication, on the other hand, involves more direct ways of expressing ourselves, like saying "I love you" and setting up time to talk and share our feelings. (Gudykunst & Ting-Toomey, 1988). Both styles of communication can be effective ways to keep relationships healthy. Our preference for using instrumental vs. affective styles of showing our care often is determined by our home culture and our individual personality. Thinking of whether you'd rather share an activity or a conversation with your partner shows whether you have more instrumental or affective tendencies in relationships.

Relational Dialectics

Relationships are constantly shifting and growing as we meet the various circumstances we face each day. Our needs and desires can vary from one minute to the next. One moment, we may feel fairly independent, enjoying a relatively light relationship, and then an emergency can shake us up and make us want to cling to our partner. We may declare our undying sense of connection one evening, and then the next morning feel a need to go off on our own for a while and do our own thing.

Dialectics are opposites that exist together. Taking a **relational dialectics** approach means that we acknowledge we have seemingly opposing needs and desires that co-exist simultaneously in relationships (Baxter & Montgomery, 1996). This approach recognizes that wanting different things at different moments is both healthy and normal in relationships. "Dialectical thinking is not directed around a search for the 'happy medium' of compromise and balance, but instead focuses on the messier, less logical, and more inconsistent unfolding practices of the moment" (p. 46). We accept that experiencing a constant shift of needs and desires is absolutely normal, and that our relational success depends on coming to intersubjective agreement on our

mutual tolerance for ambiguity and change.

Dialectics are understood by placing our seemingly opposing needs on a **continuum**, a spectrum from one opposite to the other with infinite shades of variation in between. Three basic dialectics that most of us experience are:

Figure 6.7 'Pulls and Pushes' of Relational Dialectics

1. **Autonomy vs. Connection:** We may wish to be connected and affiliated with our partner, but we also may desire freedom and a sense of individuality. These needs may vary by our stage of life, our current life circumstances, and what is going on in the moment. Can you think of something that might lead to a shift in your balance on this continuum?

2. **Openness vs. Privacy:** We may have different tolerances for sharing our complete, uncensored reality with our partner, and reserving some private space for ourselves. Think of how you feel about having the bathroom door open: sometimes you may welcome the connection; at other times you may want complete privacy. How was this dialectic handled in your home culture, and how does that balance impact you now?

3. **Novelty vs. Predictability:** Although most relationships tend to find some comfort

and stability in creating a reliable routine, falling into a rut can make us crave something new. Relationships have to find their own balance of structure and "spice" to keep things feeling stable yet also interesting.

There are several different ways that relational partners can negotiate dialectical tensions as they come up:

a. Cyclic alternation, or taking turns. "You get your way this week, I'll get mine next week."

b. Segmentation, or doing different things in different arenas. "When it comes to food, we'll do what you want, but when it comes to movies, I get to decide."

c. Selection, or choosing one over the other. "It's up to you, dear." This can create a dominant-submissive relationship structure, which can be either satisfying or unsatisfying depending on whether expectations are complementary or symmetrical.

d. Integration, which can mean somehow neutralizing differences around the issue, compromising, or finding another path altogether. "I want pizza, you want Thai food. Okay, let's go get tacos." It takes communication to be able to reframe options and/or figure out what both partners really want and can be satisfied with.

In life as in relationships, as the ancient Greek philosopher Heraclitus declared, "Change is the only constant." We can expect that both we and our partner will go through innumerable shifts in energy and circumstance. Once we come to anticipate that, we won't feel we've failed when we don't maintain an unattainable ideal.

Those who ride unicycles know that the secret to riding is to accept that you are always falling, and being able to ride that balance. In relationship, getting our two "wheels" into alignment so that we can achieve a greater degree of stability and mutual support requires clear, consistent, and skillful communication.

Communicating Skillfully in Relationships

The key to effective communication in a relationship is **empathy**—being willing to hear and understand what is going on for another person and truly caring what they are feeling. This may seem simple and obvious when we are experiencing positive feelings together. However, there are often deep-seated feelings inside us or between us that get in the way of being able to have clear communication, particularly around touchy issues. Each time we get upset about something in a relationship but aren't able to clear it, this unspoken hurt becomes like a brick in a wall that forms between us. If enough of these build up, the wall can become impenetrable, and we may go elsewhere for comfort—to other friends or relationships, to hobbies or distractions, or even to substance abuse.

It helps to have some common vocabulary to work with in order to clear the "bricks" between us while they are small and we still have space to communicate. Here are some concepts and terms that you can learn together when you are in a positive space together. They can be handy tools when challenging things occur and it is more difficult to think clearly or see eye-to-eye:

Triggers: All people have deep hurts resulting from difficult things that have happened to us. Much of this deep emotional material may be outside of our conscious awareness, and we may not even remember where it comes from. When we find ourselves having a disproportionately large emotional response to something that happens or is said, we call that a "trigger," like a trigger on a gun that releases a much more powerful reaction than the motion that set it off. **Red-flag words** often have triggers associated with them—you hear a word, and before you know it, you are boiling in anger, fear, resentment, jealousy, or indignation. You may or may not even be clear why you are reacting so strongly. Just noticing that triggers are there, and accepting that there are deep reasons for them, can be the first step to you and your partner being able to talk more clearly when they do arise.

Withholds: There are often topics we avoid addressing in a relationship, usually to prevent discomfort or pain. Perhaps we fear there is a trigger there that we'd rather not set off. Although we may feel we are being kind or polite, allowing withholds to fester can allow the wall between us to build. If we value the relationship, we want those bricks gone. Even just bringing up a withhold with someone in a respectful way communicates that we care enough about the relationship to do our part in removing obstacles between us.

Clearing a Withhold: The most important aspect of clearing withholds is your intention—if you are wanting to show care and get closer, get that clear in your mind before launching into criticism or blame. Avoid "**dumping,**" just spraying the person with more emotional material than they can handle or process.

To clear a withhold respectfully, it is best to ask the person if they are open to hearing it before launching into a speech at them. They may or may not be in the right frame of mind right then to receive what you have to say—perhaps they are tired, or busy, or irritated about something else. Asking them if now is a good time to "share a withhold" communicates that you want to build closeness by getting rid of bricks between you, but that you care enough to do it in a moment when they are ready to receive what you have to say.

"I" statements: In clearing a withhold, to avoid putting the person on the defensive, keep your language about your own experience of the situation rather than making assumptions or casting blame. Use clear, specific statements about your own feelings, such as, "When you were an hour late for dinner, I felt disregarded and frustrated because I couldn't reach you. I didn't know what to do." Express only facts (the actual timing) and your experience (your feeling of frustration), but do not make assumptions (like "you don't care about me") or sweeping generalizations (like "you're always late"). Remember that your goal is to build closeness, not prove yourself superior.

The trick to clearing withholds is to allow the listener (the recipient) to simply say "thank you" after hearing what is said. This is not the time to launch into a defense or a justification. Simply acknowledge that the speaker has given a gift of time and attention to clearing the issue, and respond with "thank you." Take time to receive it—the speaker will feel heard, and the recipient will have time to process what is really being said. Once both sides feel clear to communicate about it again, the clearing process can continue, for as many rounds as necessary. As long as both parties stay committed to clear, respectful communication, continued self-disclosure can help the relationship grow ever deeper. (Note: Self-disclosure builds closeness, not "other-disclosure" of assumptions about what others are thinking or feeling.) But even if the topic is never brought up again, sometimes just being able to say something and have it heard without excuses may be all it takes to put the issue to rest.

Paranoias or "Stories": Sometimes, based on our own fear and insecurities, we come up with stories in our heads about "what is going on" that may or may not be the actual truth. We feel paranoid that others are avoiding us, disliking us, talking about us, purposely trying to hurt us. We may be psychologically **projecting**—ascribing our own thoughts or attitudes to others. Or there may be some truth in what we are fearing.

Clearing a Paranoia: Although the secret to clearing a withhold is just listening, receiving, and letting things be aired, sometimes things need to be said that really do require a response. Perhaps we are concerned that the person is avoiding us, or that we have done something wrong, and we really do want to hear an answer about whether our fears are justified. In this case, we follow the same steps as clearing a withhold—making sure our intention is clear, and then asking permission before bringing the topic up so that the person can be in the right state of mind to receive it. But this time, we actually ask for a response. We should be ready to receive the answer, whatever it is. If our intention is truly to build the relationship through self-disclosure, hearing the other person's truth can be welcome material for self-reflection.

Curiosity: A key to maintaining one's sense of balance and poise in a difficult interaction is **curiosity**—observing how we are feeling and wondering why, without judgment or blame. Notice your feelings and thoughts, exploring yourself as if you were a detective. When you feel a strong emotion, train yourself to inquire, "Hm, I wonder what is that about?" Recognizing that our deepest growth comes through challenges, and that challenges are normal, see your partner as providing interesting material for your process.

Appreciations: If conversations bring up only challenging topics, we will come to avoid them. Who wants to wade through challenges perpetually? What humans really crave, and what keeps relationships most healthy, is expressing appreciation and praise. Whether we are willing to admit it or not, most of us welcome nothing more than when our loved ones tell us we are lovable. This is why the proportion of compliments needs to remain not only equal, but to far surpass the difficult material we share in a relationship.

Not all appreciation we feel has to be expressed verbally—in more instrumental relationships, a touch or a loving glance or a favor can serve as a powerful "thank you" or an "I love you." But with "appreciations," we make our feelings clear in words. As such, we should ask permission before we share an appreciation, to see if the person is able to receive at that moment. All the recipient has to do is listen and then say "thank you" and let the words land, but sometimes this can be hard. We may not always be ready to hear compliments and praise. But just as withholds need to be heard, so do appreciations. And if the balance is higher on the appreciations, a relationship will have a much better chance of staying healthy and nourishing for both parties.

Conclusion

The bottom line of effective interpersonal communication goes back to the Latin root of the word communication—*communis*, "to share." We benefit when we can share feelings, experiences, vulnerability, and strengths without fear.

This allows us to have **synergy**, when the interaction itself makes for an even greater outcome than the sum of the parts.

References

Altman, I. & Taylor, D. (1973). *Social penetration: The development of interpersonal relationships.* New York: Holt.

Baxter, L. A., & Montgomery, B. M. (1996). *Relating: Dialogues and dialectics.* New York: Guilford.

Gottman, J. M., & DeClaire, J. (2001). *The relationship cure: A five-step guide for building better connections between family, friends, and lovers.* New York: Crown.

Gudykunst, W. B. & Ting-Toomey, S. (1988). Verbal communication styles. In W. B. Gudykunst, S. Ting- Toomey & E. Chua (Eds.), *Culture and interpersonal communication* (pp. 99–117). Newbury Park, California: Sage Publications.

Homans, G. C., (1958). Social behavior as exchange. *American Journal of Sociology* 63(6): 597–606.

Knapp, M. L. (1984). *Interpersonal communication and human relationships.* Boston: Allyn & Bacon. Editions with Vangelisti, A. L. in 1992, 1996, 2000, 2005, 2009.

Luft, J. (1970). *Group process: An introduction to group dynamics* (2nd ed.) Palo Alto, CA: Science and Behavior Books.

Maslow, A. H. (1943). A theory of human motivation. *Psychological Review 50*(4): 370–396.

Roloff, M. (1981). *Interpersonal communication: A social exchange approach.* Beverly Hills, CA: Sage.

Chapter Seven
Small Group Communication

"A small group of thoughtful people could change the world. Indeed, it's the only thing that ever has."

—Margaret Mead

"Groups usually produce more and better solutions to problems than do individuals working alone" (Shaw, 1976). If you have not been a part of a small group thus far in your life (which is unlikely), it's a good bet that you will soon be. Everyone experiences being a member of a group at some point in life. Currently, organizations and businesses are establishing one committee after another to bring people together to collectively solve problems, enact solutions, and maintain open working relationships. Good group communication skills are a hallmark of the successful person in today's society. Employers are interested in hiring people who work well with others and are open to listening and cooperation. Acting in an open and helpful manner and supporting the efforts of others are desirable attributes.

In today's interconnected world, committees and teams lead the way in problem solving and achieving goals. Yet many people are reluctant to work in groups because they have experienced stress, misunderstanding, unequal work distribution, or other undesirable outcomes. It has been pointed out that, "smart people working collectively can be dumber than the sum of their brains" (Wald & Schwartz, 2003).

Cost/Benefit analysis (Boardman, 2006) can be applied to why we work in groups and teams. If the benefits outweigh the costs, then we will decide to do what produces the most benefits. The need for more and variable productivity or faster turn-around would lead us to think that a group can accomplish this in a more expeditious fashion with a variety of ideas. It can be true that working in a group often takes more finesse, but the benefits can far outweigh the costs. Once you have an understanding of group dynamics, groups work, group-work becomes much easier, and can be enjoyable and satisfying. Knowledge of group dynamics will help you to avoid many potential problems.

The **advantages of small groups** include having multiple people to contribute ideas and opinions, which helps to generate better ideas and solutions when brain-storming and analyzing options. Collaborating with others offers an opportunity to have contributions made by people with a wider range of experiences and strengths. Also, as the old adage goes: "Many hands make light work." With multiple people working on a project, work can be distributed and accomplished more quickly. In addition to having more minds to come up with ideas and more hands on deck, it has been found that shared decision making empowers group members to shape their own goals and provides a greater satisfaction in the outcome. **Group synergy** can occur when members combine their abilities and the outcome is greater than any individual could do on their own.

The **disadvantages of small groups** often center on group members not contributing equally. When we work in a group, we expect participants to work together cooperatively and behave in a positive manner. Of course this ideal takes work and commitment. Some individuals are bossy, complain often, talk off topic too much, are not punctual, or argue strongly to have their own way. One other disadvantage is that we don't all work at the same speed; a reality that takes ingenuity to overcome without jeopardizing the pace of the project. Making sure that people are assigned tasks suitable for them helps a group to optimize efficiency. Without a sense of coherent goals and structure, group work can feel like more effort than it is worth when we spin our wheels on group dynamics rather than being able to concentrate on the task at hand. Keeping common goals in mind and making use of some basic structural and procedural understandings can help make small groups click together and achieve more **synergy** than people working separately.

What makes a "Small Group?"

A **small group** is defined as a limited number of individuals who communicate interdependently to achieve a common goal. Groups are defined by some measure of **interdependence**, in that what each person does will impact the others in the group. This can be seen when one participant fails to do their work and consequently the rest of the group cannot proceed to the next level. A key characteristic of an effective small group is that the members have something in common, like genuine concern for their purpose.

Small groups are typically considered to be comprised between **3 and 13 people** (Shaw, 1980). As we've learned, two people in communication are considered a **dyad**, which is characterized by the directionality of interaction being focused on just one other person. As soon as you have three people in communication, you have "politics"—constant decisions need to be made in terms of positioning, gaze, agreement, attention, etc. Regardless of how many members make up a group, it is important to consider that all members have an influence on one another. "You cannot not communicate" definitely applies, because each group member's energy and engagement has a significant impact on the entire group, whether one is talking, observing, or not even in the room. How might a group member's absence be "communicating" with group members even when the person is not present?

In groups, size does matter. Typically, smaller groups can have the luxury of less formality, but as the size of the group grows, often the more formal rules are needed to structure interaction. Consider: if you have two people talking, there is one relationship. If you have three people, it becomes three relationships, and by adding a fourth person, there are six relationships. It is easy to have an intimate conversation with just one person or even two, but with an expanding group, there is much less intimacy. With greater numbers, complexity grows and more structured forms of communicating are required.

Groups also need to consider whether the number of members in their group is odd (3, 5, 7...) or even (4, 6, 8...). In some groups, particularly those that need to work quickly, voting may become necessary, and odd numbers allow for tie-breakers. However, in many groups it is important for team members to come to consensus, and an even number of group members may be preferable to balance energies and prevent groups from taking the easy way out with "majority rule." Consider what you feel would be the "ideal size" for various kinds of groups. Why do you think the American justice system requires juries to be comprised of twelve people?

Along with size and composition, groups can also be characterized by their **mandate,** or reason for being together. For example, Katzenbach and Smith (1993) provide a clear distinction between work groups and teams. A **work group** is a collection of people working in the same area or placed together to complete a task. The group's performance is the result of people coming together to share information, experience, and insights. The focus of groups is individual performance and actions are geared toward it. All teams are groups, but teams are a special subset of groups: "A **team** is a small number of people with complementary skills, who are committed to a common purpose, set of performance goals and approach for which they hold themselves mutually accountable" (Katzenbach & Smith, p.112). Teams require both individual and mutual accountability, whereas groups do not. In groups, members are most interested in and responsible for individual accountability. By understanding the similarities and differences between these two concepts, we can begin to create an appropriate environment for each and determine the conditions in which each is effective.

Teams have clear goals from the beginning, and rules and operating procedures are discussed and developed to aid in the group's collaboration. In current organizations, self-directed work teams exist and are responsible for their own work. Self-directed work teams have proliferated in the last few decades in a variety of organizations and industries. In a small group, roles are not explicit. They will develop according to the needs of the task, and the responsibilities will be governed by needs and who can fill those needs as well. Rules are not typically established, but evolve as group expectations and preferences come forward.

Types of Small Groups

The likelihood of being in a group is compounded by there being so many types of small groups, which vary by purpose, function, composition, and duration. Because the way we behave in groups depends on why we are there, it is helpful to consider the different roles and responsibilities we experience in different groups: **primary, social, therapy/self-help, learning, service, public, work, civic, focus, virtual, study, community,**

task, and problem-solving. With which types of groups do you have personal experience? Which types do you find most comfortable, or most challenging? Why?

A **primary group** satisfies one's basic human needs; members have an intimate relationship. Primary groups include your family and close friends.

A **social group** includes members who share a common interest or engage in a common activity, such as a book club, gaming group, religious congregation, fraternity or sorority, an intramural sports team, etc. While close relationships can evolve among members of a social group, it is the common activity or interest that keeps them together.

Therapy/Self-help groups are one in which individuals convene to share their troubles and take solace in others who have experienced similar situations. Self-help groups can help us relate better, find resources, overcome addictions, experience healing, and develop spiritually or psychologically.

A **learning group** includes members who desire to enhance their skills, abilities, cognitive processes, gain knowledge, or improve a behavior. Examples of learning groups include enrolling in a swimming class, taking a birthing class when expecting a baby, attending classes with a religious or spiritual group, or taking a communication course in public speaking to overcome shyness.

A **service group** is primarily composed of volunteers who donate their time, energy, and effort to help others who lack something that would help them lead a functional life or are in need of a particular service. Often organized by religious congregations

or community centers, working together on service can be a satisfying way to engage in bettering one's world.

In a **public group**, members interact for the benefit of an audience. An example of a public group is a panel discussion, in which an invited group engages in a discussion about a topic in front of an audience that can learn from the dynamics of their interaction. Another example is a symposium in which each group member presents a speech on one aspect of a topic.

A **work group** occurs within an organizational context. The members of a work group complete a common task on behalf of an organization whose members take collective responsibility for the task. Work groups are differentiated by the physical and intellectual abilities needed by group members, the amount of time the group dedicates to task completion, the task structure, the resistance that group members encounter when attempting to complete the task, the degree to which task completion depends on technology, and the health risks assumed by group members as they engage in task completion (Devine, 2002).

Civic groups are local government and education groups that operate within the official structure of public institutions. A civic group might include a school committee or board of selectmen. A board of selectmen makes decisions on local laws, local budgets, and safety issues.

Focus groups encompass a wide variety of groups such as social research, urban planning, usability engineering, and marketing. Often, focus groups are convened by organizations to solicit feedback

Forming

Team acquaints and establishes ground rules. Formalities are preserved and members are treated as strangers.

Storming

Members start to communicate their feelings but still view themselves as individuals rather than part of the team. They resist control by group leaders and show hostility.

Norming

People feel part of the team and realize that they can achieve work if they accept other viewpoints.

Performing

The team works in an open and trusting atmosphere where flexibility is the key and hierarchy is of little importance.

Adjourning

The team conducts an assessment of the year and implements a plan for transitioning roles and recognizing members' contributions.

Figure 7.1 The stages of group development.

on programs, policies, or products. For example, a marketing focus group might examine new packaging for pizzas and discuss design, determining which one would appeal to them the most.

Virtual groups function through mediated communication to allow people to work, play, or socialize interdependently from different locations. From corporate teleconferences to multiplayer online role playing games, virtual groups tend to allow for less nonverbal interaction, which places more emphasis on the verbal content of people's contributions. It is also possible to communicate through avatars, created to highlight chosen aspects of a character's identity.

Study groups are formed to help students learn course material, work on projects, or prepare for exams. Working together gives students an opportunity to discuss the information more thoroughly and deepen the learning

experience. These differ from **learning groups** in that learning groups have more of a fixed, lasting duration, whereas study groups can be convened around particular tasks.

Community groups, whether geographic or interest-based, draw people together around shared interests, allowing participants to interact, share information, and coordinate action. From local neighborhood associations to

Type	Purpose
Executive	Plan/direct
Command	Coordinate
Negotiation	Deal/persuade
Commission	Choose/investigate
Design	Create/develop
Advisory	Suggest/diagnose
Service	Provide/repair
Production	Assemble/build
Performance	Enact
Medical	Treat/heal
Response	Protect/rescue
Military	Protect/neutralize
Transportation	Haul
Sports	Compete/win

Source: From Devine, D. J. (2002). A review and integration of classification systems relevant to teams in organizations. *Group Dynamics: Theory, Research, and Practice, 6,* 291–310. Copyright © American Psychological Association.

arts organizations to groups that support particular causes, community organizing can make the fibers of a community stronger.

Task groups convene to work on a particular task. Often assigned to work together within or between organizations, task groups are less social in nature and often disband once the task is completed. They can be called together within any context, from a school association fundraising for a field trip to a marketing team coming up with a campaign to introduce a new product line. The main characteristic of the task group is that they disband once the task is completed.

Problem-solving groups may be temporary or long-standing. They are brought together to coordinate action, overcome obstacles or impediments, or pool resources toward a desired goal. Problem-solving groups may last until a problem is resolved. Coordinating action on issues like environmental sustainability, crime or violence prevention, or meeting needs of the most vulnerable members of a community may or may not ever come to a natural "end."

Stages of Group Development

At first, being unsure of how group dynamics will emerge is perfectly normal. The anticipation of how you will get along with members is all part of the social process inherent to community life. One thing for certain is that good communication skills are a must. Making sure you listen, choose your words carefully, observe non-verbal communication, and work on creating a polite and productive atmosphere, showing respect to each and every member, will help to make sure goals are achieved satisfactorily. Seeing the larger view of how groups function can help give a sense of structure and help us see the trajectory of the work. Groups move through these classic phases: **Forming, Storming, Norming, Performing,** and **Adjourning** (Tuckman, 1965).

During the **Forming phase,** as members try to get oriented, they are nervous and unsure of how to proceed. This can be a tentative time during which members hesitate to express themselves. Members are concerned about how they are perceived, as well as trying to discover who their co-members are. Wondering who will be in charge and how work will be distributed, they look for a way to move forward. Once individuals feel accepted, they can begin to identify with the group and find their niche.

In the **Storming** phase, conflict may arise as members try to establish where they fit in, discover the roles they may play, and argue their positions. Group members may vie for leadership roles, based on members' strengths and their involvement. Many groups are not limited to only one leader, so being open to everyone's needs and creative about distributing resources and responsibilities can be crucial to both success and satisfaction.

During the **Norming** phase, acceptable and unacceptable behavior has been established, guiding behavior and interaction. Roles have been established, as well as norms. Examples of this could be anything from how timely one needs to be, the type of language used in a meeting, dress or the specific parameters regarding meetings, such as the order of business, how often meetings would take place, time frame, etc. During this phase, the group begins to work cooperatively and make decisions on how to move forward to achieve their goal. Cohesion emerges and members are comfortable enough to express themselves.

In the **Performing** phase, the focus is on accomplishing the goal. Roles change as required by altered circumstances. There may be several tasks that need to be achieved as part of reaching the overall goal. Members must work together to overcome obstacles in their path. This is the time when individual members' various talents will come into play. For example, if your group is preparing to have a golf tournament to benefit a particular charity, there would be many facets involved to make it happen. You might want to figure out how you would promote the event, what food would be served, where your golfers were coming from and fundraising for t-shirts, prizes and other costs. Even producing t-shirts can break down into a list of items: What colors should they be? What is the logo? How many do you buy and what sizes? Do you requisition a professional to design the logo and pay for it, or do you have a member who is a talented artist design it? Decision-making is a large part of achieving goals.

After groups finish a project or end a particular phase, the **Adjourning** phase provides some kind of closure before members disperse. The final product of the work may be compiled and presented in some way. A final party may provide punctuation and a satisfying ending to the group effort. Sometimes people make lasting connections, and some groups determine to have a reunion. Reunions often bring special closure to long and arduous work.

Success in Small Groups

There are two main ways to consider success of a small group: 1) the quality of whatever "outcome" is desired, and 2) group members' satisfaction with the process itself. According to Steiner (1955), "Actual productivity, what a group does in fact accomplish, rarely equals potential productivity" (p. 276). Because there are so many elements that can lead to unsatisfactory group processes that can lead to unsatisfactory outcomes, Steiner's rule is:

Actual Productivity = Potential Productivity—Losses Due to Faulty Process

In a group, "faulty process" can be due to either poor coordination, or sheer motivation loss by members, which can happen for many reasons. There may be unclear expectations, interpersonal conflicts, scheduling issues, or simply unwillingness to work with others. Motivation loss, sometimes known as "**social loafing**," has been described as the "decrease in individual effort when performing in groups as compared to when performing alone" (Latan, Williams, & Harkins, 1979, p. 822). Groups that "gel" and produce satisfactory outcomes tend to establish a positive group climate quickly so that "faulty process" doesn't detract from the group's potential synergy.

Norms are recurring patterns of behavior or thinking that come to be accepted in a group as the "usual" way of doing things (Scheerhorn and Geist, 1997) or, in other words the limits of allowable behaviors of individual members of the group. These guidelines designed to regulate the behaviors of group members can be either stated or unstated; they arise socially as part of the group process. For example, when Bethany, in her enthusiasm, kept talking at the same time as her group members, she received discouraging looks from her group. Eventually, she realized that the preference was for each person to talk for no more than one to two minutes, taking turns, with discussion ensuing later. At this point, she began to **self-monitor** (paying attention to her communication and behavior), exhibiting patience, discipline and speaking at the appropriate times.

Rules are explicitly stated procedures. For example, your syllabus for each course is a collection of procedures to follow for your success in the course. Rules are typically written or clearly stated and tend to endure over time. Changing them successfully requires consent from all involved.

Gatekeeping in a group context is the process of coordinating discussion so that all members have an opportunity to contribute. It might occur when someone suggests to another member that they haven't been heard yet, or perhaps setting a maximum amount of time each member can talk about a specific subject. Jill, being slightly reticent to speak, sits quietly while the group chats about the pros and cons of hiring a DJ for their function. John might urge Jill to comment on the DJ she had recently used at her work celebration. Encouraging members with praise and positive reception of their contributions also keep members buoyed and confident. Finally, one important part of group work is mediating when conflict arises. Conflict can be both healthy and unhealthy. It can be a normal part of group processes, contributing to more thorough analysis of the information available. Unfortunately, if it continues to escalate, it can be disruptive and uncomfortable.

Mediation works to resolve conflict in an open, productive manner so that the necessary feelings and information can be aired without shutting down the group process. When people in a group don't get along, attention can be directed away from personality conflicts and focus on the issues instead. We cannot always choose who will be in a group with us, but we can always choose our attitude and orientation toward the task at hand. Like a car engine, keeping individual gears and parts "well-oiled" can make the system's functioning smoother, more effective, and more pleasant for all concerned.

When members of groups work together, it has been shown that supporting each other's endeavors has a profound effect. Working together and creating a climate of trust and reliance makes for better productivity. **Group cohesion** happens when group members feel: 1) a degree of **interpersonal attraction**, genuine liking and trust among them, 2) a **shared commitment** to the task itself, and 3) **group pride**, or a sense of "we-ness" and belonging within the team. Cohesive groups tend to create supportive climates that achieve higher success, fostering optimism and self-confidence. When groups are confident, they are better able to overcome problems and make decisions.

Cohesiveness is recognized by how well the group gets along, by their mutual admiration, and their devotion to their purpose. Longevity can also be a characteristic of a cohesive group in that they will often stay together longer.

Committing oneself to the goal of the group and establishing **mutuality of concern** makes for a less bumpy ride. Mutuality of concern is the degree to which members share the same level of commitment to a group. Enthusiasm for the group focus helps to create better cohesion amongst members. Gouran and Hirokawa (2003) provided several suggestions for ways to create group cohesiveness. These involve speaking respectfully to other members, being friendly and courteous, showing cooperation, being sensitive to others, showing value in group members' contributions and opinions, staying on task, cooperating with others, and not competing. This does not mean that one must always agree or take everything at face value. Questioning and reasoning never go out of style. Certainly, a sense of

Figure 7.2 Groupthink.

justice, versatility, cheerfulness, enthusiasm, confidence, perspective, egalitarianism, and other such traits are important to create an underlying fabric of cohesion that can help the group withstand challenges.

Groupthink

Although group cohesiveness can have positive effects, it can also have a significant downside if not taken cautiously. Members can become so comfortable with and accepting of each other that they become sidetracked or fail to analyze information carefully. They may believe in their team to the point that they assume their outcomes will be positive. What can emerge is a group that is so cohesive that it forgets to do critical thinking—a potentially dangerous mode of processing known as Groupthink (Janis, 1971). **Groupthink** is a psychosociological phenomenon that happens when group members try to minimize conflict and reach a **consensus** (general agreement) without critically evaluating alternative ideas or viewpoints. It happens within groups of people when the desire for harmony or speed overrides a realistic appraisal of alternatives. Communication scholars have found evidence of Groupthink behind policy disasters ranging from the Bay of Pigs invasion to the 1984 Space Shuttle Challenger disaster (t'Hart, 1990).

To evaluate a group process, consider the following **factors that lead to Groupthink**:

1. **Homogeneity**: Are group members basically coming from the same perspective? Are there any ways to encourage the expression of alternate viewpoints? Does the group have such a strong sense of "we-ness" that people may not feel comfortable expressing different ideas or experiences that run counter to the group norm?

2. **Structural factors**: Is the group insulated from fully engaging all relevant information? Is the leadership of the group biased in some way? Are there clear decision-making procedures that ensure that the perspectives of all group members are truly heard? Does everyone in the group feel that they have equal access to contributing fully? Are minority perspectives protected or valued within the group process?

3. **Stressful context**: Are there any factors external or internal to the decision-making context that might be putting the group under stress that could cause them to want to speed along their process? Are people tired, hungry, or uncomfortable? Is there an imminent deadline? Is anything going on between group members that could cause enough stress to make group members want to be done with the work before considering the full range of alternatives?

To prevent Groupthink, it is important to provide for oversight and control by having clear, commonly-agreed-upon rules and procedures that provide for a thorough process. Group members should agree to a timeline that allows for thorough **brainstorming**, considering all possible options together as a group, before launching into evaluation and selection between alternatives. There needs to be a built-in way to allow for objection and protect dissenters, sort of a **"devil's advocate"** that can present alternative views for the sake of considering a wide range of alternatives. The group needs to set up work time and space so that members are not exceedingly tired, hungry, or stressed. (This is one reason many groups arrange for working meals, so people can eat and not be rushed.) Finally, there needs to be a clear decision-making structure, whether voting by majority, coming to consensus, or some other formula. Everyone needs to know how the final decision will be made so that they can weigh in appropriately at the appropriate time.

Examining and discussing differing viewpoints are essential to coming to a sound conclusion. A devil's advocate can be just what is needed for flushing out a topic and brainstorming for better ideas.

When groups fail to look at the pros and cons of an idea, they limit the creative process and thus may inhibit the development of ideas. Although it is important to be enthusiastic and complimentary, it is necessary to be analytical thinkers and to evaluate carefully to ensure that Groupthink does not sabotage the full potential of a group's process.

Approaches to Leadership

When undertaking a complicated project, there are many responsibilities and tasks to complete to get the job done on time. Leadership roles may trade off based on members' strengths and their involvement; groups are not limited to only one leader. Good leaders are usually good facilitators, making sure that all members are encouraged to contribute and to keep efforts moving forward.

There are **three basic approaches to leadership** that a group might take on in order to structure their group process:

Figure 7.3 Functional leadership.

1. **Traditional leadership** typically involves one central person who holds the main responsibility for the group's functioning. Within this traditional notion of leadership, there are three ways a leader might operate: **A) An authoritarian leader** takes charge and holds the ultimate responsibility for the completion of a task in command-and-control style. Often, authoritarian leadership emerges when one person with a dominant personality or obvious experience or opinions related to the topic steps forward. In cases when a task needs to be completed quickly or with minimal communication, authoritarian leadership can be the most streamlined, although the depth and richness of a broader group process may be sacrificed. **B) A democratic leader** emerges through some sort of voting or consensus-building process through which members agree to structure participatory leadership. This takes more time, structure, and communication, but allows group members more involvement in selecting and supporting their chosen leader. **C) A laissez-faire leader** does very little to direct the group. Although they may be appointed in some way to bring the group together, the laissez-faire leader does not propose structure or solutions, but simply holds the role to create the container for the group's process to emerge as it will. This kind of open process can be organic

and low-stress, but when a task needs to be completed, it offers little to keep the group on track or offer ac-countability for outcomes. Support groups in which the group process itself is the only goal can be very suitable for laissez-faire leadership.

2. **Shared leadership** means that all group members hold some of the responsibility for the outcome, often through some process of voting and/or consensus-seeking. Although there may be one or more individuals who serve as facilitators, the sense of accountability is shared equally among everyone in the group. This requires more communication, but can be very worthwhile to leverage the contributions of all group members. Shared leadership works best when there is equal commitment from all members of a group, and when the group process itself is one of the goals of the group. It is an empowering group structure that requires conscious focus from all, but can be an excellent growth experience for everyone in the group.

3. **Functional leadership** means that different group members take responsibility for differ-ent aspects of the work. Each person may be responsible for producing a particular piece of the final product accord-ing to their strength or area of expertise. The functional leadership approach views each member of the group as a unique contributor to both

Figure 7.4 Authoritarian Leadership

the process and product(s) of the group. Particularly when various individuals (or de-partments) are being brought together to represent their respective areas of contribu-tion, a functional approach can be useful to empower each member of the group to hold accountability for the aspect of the process that they are expected to bring.

There are **two main types of functional leadership** that con-tribute to a healthy group process: **Task leadership** and **Process leadership**. **Task leadership** be-haviors deal with the facilitating progression of the group's overall goal. Structuring conversation, as-signing roles, taking notes, doing research, delegating tasks, etc. all have to do with moving the neces-sary work forward to keep the group on task and get the job done. **Process leadership** deals with the group's well-being and making the group process comfortable so that members can contribute freely and fully. Maintaining a positive

group climate is necessary to keep the group moving along productively. Sometimes when arguments get intense, a process leader might make a joke or use a calm voice to redirect the conver-sation or suggest a break. Because of the diversity in a group, there will be all kinds of personalities and experiences. Sensitive people who can pick up on interpersonal vibes and make appropriate sug-gestions to "grease the wheels" between people keep the group process positive and smooth. The value of what we know can only be appreciated when members share their knowledge and experi-ence with everyone. It is harder for some group members to speak out than others, so creating a posi-tive group climate that supports everyone in participating is an important process function that makes group work pleasant and productive. Acknowledging both task and process leadership as important to the group's outcome means considering a variety of group roles as important to the process.

Group Roles

We bring our unique talents and personality traits to a group. The make-up of the group may influence the various roles that you and other members play. Who you are and who they are will dictate what roles you adopt, and how you contribute to the group. Three categories of group roles were originally defined by Kenneth Benne and Paul Sheats in 1948: **Task Roles, Maintenance Roles,** and **Individual (Dysfunctional) Roles**. The two functional categories include **Task** and **Maintenance Roles** that get the work of the group done and make the group climate smooth and productive. The dysfunctional category is comprised of **Individual roles** that display the personality traits of particular group members that are put above the group's intentions. These tend to be disruptive of the group, weakening its cohesion. Roles are often shared; the challenge is for each group member to take as many different roles as are appropriate to the group's needs in the various phases of its process toward achieving its purposes.

1.   **Task Roles**

   a. Initiator/contributor—offers new ideas or approaches.
   b. Information seeker—asks for clarification of facts.
   c. Opinion seeker—asks members to share opinions.
   d. Information giver—provides facts, statistics, and examples.
   e. Opinion giver—offers opinion or belief statements.
   f. Elaborator—provides comments or example to extend ideas.

   g. Coordinator—clarifies and notes relationships among ideas.
   h. Orienter—summarizes ideas and seeks to keep the group focused on task.
   i. Energizer—spurs group into action by giving motivational statements.
   j. Procedural technician—handles tasks like writing ideas on the board.
   k. Recorder—makes a written record of the group's progress.

2.   **Maintenance Roles**

   a. Encourager—offers praise, support, and positive feedback.
   b. Harmonizer—manages conflict and mediates personalities.
   c. Compromiser—manages conflict by mediating ideas.
   d. Gatekeeper—invites less talkative people to contribute and vice versa.
   e. Follower—goes along with suggestions and ideas.
   f. Expresser—articulates consensus feelings of group members.
   g. Observer—summarizes the group's progress or lack thereof.
   h. Tension reliever—provides humor and suggests breaks where appropriate.

3.   **Individual/Dysfunctional Roles**

   a. Aggressor—attacks people, not ideas; steals credit.
   b. Blocker—stubborn and disagreeable, shooting down ideas.
   c. Recognition Seeker—wants credit for everything.

   d. Self-confessor—self-discloses personal information to gain group sympathy.
   e. Joker—focuses on fun, jokes, and stories to the point of distraction.
   f. Dominator—takes control of agenda and conversation.
   g. Special interest pleader—has a hidden or personal agenda to fulfill.
   h. Help seeker—seeks to evoke sympathy due to low self-esteem.

It is common for group members to hold multiple roles and move between them, sometimes facilitating the group process, and sometimes holding it back. It helps to know all of these possible roles so that we can pay attention to our own behavior and bring out our best contributions in the ways that serve both ourselves and the group most effectively. Think for a moment about your own tendencies in groups, and that of others with whom you've worked. Why do you think particular roles are more or less comfortable for particular personality types? How do we learn and step into new roles as needed? How can we politely call attention to particular role patterns as they emerge and impact the group process? Are there new skills and roles that you'd like to cultivate the next time you work in a group?

Situational Leadership

It is crucial to recognize that there is not one best way to lead or participate in a group. Each group experience will be unique and require different skills, from day to day or even minute to minute. This is why it is important to bring strategic flexibility and a wide repertoire of possible behaviors and contributions, so that you can know when to speak up and when to hold back, and to become a more skillful observer of the group's flow and progress.

One way to understand how important it is to invoke different leadership styles and role behaviors is through the lens of **situational leadership** (Hersey & Blanchard, 1969), in which we utilize different styles of interaction depending on the situation. When the task orientation is high (we have something we must accomplish, and perhaps not much time to do it), a good leader needs to invoke **directive behavior**—telling people what to do and how to do it. Think of a firefighter in an emergency situation, needing to give clear guidance quickly without much group process. However, in a situation when the group process is very important, a good leader will invoke **supportive behavior**—listening to group members, considering their feelings, and spending much more time around the process itself. For example, in a group therapy session or a focus group around a new office policy, the entire reason for drawing people together is to listen and consider their feelings and opinions. In that case, directive behavior would be highly inappropriate, and we would need a repertoire of supportive behaviors to draw on.

To understand the choice of situational leadership behaviors we may utilizie, we draw axes of high and low supportive versus directive behavior. If our involvement is not crucial to the group process (either in terms of direction or support), we may choose a style of **observing/delegating**. If we need to give strong guidance, and there is not much need for supportive behavior, we may choose a style of **directing/telling**. When the need to offer support is higher than the need to offer direction, we would choose a **supporting/participating** approach. And when our need to provide both support and direction is high, we need to be equipped with

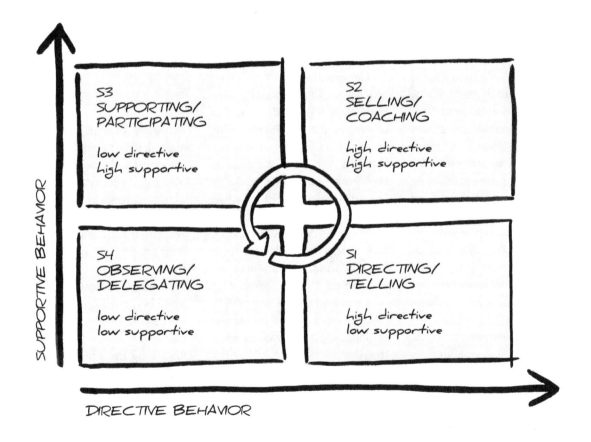

Figure 7.5 Situational Leadership

a **selling/coaching** style in which we can both offer our expertise and support group participants in understanding why particular choices are made. What situations can you think of that would be most suitable for these different styles of leadership?

Conclusion

Small group communication can be one of the most valuable and productive experiences of our professional and personal lives, but can also be one of the most challenging. Effective small group participation requires us to have a broad skill set, as well as high motivation to bring our best contributions to the experience. We need to combine skills in verbal and nonverbal communication, effective listening, with a high degree of interpersonal awareness and sensitivity. We need to possess a sense of our strengths and be willing to developing new ones, while also noticing and being able to rely on the strengths of others, as well. Because the range of skills and behaviors we need for successful group communication is so broad, it is very helpful if our motivation to participate is high so that we can keep our energy and focus through the process. This is why maintenance roles and supportive behaviors are just as important as directive roles and task behaviors—they keep the group environment open, supportive, fruitful, and fun.

No matter how detailed, models are nothing more than representations (often graphical representations) that illustrate theories about the world. They are, in a sense, maps. Heeding Alfred Korzybski's (c.f. General semantics) warning that the "map is not the territory," we should always be careful in applying models to the world, because no model can account for all cases. In other words, there are always going to be exceptions to the "rules" implied in any model, including the Thomas-Kilmann model. As a map, that interaction model will not always guide us toward the most sound advice. This is especially the case when a win-lose scenario or zero-sum game appears to be emerging. Let's take a look at each section of the model and consider a situation in which each scenario may not be the best course of action.

Avoidance: When one party is aggressive, agitated, or violent, it is probably best to walk away. You may attempt to resolve the conflict at a later time, when the individual is (hopefully) more accepting of or amenable to a civil discussion.

Competition: In an emergency situation, often one person must make a quick decision that others might not agree with. Think about a fire or hostage situation. Very often someone on the "front line" has to make an immediate decision that others may not agree with. The decision is sometimes based on knowledge and experience and sometimes not. Unfortunately this does not always mean that the correct decision was made. Lives may still be lost. However, something had to be done quickly to avoid a greater tragedy.

Accommodation: When one person is very passionate about a decision and the other is much less so, the less passionate person may choose to accept the other person's way of addressing the conflict and get on to the "next more," so to speak.

Compromise: As discussed in Chapter 6 ("Interpersonal Communication"), one good strategy to help build and maintain a successful and rewarding relationship is through compromise. Consider, for example, something as simple as splitting decisions regarding what to do on a date. The couple may compromise, so that one person decides what to do on Friday night and the other makes plans for Saturday night, or perhaps the following Friday.

Collaborating: Described as a win-win situation, this occurs when individuals work together to identify a solution that satisfies both. One downside of collaboration is that there is no immediate solution. It takes time and effort to collaborate.

Strategies to Resolve Conflict

Maintain Awareness: It is always a good idea to remain aware of your personal objectives and the objectives of others.

Offer Respect: Respect the thoughts and views of others. If you give them a chance to explain their reasoning, you may find that they can offer good solutions.

Control Emotions: Try to avoid becoming angry or agitated because you are in a disagreement with someone. Take turns discussing the pros and cons of each option.

Manage Stress: To manage stress during a conflict, remember to take deep breaths to help you relax if you feel tense. Make eye contact—positive face-to-face connections—during your discussion. Suggest taking a break and grabbing a coffee or a bite to eat. Sometimes a change of scene can be helpful.

References

Benne, K. D., & Sheats, P. (1948). Functional roles of group members. *Journal of Social Issues, 4*, 41–49.

Boardman, N. E. (2006). *Cost-benefit analysis, concepts and practice.* (3rd ed.). Upper Saddle River, NJ: Prentice Hall.

Devine, D. J. (2002). A review and integration of classification systems relevant to teams in organizations. *Group Dynamics: Theory, Research, and Practice, 6*, 291–310.

Festinger, L., Schachter, S., & Back, K., (1950). "The spatial ecology of group formation," in L. Festinger, S. Schachter, & K. Back (Eds.), *Social Pressure in Informal Groups.* Palo Alto, CA: Stanford University Press.

Gouran, D. S. , & Hirokawa, R. Y. (2003). *Effective decision making and problem solving in groups: A functional perspective.* In R. Y. Hirokawa, ed., R. S. Cathcart, ed., L. A. Samovar, ed., & L. D. Henman (Eds.), *Small group communication theory and practice: An anthology (8th ed., pp. 27–38).* New York: Oxford University Press.

Hersey, P. and Blanchard, K. H. (1969). *Management of organizational behavior: Utilizing human resources.* New Jersey: Prentice Hall.

Janis, I. L. (November 1971). Groupthink. *Psychology Today* 5 (6): 43–46, 74–76.

Katzenbach, J.R. & Smith, D.K. (1993). *The Wisdom of Teams: Creating the High-performance Organization.* Boston: Harvard Business School.

Scheerhorn, D., & Geist, P. (1997). Social dynamics in groups.

In L. R. Frey & J. K. Barge (Eds.), *Mangaging group life: Communicating in decision-making groups* (pp. 81–103). Boston: Houghton Mifflin.

Shaw, M. E. (1980). Group dynamics: The psychology of small group behavior (3rd ed.). New York: McGraw-Hill.

Steiner, I. D. (1972). *Group process and productivity.* New York: Academic Press.

't Hart, P. (1990). *Groupthink in Government: a Study of Small Groups and Policy Failure.* Amsterdam; Rockland, MA: Swets & Zeitlinger.

Tuckman, B. (1965). Developmental sequence in small groups. Psychological Bulletin, 63(6): 384–399.

Wald, M. L., & Schwartz, J. (2003, 08 04). Shuttle inquiry uncovers flaws in communication. New York Times. Retrieved from http://www.nytimes.com/2003/08/04/science/04SHUT.html

Chapter Eight
Intercultural Communication

Introduction: Why Study Intercultural Communication?

Globalization and Diversity

It is imperative to study intercultural communication in order to function in today's global society. People have always moved across the globe. For example, history regales us with the adventures of Alexander the Great and Marco Polo; in ancient times, Chinese merchants traveled to India and even as far as Africa and the Mediterranean. In addition, anthropological theories suggest that the Native Americans who populated the Americas may have had their origins in places as far away as Siberia, Southeast Asia, and Eurasia (Dulik et al., 2012). More recently, several nation-states—including but not limited to Great Britain, France, and Spain—engaged in **colonization**, invading and ruling over distant lands in the Americas, Africa, and parts of Asia, where they often suppressed the native populations. The creation of such colonies facilitated the movement not only of people but also of massive amounts of goods and capital. The history of the United States has its basis in European colonization and the systematic genocide of Native Americans, the involuntary importation of more than 10 million African slaves, and the annexation of Mexican territory. As a result, racial and ethnic diversity became an integral part of our history.

Although the era of territorial colonization has largely (though not completely) ended, its influence on the world has been significant and enduring, especially in terms of the spread and blending of languages and cultures. It ushered in a new period of **globalization,** involving the worldwide flow of technologies, media, ideas, and people (Appadurai, 1996) and creating new opportunities and innovations. Think about the film *Slumdog Millionaire*, a British movie that is set in India and revolves around the Indian version of the popular television game show *Who Wants to be a Millionaire,* which originated in Britain. It stars Dev Patel, a British actor of Indian origin whose parents were born in Nairobi, Kenya, where a significant Indian population resides. This film won eight Oscars, including Best Picture, and four Golden Globe awards. It has grossed more than $140 million within the United States and more than $375 million worldwide (www.boxofficemojo. com). The movie epitomizes the era of globalization and has made an immense contribution to popular culture.

But globalization also poses challenges. Let's return for a moment to the movement of people, otherwise known as **migration**. Over the last several decades, people have been voluntarily moving around the globe in unprecedented numbers. According to the United Nations, in 2015, there were 244 million international migrants, or persons living in a country other than the one in which they were born; this figure includes about 20 million **refugees**, or persons displaced from their homelands because of armed conflict and/ or political persecution ("244 million international migrants"). Owing to historical factors that stem from the legacy of colonialism, the United States, Great

Britain, and Continental Europe are common destinations for migrants. Therefore the diversity within these nations is growing at a rapid pace. One consequence of high levels of migration is the rise of **xenophobia**, or sentiments and actions that target in a negative way those who are perceived as foreigners. This can be seen in the discussions leading up to the 2016 decision by the people of the United Kingdom to leave the European Union. Similarly, there was U.S. President Donald J. Trump's highly criticized decision of 2017 to ban immigration and refugee resettlement from specific nations and to prioritize Christians over Muslims; this harkens back to other xenophobic periods in U.S. history, such as the time during which, in an effort to maintain racial homogeneity, all Asians were excluded by immigration policies that directly or indirectly gave preference to immigrants from northern and western Europe. Such decisions have important implications for people's lives as well as for human rights in general.

The history of colonization combined with contemporary global migration has resulted in the diversification of populations across the globe. Communication and interactions with diverse populations in the personal and professional aspects of our lives is inevitable. Moreover, despite the negative representations of these diverse populations, often through the media, diversity is generally considered desirable because of the ways in which it broadens our horizons, expands our worldviews, and enriches our lives. Imagine never interacting with anyone who was different from you; your frame of reference for understanding the world would be very narrow. According to the **intercultural contact hypothesis**, the best way to improve our relations with people from other cultures is to interact with them more. Unfortunately this is not always true; various conditions affect the validity of this hypothesis, such as the nature of the relationship between the parties, the amount and quality of their interactions, and the context in which they interact (Allport, 1979). At some level, it makes sense that the more positive your intercultural interactions are, the more positive your overall perceptions of intercultural communication will be (and vice versa). Hence the more we learn about intercultural communication, the better communicators we will become, thereby improving our overall intercultural interactions.

Social Justice

Social justice, or the aim of improving the treatment of and opportunities for marginalized groups of people, is another important reason for studying intercultural communication. Despite the advances that many nations have made in advancing equal rights, many cultural groups based on race, ethnicity, gender, class, and/or sexual identity (among others) continue to struggle to obtain just treatment and achieve equal rights.

Prejudices—preconceived, usually negative perceptions that one may hold about another cultural group (Allport, 1979)—can negatively affect the experiences of people targeted by them. When these prejudices are held by people in power, access to opportunities can also be limited. For example, a recent study demonstrates that upper-class white males were more likely to be called for job interviews by law firms than equally qualified upper-class white females and lower-class white males or females because they are seen as a better fit in the "elite culture and clientele of large law firms" (Rivera & Tilcsik, 2016, p. 1100).

It is important to remember that such prejudices are not always conscious, nor do they have to be explicit. They can also be cultural or **systemic** (i.e., built into the way our institutions function). Consider, for example, the following information about black males:

1. Police officers are more likely to stop black drivers than white ones. Once pulled over, people of color are more likely than whites to be searched, and blacks are more likely than whites to be arrested (Ghandnoosh, 2015).

2. Some 49% of African American men have been arrested at least once by the age of 23 (Ghandnoosh, 2015).

3. African Americans now constitute nearly 1 million of the total 2.3 million people who are incarcerated (Criminal Justice Fact Sheet, 2017).

These statistics do not reflect any inherent criminality in black males, just as they do not necessarily reflect the prejudices of all individuals involved in the judicial system (police officers, district attorneys, judges, etc.). Instead, they point to a criminal justice system based on systemic racism; the laws and institutions of our society necessarily lead to a particular result: the disproportionate stopping, arresting, and incarceration of black males. This creates a vicious cycle that has a negative effect on the lives of and opportunities of many black males, leading to lasting social and material consequences. Such inequalities pervade institutions across nations in varied ways. They also affect the ways in which members of different cultural groups experience these institutions. This is why different racial groups within the United States have reported varying perceptions of Black Lives Matter, a movement that works against the "extrajudicial killings of Black people by police and vigilantes" (About the Black Lives Matter network, 2017). That is, members of different racial groups experience the judicial system differently. According to a recent study conducted by the Pew Research Center, 28% of white Americans oppose Black Lives Matter, compared with only 12% of black Americans. On the other hand, 40% of white Americans support the movement, compared with 65% of black Americans (Horowitz & Livingston, 2016).

Therefore an important aspect of intercultural communication is to understand that these diverse perceptions are based on wide-ranging lived experiences and worldviews. Such understanding can help to improve not only the nature of our intercultural interactions but also the ways in which our institutions function. This reflects the need to study intercultural communication for ethical reasons, to improve the world around us. The goal of this chapter, then, is to provide a brief overview of some important ways of understanding intercultural communication and give you some basic tools for improving your intercultural competence.

Three Perspectives on Intercultural Communication

There are three major perspectives within the field of intercultural communication: social scientific, interpretive, and critical. These perspectives vary in several ways. First, what is intercultural communication exactly? Different scholars of intercultural communication would likely define it in different ways based on their particular perspectives. Second, these perspectives also reveal differences in defining what constitutes "culture." Third, recall the transactional model of communication that you read about in Chapter 1. Where would you locate the role of "culture" in this model? The best answer is probably that culture is relevant to the entire model. However, each of the three broad perspectives within the field of intercultural communication emphasizes the role of culture in a different part of the model. Finally, based on all of these three aspects, each of the different perspectives has a different goal when it comes to studying intercultural communication. In this section, we examine each of these three perspectives in order to gain a complete understanding of intercultural communication.

The Social Scientific Perspective

The social scientific perspective is the most traditional approach to intercultural communication. After the end of World War II, U.S. diplomats were heavily criticized for their failure to know even the language, much less the culture, of the countries to which they were assigned, contributing to the coining of the term *the ugly American* (Rogers et al., 2002). The field itself arose during the 1950s among scholars working at the Foreign Services Institute (FSI), which provided training to U.S. diplomats. The U.S. Congress established the FSI in 1946 to provide better training to the nation's diplomats. Linguists were hired to teach them language skills, and anthropologists were hired to teach them about different cultures. However, the trainees wanted "to understand how to communicate effectively with individuals who had a different culture than their own" (Rogers et al., 2002, p. 9). Scholars at FSI then started focusing on communication across cultures and on the fact that we are often unaware of our cultural behaviors. From this history emerged the foundations of intercultural communication, defined as the communication between people whose cultural orientations are distinct enough to alter the communication process because of mutual differences in rules, norms, values, interpretations, or contexts (Oetzel, 2009).

There are two important things to note in this definition. The first is that the focus is on *people* of different cultures. Within the communication model, then, social scientists locate culture in the sender and receiver. Second, this approach refers back to the definition of "culture" that was discussed in the first chapter as "norms, practices, or beliefs that define a particular grouping of people." According to the social scientific perspective, therefore, intercultural communication occurs when cultural behaviors and patterns inherent in the sender and receiver affect their communication in distinct ways. For example, in Chapter 4, you read about how different cultural groups may have different norms when it comes to physical contact. Imagine for a moment being approached by someone from a different culture who is accustomed to a greater level of physical touch than you are. If you know these cultural differences in advance, you are more likely to *understand* the other person's behavior and less likely to have a personal conflict with the person over your differing norms or perceive their touching as invasive. In fact, you might even be able to *predict* this behavior and therefore not be caught off guard by it. Finally, you may be able to *adapt* your behaviors to the cultural context so that you do not offend others by appearing distant and rude.

In the 1960s, Geert Hofstede (2011) came up with a series of *cultural dimensions* on the basis of which national cultures can be evaluated. Three of these are:

1. Power distance: This is the extent to which people accept variations in levels of power. It is premised in the idea that all societies are unequal but that some are more unequal than others. In a large power-distance culture, for example, children may be expected to be highly obedient and to give great deference, or respect, to their elders. Political leaders may be autocratic, while subordinates within any institution are expected to simply follow directions. On the other hand, in a small power-distance culture, parents and children may have more of an equal relationship, as may bosses and subordinates. Elders may not be respected or feared. Power distances tend to be larger in eastern European, Latin, Asian, and African countries. They tend to be smaller in Germanic and English-speaking countries.

2. Individualism vs. collectivism: This dimension relates to the level of integration of the people within a society. In individualistic cultures, the emphasis is on individuals looking out for themselves and/or their immediate families. People tend to highly value their privacy and the right to voice their personal opinions. In collectivistic societies, the emphasis is on one's belonging within larger groups, including one's extended family. People tend to value relationships first and foremost, prioritizing the maintenance of harmony over voicing personal opinions. Highly developed and western countries tend to be more individualistic, whereas less developed and eastern countries tend to be more collectivistic.

3. Masculinity vs. femininity: This dimension has to do with the extent to which a society prioritizes "men's" and "women's" values. Masculine cultures tend to value strength, assertiveness, and ambition. Moreover, there is a wide differentiation in terms of gender roles: men should be logical, willing to fight, and decisive, whereas women can be more emotional. Feminine cultures, on the other hand, do not differentiate as much between the genders. Both genders should be caring and can be emotional, just as both can be logical at times too. Some German-speaking and Latin countries tend to be highly masculine, while Nordic countries and the Netherlands tend to be very feminine.

These dimensions are useful in understanding some of the communication differences between people from different cultures. For example, collectivistic cultures see conflict as a threat to interpersonal relationships and may therefore minimize or avoid conflicts. Individualistic cultures, on the other hand, may see conflicts less as a threat and more as a healthy way of asserting one's identity in interpersonal relationships. To understand this, think about grapes as compared with an apple. With grapes, you can pull one grape off the bunch, and there's no real problem for either the grape or the bunch because each individual grape has its own skin. In contrast, if you were to take a bite of an apple, it wouldn't be long before the bitten-off piece and the remaining apple would start to turn brown.

Think about the way in which you were raised. Do you see yourself as a grape within your community or relationships, part of a bunch but still with your own distinct identity? Or do you see yourself more as an apple, so that what happens to one person in your community or circle of relationships affects everyone?

Perhaps you see elements of both? If so, you have identified a major drawback of the cultural dimensions approach, which assumes homogeneity, or sameness, within clearly defined and static (unchanging) cultures. Think about your home country. Is everyone within your nation the same? Do they all act the same? Has the culture stayed the same throughout the years and generations? Do you behave in the same way as your grandparents did, for example? You would probably answer each of these questions with a resounding no. The truth is that within any nation there are differences according to various influences, such as region, family, or even individual personalities, and also in terms of time. Therefore, although there is some validity to the claim that the United States is an individualistic culture compared with many other national cultures, it is not valid to claim that all Americans are always individualistic in exactly the same way.

This illustrates the difference between *generalization* and *stereotyping*. **Generalizations** are broad claims made about a group of people based on credible research about the preponderance of beliefs within that group. They can help us hypothesize about someone's behavior. **Stereotypes**, on the other hand, are assumptions that all members of a cultural group share certain characteristics (Bennett, 1998). Whether positive (e.g., "All Asians are smart" or negative ("All Asians are bad drivers"), stereotypes are harmful because they deny a person's individuality (Tatum, 1992). It is easy to see how valid generalizations can lead to stereotypes if we are not careful. To avoid this trap, it is important to remember that there

are variations within cultures and that no cultural dimension characterizes every individual or every communication behavior. For instance, being from the United States, you might privilege an individualistic perspective in certain ways, but this does not mean that you lack all concern for community or the people around you.

The Interpretive Perspective

Because the social scientific perspective relies so much on generalizing about large groups of people, another perspective arose that focused on acquiring a more in-depth understanding of people's experiences. According to the interpretive perspective, intercultural communication is defined as the way in which people from different cultural backgrounds use symbols to create, maintain, repair, or transform reality.

The most important thing to note in this definition is that it emphasizes the use of *symbols*. Within the model of communication, messages (and feedback) are always made up of symbols; this is where interpretive scholars locate culture. The interpretive approach emphasizes the idea of **social construction**—that we construct our society based on the way in which we use our symbols. Remember that the relationship between a symbol and the thing it represents is arbitrary, meaning that there is no necessary connection between the two. However, people within a society must agree upon its meaning in order to communicate with one another. This agreement is not necessarily straightforward;

many factors play a role, such as the material needs of a society, relationships, lived experiences, contexts, etc. All of this constitutes culture, which is defined here as the learned and shared contextual meanings of a society. According to interpretive scholars, understanding the ways in which symbols are used within a society can help us to understand more about the culture.

Let's consider the example of the college classroom as a cultural group that we might want to study. What are some of the symbols you might observe in a college classroom? Let's consider three different situations.

Classroom A: The instructor is standing at the front of the room while students enter and take their seats in rows facing him. The instructor speaks primarily from lecture notes but may smile, make eye contact, and interact with the students as the class progresses. As students wish to speak, they generally raise their hands and wait to be called on by the instructor, though they may occasionally call out answers to questions. Students are generally dressed in blue jeans or shorts, while the instructor wears a nice shirt and slacks.

Classroom B: Students enter a large classroom and find their seats first. Then they stand up when the instructor enters, and she walks straight to the front of the classroom, making little to no eye contact with the students. As the students sit down again, the instructor opens her lecture notes and begins to read them out loud while the students take notes. As students wish to speak, they generally raise their hands and wait to be called upon by the instructor; they never deviate from this norm. Moreover, students rarely raise their hands to speak. The professor is dressed in a formal suit, while students are generally dressed in nice shirts and slacks.

Classroom C: Desks are arranged in a large circle where both students and the instructor sit. The instructor has some notes but rarely looks at them, instead talking to the students and making eye contact with them. Students almost never raise their hands to speak; instead, they rely on nonverbal cues to know when it is their turn. Both the instructor and the students are dressed in blue jeans or shorts. Laughter is commonly heard during the course of the conversations.

This process of observing the usage of symbols to understand cultures is referred to as the **ethnography of communication**. In each of these three scenarios, each classroom constitutes its own culture because its members have been socialized into a particular system of meanings, as exemplified by their awareness and compliance in terms of how they use particular symbols (Philipsen, 1992). For example, Classroom A demonstrates a relatively moderate hierarchical relationship between students and instructor, while Classroom B depicts a more intensely hierarchical relationship. What conclusions would you draw about Classroom C? It is important to note that members of the culture in each classroom (students and instructor) have learned these meanings, even though they may not be aware of it. More importantly, every time they enact the symbols described, they reproduce that particular culture.

Interpretive scholars learn about culture by focusing on the symbols that are being used. Unlike social scientists, they are not interested in comparing but may focus on a particular cultural group and find out as much about it as they can. As shown by the preceding example, a single classroom can have its own culture! But you may also consider how each of these examples reflects, for example, the cultural dimension of power distance, as already discussed. This approach to intercultural communication is always **inductive**, meaning that we take a particular instance and draw larger conclusions from it about how that cultural group views, for example, power distance and hierarchy. Therefore interpretive scholars may also interview members of cultural groups to learn more about them from their own perspectives. These approaches are useful in terms of gaining highly in-depth knowledge, but they also have a huge drawback. When you focus on such micro-levels of culture, it becomes much more difficult to identify larger cultural patterns in the same way that Hofstede did in the 1960s.

The Critical Perspective

The critical perspective draws from the intercultural perspective; it picks up the notion that we use symbols to construct our realities. However, it also asserts that power and social hierarchies have material consequences for the ways in which those symbols are used. Within the communication model, culture is not confined to any specific component but rather exists within the larger communication context. No communication that takes place is ever devoid of a sociohistorical context.

Historically, certain groups have always held power and have sought to maintain that power. Empirical data, for example, show that white males continue to hold the greatest number of federal and state judgeships (Torres-Spelliscy, Chase, & Greenman, 2010), executive offices (Kohli, Gans, & Hairston, 2011), and CEO positions of Fortune 500 companies (Burns, Barton, & Kerby, 2012).

From a communication perspective, however, it is important to remember that power is not defined purely by numbers. A group can be in the numerical majority and still not hold power. Can you think of any examples of this? (*Hint*: If not, look back to the first page of this chapter.) Instead, power is defined by the ability to make meanings, which in effect creates our society. If you had the power to make meanings, wouldn't you make them in such a way as to maintain your own power? You would create a culture in which everything about yourself was good and desirable! Remember that meanings are communicated through the use of symbols, and symbols are social constructs; therefore their meanings depend on social processes. What happens if an army disregards a red cross and bombs a hospital? What kind of power is necessary to get people to agree upon and comply with set meanings?

But in general, you and I personally do not get to construct meanings; instead, we operate within a system that has already constructed them. To the extent that we can rely on those meanings that are positive and beneficial for us, we have **privilege**. Privileges can certainly be earned, in the sense of hard work; but in the context of this chapter, we are talking about *unearned* privilege. For example, you may have heard the term *white privilege*. This refers to such things as never being asked to speak on behalf of all people in your racial group or people not being suspicious that you got your job "only" because of affirmative action (McIntosh, 1989).

Moreover, those with many privileges tend to be networked with others who also have many privileges, further increasing their ability to access opportunities. The value of our social networks in terms of facilitating certain actions or achievements that would otherwise not be feasible is known as *social capital* (Coleman, 1988). The concept of social capital has been described in western philosophy since the latter part of the 20th century, but was more recently defined by Szreter (2000) as "the social relationships between people that enable productive outcomes." It is fitting that this term should come into vogue around the turn of the 2000 millennium because of the proliferating power of the Internet in the formation of social networks and the exercise of social capital. Modern structures of mass communication are shifting rapidly as people's direct ability to disseminate messages and broaden diverse social networks expands exponentially. One important thing to note about social capital is that it is very much bound within context.

However, it is important to remember that everyone is privileged and not privileged in various ways; certainly not all white people are privileged in the same ways. For example, white heterosexual males may experience privilege differently than white homosexual males.

This is because our identities are **intersectional**, meaning that race, ethnicity, class, gender, sexuality, etc., all play into our identities and affect our levels of privilege in different ways. Power and privilege can be based on the context of when, where, and with whom you are interacting. A black male may experience a different level of privilege in interacting with a white male as opposed to a white female. Someone who does not fit into a privileged category in a specific interaction would naturally be disempowered to some extent; therefore they might contest, or challenge, the meanings that have been created and that contribute to their disempowerment. Unlike the case in the interpretive perspective, culture is not an agreed-upon set of shared meanings but rather a site of contested meanings that is constantly being shaped and reshaped through communication processes that are marked by power. Critical intercultural scholars will focus on questioning or challenging presumed cultural norms by looking specifically at how communication and the symbols that we use either maintain or challenge certain hierarchies and power structures in our society.

Let's take a look at a hypothetical example. Anita is a Mexican American college student in the United States. Her family is from the Rio Grande Valley in Texas and has lived there for at least ten generations, dating back to before the territory belonged to the United States. She identifies as an American but also take great pride in her Mexican heritage and speaks Spanish fluently. During a class discussion one day about immigration, another student proclaims, "Mexicans are lucky to live in this country! They

should all just speak English and become American." Anita is very upset by this comment, given her family history and her identity. How might Anita respond to this incident?

One example of a critical approach to intercultural communication is **co-cultural communication theory,** which "explores the process by which co-cultural group members select certain communicative practices when interacting within the structures of dominant society" (Orbe, 1994, p. 14). The term *co-cultural group members* refers to groups who occupy marginalized positions within a given societal structure. It is premised on the idea that, in communicating with others who occupy more dominant positions, co-cultural group members make tactical decisions about how to communicate for a variety of reasons, such as feelings of apprehension, powerlessness, disappointment, or of being silenced.

Such decision are often based on several important factors:

1. The preferred outcome of their communication. Are they looking to assimilate or just fit in with society's expectations? Are they looking to accommodate or to find their unique place within the multicultural society? Or are they looking to separate by refusing a connection with cultural others?

2. The situational context, or the specific circumstances of the communication. For example, like anyone else, co-cultural group members may use different strategies depending on whether they are at home or at work.

3. Perceived costs and rewards. This may remind you of the social exchange theory, where costs and rewards are evaluated in making choices about interpersonal relationships. Similarly, here co-cultural groups members make decisions about how to communicate based on what they perceive to be consequences of potential strategies.

4. Communication approach. This refers to assertive, nonassertive, or aggressive communication practices. Assertive communication practices are those where a person expresses himself or herself while taking into account the other person's needs or feelings. Nonassertive communication practices are those where a person remains nonconfrontational. Aggressive communication practices are often hurtfully expressive.

Let's return now to Anita's story. She has to make a decision about how to respond to her classmate's insensitive comment. She has to evaluate how her response might be received in the class. In order to do this, she might think about whether she is likely to receive support from her professor or other classmates. She might think about her own comfort level in responding out loud. She might consider her desire, or lack thereof, to bring attention to herself by responding out loud. She might also think about the need to maintain a certain level of professionalism within the classroom context. What are some other things she might contemplate before making a decision? Based on different

answers to these questions, what are some possible ways that she might respond to this classmate? The point here is not to judge each of these responses as right or wrong but to try to understand why a person from a co-cultural group might make any of these decisions.

Critical intercultural scholars are driven by the goal of empowering disempowered cultural groups in order to attain social justice. If our society is produced through communication, then changes to that communication can help to promote social change. However, an important drawback of this approach is that it always assumes an inequality of power that must be rectified. The extent to which you perceive that to be a drawback depends largely on the extent to which you believe that unequal power relations shape our society.

Although achieving social justice will likely remain an ongoing objective for the foreseeable future, in the next section, we look at some specific ways that you can work toward improving your own intercultural communication competence.

Building Intercultural Competence

According to Milton J. Bennett's (1979) developmental model of intercultural sensitivity, building intercultural competence means moving away from ethnocentric mindsets to ethnorelative ones. **Ethnocentrism** refers to the notion that one's own cultural patterns, values, and beliefs are normal and/or preferable to any others. During the era of colonization, for example, the act of colo-

colonization was often justified based on ethnocentric beliefs that white, western cultures were more civilized and modern than the "backward" peoples over whom the the colonizers were ruling. Hence colonization was fulfilling the "white man's burden." This negative view of other cultures was an obvious version of ethnocentrism. A more subtle form of ethnocentrism would include such statements as "We're all just human" or "I don't see race." These types of statements imply the nonexistence of difference and consequently reduce the significance of perspectives or experiences that differ from one's own. You may seemingly tolerate other cultural viewpoints, but your own cultural positions and viewpoints remain the norm. **Ethnorelativism**, on the other hand, includes moves toward not just "tolerating" difference but valuing it positively and actively seeking to incorporate it in our own lives, experiences, and frames of reference. For example, one consistent way of challenging your ethnocentrism is to immerse yourself in a new culture (Turk, 2001). Study abroad is one terrific option that college students have, enabling them to travel to different countries. However, the ability to take advantage of this opportunity depends on a lot of factors. Aside from international travel, then, let's discuss a few other ways of moving toward ethnorelativism.

Even though "tolerance" itself tends toward ethnocentrism, developing a **tolerance for ambiguity** can be very useful in ethnorelative intercultural interactions. Think about each time you start a new semester. Do you like to know as soon as possible everything that the class will cover, all assignments, all due date, all tests, etc.? Or do you prefer to just get the basic information you need to know at that point and figure that the rest of the information will come as you need it? If you fall into the second category, you may have a high tolerance for ambiguity, meaning that you are comfortable with the temporary state of "not knowing."

Consider how this could be helpful in intercultural interactions. Although there is definitely some value to learning about different cultures, it is simply not possible to know everything about every culture. Therefore, during an intercultural encounter, you are likely to have moments where you are uncomfortable or do not understand the behavior of the other person. For example, imagine a business meeting where you want to focus on the task at hand, but the other person keeps asking distracting questions about your family. You might instinctively retreat to an ethnocentric position by thinking that the other person is annoying or not a valuable business partner. However, tolerance for ambiguity would allow you to consider that the other person may be communicating from a different cultural perspective, even though you may not immediately know what that perspective is. (In this case, the other person may be communicating from a collectivist cultural dimension.)

Building **empathy** is another important tool in moving toward ethnorelativism. Empathy should be distinguished from the notion of sympathy, which is based on one's personal views and is therefore ethnocentric. Empathy, on the other hand, is the ability to see a situation from another person's perspective (Bennett, 1979). But how exactly does one do this? As

discussed earlier in this chapter, different cultural experiences lead to people having very different perceptions of the same situation. Recall the example of the Black Lives Matter movement. We discussed how different experiences with the U.S. criminal justice system have led to different perceptions of the movement itself. But even if all of your experiences with the criminal justice system have been positive, empathy would involve looking beyond those personal experiences in order to try to understand why others might have a different point of view. At the same time, it is important to realize that one can never *fully* understand another's experiences and perspectives. Hence, think about empathizing as an ongoing communication process that can help in intercultural interactions by allowing people from different cultural backgrounds and worldviews to negotiate shared meanings (Broome, 1991).

Empathy in the context of intercultural communication also cannot be understood outside of power dynamics. As Turk (2001) explains, the perspectives of dominant group members tend to be universally known; however, those same dominant group members tend to be less aware of the perspectives of nondominant group members, who tend to be silenced more often. Hence, when there is a power imbalance between cultural groups, the more dominant group members may need to make a stronger outward effort toward empathy.

Conclusion

Effective and successful intercultural communication is a

challenging goal for even the most interculturally aware people. We have all been socialized into our own cultural norms, with which we are comfortable and familiar and which include stereotypes and prejudices. Temporary retreats to ethnocentrism are normal and even welcome when an intercultural challenge becomes overwhelming. Therefore no one is to be blamed or shamed for the occasional intercultural faux pas or lack of sensitivity, just as we should feel guilty for our privilege or access to social capital. At the same time we all need to take responsibility for improving our intercultural communication skills, breaking cycles of oppression, and broadening our perspectives when it comes to other cultural groups.

References

244 million international migrants living abroad worldwide, new UN statistics reveal. (2016, January 12). Retrieved from http://www.un.org/sustainabledevelopment/blog/2016/01/244-million-international-migrants-living-abroad-worldwide-new-un-statistics-reveal/

About the Black Lives Matter network. (2017). Retrieved from http://blacklivesmatter.com/about/

Allport, G. W. (1979). *The nature of prejudice*. New York, NY: Basic Books.

Appadurai, A. (1996). *Modernity at large: Cultural dimensions of globalization*. Minneapolis, MN: University of Minnesota Press.

Bennett, M. J. (1979). Overcoming the golden rule: Sympathy and empathy. In D. Nimmo (Ed.), *Communication yearbook 3* (pp. 407–422), Beverly Hills, CA: Sage.

Bennett, M. J. (1993). Towards ethnorelativism: A developmental model of intercultural sensitivity. In R. M. Paige (Ed.), *Education for the intercultural experience* (pp. 21–71). Yarmouth, ME: Intercultural Press.

Bennett, M. J. (1998). Intercultural communication: A current perspective. In M. J. Bennett (Ed.), *Basic concepts of intercultural communication: Selected readings* (pp. 1–34).

Broome, B. (1991). Building shared meaning: Implications of a relational approach to empathy for teaching intercultural communication. *Communication Education, 40*, 235–249.

Burns, C., Barton, K., & Kerby, S. (2012). The state of diversity in today's workforce: As our nation becomes more diverse so too does our workforce. Center for American Progress, Washington, D.C. Retrieved from https://cdn.americanprogress.org/wp-content/uploads/issues/2012/07/pdf/diversity_brief.pdf

Coleman, J. S. (1988). Social capital in the creation of human capital. *American Journal of Sociology, 94*, S95–S120.

Criminal Justice Fact Sheet. (2017). Retrieved from www.naacp.org

DeTurk, S. (2001). Intercultural alliance-building: Myth, competency, or possibility for alliance-building? *Communication Education, 50*(4), 374–384.

Dulik, M. C., Zhadanov, S. I., Osipova, L. P., Askapuli, A., Gau, L., Gokcumen, O., ... et al. (2012). Mitochondrial DNA and Y chromosome variation provides evidence for a recent common ancestry between Native Americans and indigenous Altaians. *The American Journal of Human Genetics, 90*(2), 229–246. DOI: http://dx.doi.org/10.1016/j.ajhg.2011.12.014

Ghandnoosh, N. (2015). Black lives matter: Eliminating racial inequity in the criminal justice system. Washington, D.C.: The Sentencing project. Retrieved from www.sentencing project.org

Hofstede, G. (2011). Dimensionalizing cultures: The Hofstede Model in context. *Online readings in psychology and culture, 2*(1), 1–26.

Horowitz, J. M., & Livingston, G. (2016, July 8). How Americans view the Black Lives Matter movement. PEW Research Center, Washington, D.C. Retrieved from http://www.pewresearch.org/fact-tank/2016/07/08/how-americans-view-the-black-lives-matter-movement/

Kohli, J., Gans, J., & Hairston, J. (2011). A better, more diverse senior executive service in 2050: More representative leadership will improve the effectiveness and efficiency of the federal government. Center for American Progress, Washington, D.C. Retrieved from https://cdn.americanprogress.org/wp-content/uploads/issues/2011/09/pdf/ses_paper.pdf

Oetzel, J. G. (2009). *Intercultural communication: A layered approach.* New York, NY: Pearson.

Orbe, M. P. (1998). *Constructing co-cultural theory: An explication of culture, power, and communication.* Thousand Oaks, CA: Sage.

Philipsen, G. (1992). *Speaking culturally: Explorations in social communication.* Albany, NY: SUNY Press.

Rivera, L. A., & Tilcsik, A. (2016). Class advantage, commitment penalty: The gendered effect of social class signals in an elite labor market. *American Sociological Review, 81*(6), 1097–1131.

Rogers, E. M., Hart, W. B., & Miike, Y. (2002). Edward T. Hall and the history of intercultural communication: The United States and Japan. *Keio Communication Review, 24*, 3–26.

Tatum, B. D. (1992). Talking about race, learning about racism: The application of racial identity development theory in the classroom. *Harvard Educational Review, 62*(1), 1–24.

Torres-Spelliscy, C., Chase, M., & Greenman, E. (2010). Improving judicial diversity. Brennan Center for Justice at New York University School of Law, New York, NY. Retrieved from https://www.brennancenter.org/sites/default/files/legacy/Improving_Judicial_Diversity_2010.pdf

Chapter Nine
Mediated Communication

"The new electronic interdependence recreates the world in the image of a global village."

—Marshall McLuhan

Our World Community

Like any other adaptive species on the planet, humans function as communities. "Community" can mean many things—the neighborhood where you live, the family or tribe you are born into, an institution you are part of, or a grouping of people who share your interests. We use terms like "our campus community" or "the gaming community" or "a spiritual community" to describe concepts around which we organize ourselves. Think of all the communities to which you've belonged over the course of your life. How do you know what makes someone a "member" of any one of these communities? And, what are the connections between "community" and "communication"?

Indeed, with the far reach of modern communication, an always-increasing proportion of the world's population live in a 'global village,' as Canadian medium theorist Marshall McLuhan observed. News of a natural disaster, the toppling of a government, a bombing in a city center, the foibles of a new president, or even the untimely death of a pop star tends to reach us just as quickly as (and often more quickly and in greater detail than) it does inhabitants of the place where the event actually transpired. If you think about it, the planet we live on is also a community, and increasingly fosters the experience of inhabiting one massive village where everybody knows everyone else's business. This is the essence of the Global Village idea McLuhan coined. Of course, our collective involvement is not merely a matter of connectivity. An occurrence in one part of the world can significantly affect the

systems we inhabit—economically, socially, and biologically. Our environment is a planetary one, where impacts on air and water and earth affect entire ecosystems. Conflicts are waged, not only over land and resources like petroleum or precious metals, but also over life-giving resources like water and even airspace. In 1950, the world's population was 2.5 billion; by 2011 it had reached 7 billion, and by 2050 the global population is projected to reach 10 billion. With almost all the population growth occurring in emerging economies, by 2030 some 2 billion people will have joined the global middle classes. Economist Dambisa Moyo predicts, "in less than 20 years we will witness the creation of a middle class of roughly the same size as the current total population of Africa, North America and Europe ... This means that global demand for food and water is expected to increase by 50% and 30% respectively by 2030;" (Altkenhead, 2012).

Figure 9.1 The Global Village: This image helps us envision a 'global village' where the transmission, reception, and exchange of information by fiber optic cables carrying digital signals across the planet's surface, as well as exchanged between satellites and between satellites and the surface has almost entirely defeated the limitations of both time and space. Indeed, according to NASA.org (2017), among the approximately 20,000 pieces of human-made objects circling the earth in low and geosynchronous orbit, approximately 2,750 are functional communication satellites of various kinds that allow near-instantaneous global communication to occur "24/7."

Mediated Communication

One of the world's most influential media scholars, Canadian Marshall McLuhan, famously said, "The medium is the message," noting the ability of the media themselves to not only convey and define messages, but also to structure our ways of thinking and being in the world (McLuhan, 1964). With the tools of technology, our roles as members of a truly interconnected global society are more important to consider than ever before. **Mediated communication**, the various processes of transferring messages through devices and systems, is transforming human communication in the 21st Century. These innovations are changing the ways we interact, learn, shop, entertain ourselves and each other, engage in civic life and participate in politics. The lines continue to blur between what was previously described as **mass communication** and **computer-mediated communication** (CMC). Today, we see almost daily innovations in how messages are developed, disseminated, shared, linked, and transformed in fast, interlaced streams of cultural meaning-making. Modeling the interlinked, rapidly changing processes of mediated communication is becoming an ever-increasing challenge.

The term **mass communication** refers to media such as radio, television, film, newspapers, magazines, etc. that transmit messages rapidly or even simultaneously to large numbers of people. Although the sender is typically in one place and time, the audience/receivers may be in thousands of locations, and in many different time zones, often in multiple countries. Think for a moment about the challenges all of that represents to us as communicators: if the first rule of communication is "Know Your Audience," how can we "know" millions of people? How do we create messages that are meaningful, that strike a resonant chord with our receivers, when we are trying to communicate with "masses" of people? Questions like these have prompted media analysts to investigate the extent to which new communication technologies are neutral conduits that simply increase the speed and scale of content transmission or, conversely, more active symbolic and cognitive systems that prohibit or allow, enhance or degrade, or otherwise alter content which, in turn, will tend to bias audience interpretations of that content. Consider, for example, the structural differences between newspapers, radio, and television. Such questions should prompt us to wonder if, for example, FDR would have been elected in the early 1950s (as opposed to the early 1930s), in the "AT era" (after Television began to surpass Radio as the electronic communication medium of choice for news and entertainment). Given that Roosevelt suffered from polio as a younger man and was more or less wheelchair-bound throughout his 16 year tenure, it has been theorized that he may not have been able to sustain public support were his disability been the subject of popular conversation. Such questions should also prompt us to wonder if Barrack Obama or Donald Trump would have been elected in the "BT era" (before Twitter), as both candidates – especially Mr. Trump – made expert use of Twitter as a communication medium to reach their advocates and gather new ones.

Computer-mediated communication (CMC) refers to sharing messages through the use of networked computers or other devices. Although the term grew from communication transactions that occur through computer-mediated formats such as email, chat rooms, and instant messaging (IM), it now includes additional forms of mediated interactions such as social networking,, gaming, and text messaging. As technologies develop and the ability to share text, images, links, videos, and all manner of information becomes more and more seamless, we now must refer to any communication that takes place through a device as **mediated communication**. This blended field now encompasses elements of interpersonal communication, group communication, and mass communication. Having strategic flexibility, some basic media, information, and technological literacy skills, and a sense of perspective can help us to use mediated communication in more effective ways. This can simultaneously increase our social capital and ability to communicate effectively in the world, both locally and globally.

A Brief History of Mediated Communication

The next page or so offers just a quick scan of what is, in fact, a very complex media history. That history, through the discussion of a number of specific, is then elaborated on in the section entitled 'Understanding Our Media Ecology.' There we consider some key similarities, as well as some important differences, between our mediated past and present that will put us in a good position to make some educated guesses as to what our mediated future might look like. We begin with a brief history of mediated communication.

The development of written alphabets and glyph systems in ancient Mesopotamia, Mesoamerica, China, Egypt, and India moved much of humanity from oral culture to written culture. Over thousands of years, humans learned to write—and in turn, to store, save, repeat, and share information over vast distances. This break from oral traditions meant that information could reach many people in the same (written) form, rather than relying solely on word of mouth and storytelling. Power moved from known individuals, the storytellers of a community, to the written words themselves, and control of information and ideas became a major currency of power, which was held tightly by monarchs and monasteries alike.

In the mid-15th Century, Johannes Gutenberg's moveable type press made possible the more rapid and less expensive duplication of information; this in turn enabled easier storage, putting books in the hands of many people. For the first time in history this made large amounts of information accessible to people typically considered to be outside the educated and privileged classes. In the form of books, and later newspapers and magazines, information was now portable and storable, available to influence mass consciousness and impact societies in much more significant and far-reaching ways.

These early mass media were followed in the 19th and 20th centuries by telegraphy and the wireless (later called "radio"), and by photographic and electronic media—from still photographs to film and later video and digital imagery. The concept of "mass" broadcasting brought about by the growth of major broadcast networks during the World Wars and through the middle of the 20th century began a trajectory toward more market-driven individualized programming with the advent of video recording devices, cable networks, and of course the Internet.

The groundwork for and basic structure of the **Internet** was actually developed in the 1960s and 1970s under the direction of the U.S. Department of Defense's Advanced Research Projects Administration (ARPA), known as the ARPANET. This was an internal system of file transfer between military institutions and research universities around the country. In the 1980s, the concept of a Worldwide Web was developed, but the Internet as we now know it did not enter mainstream public use until the 1990s (NewMedia.org, 2014). By 2014, there were over 3 billion Internet users, the largest percentage of which (almost half) was in Asia (Internet World Stats, 2015).

Today, by leveraging new methodologies like data-mining, meta-data analysis and the whole 'Big-Data' movement under which these and other related practices are generally described, the communication industries' ability to monitor "hits," views, and trends in real-time by way of these and other Internet user tracking mechanisms is changing the notion of what we considered "mass communication" in the 20th century. Today, all of this is typically referred to as "networked communication" in industry parlance. Throughout this same time period the term "broadcasting" is turning into a very different business often called "narrowcasting," a term coined by public broadcasting advocate J.C.R. Licklider, who in a 1967 report envisioned a multiplicity of networks aimed at serving the needs of smaller,

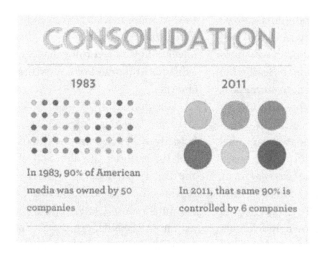

Figure 9.2 Media Consolidation

Media Consolidation, source: http://www.frugaldad.com/media-consolidation-infographic/

more targeted audiences (Parsons, 2003). Every time your clicks and preferences are captured and you are delivered targeted marketing, like the coupons the register spits out at the grocery store, or those ads that appear along the side of your web browser, or the uncanny suggestions offered up at Amazon.com or Netflix, you are being delivered as a "product" of **narrowcasting** to advertisers, corporations and other interested parties, whether you choose to be or not. Narrowcasting is related to **audience segmentation**. Some media commentators have suggested that audience segmentation will soon bring the end of Mass Communication as we know it since these two practices are allowing a much more focused and fine-grained ability on the part of media producers to effectively target and reach particular demographics. These processes, in turn, add credence to a kind of truism in the field of Mass Communication which suggests that the real content of, say, the medium of commercial television is the commercials, and the product of that medium is the audience those commercials are aimed at.

As newspaper and magazine readership continues to decrease, more people worldwide are getting their news from online and television news sources. Many are abandoning news and information programming and sources entirely in favor of sports and entertainment news and programming. At the same time we are limiting our information sources as consumers, the growth of media empires and conglomerates means that fewer professionals are responsible for the information we are getting. One large multinational corporation may own hundreds of media outlets—newspapers, broadcast and cable television and radio stations, satellite networks, magazines, web sites, movie studios, and distribution networks. Having only a few large corporations owning most of the communication media means that we are exposed to news and information from fewer sources,

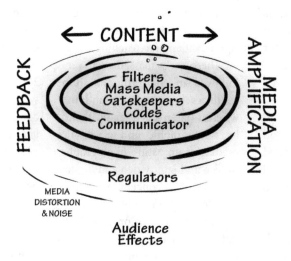

Figure 9.3 HUB Model of Mass Communications.

and are less likely to know the source of our information.

In other words, we are in the midst of a vast communication revolution that is disrupting long-held assumptions and understandings of the mass communication industry, and the processes underlying it. Mass Media in the early 21st Century operates at an unprecedented speed and scale. Indeed, we have never seen anything like this before in the history of human communication. Electronic and digital media now allows access to more information, news, entertainment and pretty much any other kind of content we might want, across greater distances and faster and more efficiently than ever before. We are now presented with a dizzying array of choices and challenges. As media producers and consumers, and as communicators in general, we have been granted powers that were almost impossible to imagine just 50 or 60 years ago. But as has always been the case, great power calls for great responsibility. Whereas social capital used to be held mainly in the hands of highly capitalized (well-funded or otherwise powerful) sources and networks, today anyone with a communication device can gain followers and develop tremendous social capital, almost overnight. Modes and means of power are shifting, and much of the news and information we encounter is not always generated by "media professionals."

We are no longer merely passive media consumers, who simply turned on the television and watched one of the three available channels, or tuned in to our favorite radio station and listened for hours, or who faithfully read the daily newspaper delivered to our doorsteps. We are now, to varying degrees, participatory media consumers. In the 21st Century, Mass Communication creates the potential for mass participation. "Potential" is the key word in that sentence because, indeed, mass participation is more often a matter of possibility than reality. In this new context, modern media users more freely choose what information they expose themselves to on a minute-by-minute basis. Every time we view or click on something, our choice contributes to shaping our rapidly-shifting mediated world.

The HUB Model of Mass Communication

Consider your position—if you generate or consume messages, purchase devices or subscriptions, or tend to operate as a common consumer in our society, you are an active participant in driving the flow of **capital** (money) in our mediated world. Every time you click on a link, respond to an ad, post a comment, watch a video, play a game, or just communicate with others through mediated devices, you are shaping the flow of goods and services that shapes our society. Even though it was developed in 1974, well before the mainstream proliferation of the Internet, the **HUB Model of Communication** (named for the three communication scholars who developed it: Hiebert, Ungurait, and Bohn) is still a useful tool for understanding our place in the complex web of forces involved in mediated communication. The HUB Model can help us **leverage our power** mindfully, and in ways that we feel best serve us and our society.

There are different paradigms under which media operate, which can broadly be classified as **authoritarian** (government-controlled) systems and **libertarian** ("free press") systems (Siebert, Peterson, & Schramm, 1956). Within the libertarian ideology, there are two basic models for how media can best operate: a social responsibility paradigm, and a commercial paradigm. A **social responsibility paradigm**, best typified by public broadcasting, views media as a public service, and is therefore paid for by some combination of pubic (tax) money and donations from supporters. A **commercial media paradigm**, on the other hand, is primarily paid for by advertising, so the economic process behind it is much more subtle. Money is given by advertisers to media organizations based on the number and kind of consumers they can "deliver." Indeed, according to the commercial paradigm, the audience is the product being sold.

The HUB Model describes the process of mass/mediated communication as a set of concentric interacting ripples that form whenever a message is disseminated, dropped like a pebble into a pool. Depending on its importance and penetration, the message may cause ripples that expand outward through society, then bounce back towards the center, affected by many socio-cultural factors along the way. Under a **commercial media paradigm**, there are many philosophies and structures that are all created and maintained in various ways by the people who support them—and that means all of us. Consider how your social capital may interact with our mediated world through the following "ripples":

Communicators: At the center of the HUB Model are communicators. Unlike most of our daily personal communications in relationships or at work, the communications we receive from the mass media come from sources we do not know and who do not know us. They are paid professionals, working for large national and often multi-national corporations and conglomerates. Their job is to create and deliver the messages (programs, stories, web pages, advertisements, etc.) that will earn the most money for the ultimate senders—the parent companies and their shareholders. At the top levels, these are individuals who are often not media communication professionals but rather financial and business experts, who are far removed from their audiences.

Although it may be comforting to think that the media exist simply to inform or entertain us, the fact is that with only a few exceptions (i.e., public broadcasting), commercial media exist for one purpose: economic profit. To reiterate, the basic operating logic of commercial television is not to "deliver programming" to consumers but rather to "deliver audiences" to businesses and advertisers. The commodity being bought and sold is our attention— our eyes, ears, and total cognitive and perceptual system. We do indeed appear to live in the 'attention economy' computer scientist, economist, and philosopher of technology Herbert Simon saw emerging in the last quarter of the 20th Century. This places pressure on communicators to be as efficient as possible in getting attention for their messages in the marketplace of ideas so that they can generate the revenue that pays their salary. How do consumers' decisions impact the trends that decide where careers can be made in communication?

Codes: Communicators are trained in using the "codes" or means of expression particular to their industry and to the business of mediated communication in general. As with spoken and written language, these codes and conventions constitute **media grammars** (or 'logics') intrinsic to specific media. Professional training, style guides, community norms, technological capabilities, business standards, and the interaction that goes on around the planning, design, generation and editing of content, all play a role in the accepted "grammars" that communicators use. We need to examine not just what we do see, read, or hear, but also what we **do not** see, read, or hear. What pops up first on your news feed each day? As communication scholars Maxwell McCombs and Donald Shaw (1972) famously noted, professional media have an **agenda-setting function**—they can't always manage to tell us what to think, but they do manage quite effectively to tell us what to **think about**.

Professional codes, business realities, and constraints of the media themselves limit the palette of colors a communicator can use in covering ideas and information. For example, we tend to see much more news and information from places where big media networks have bureaus placed, and very little information about other parts of the world. How might logistical realities limit the codes by which news and ideas are communicated? Can you think of ways that audience members can impact decisions and drive changes in how issues are covered and framed? Further, what is the role of the audience in the content shift resulting in less hard news and significantly more entertainment, celebrity, and sports information in the 21st century?

Gatekeepers: Most of the mass communicated messages we receive come to us through layers of **filters**—people and/or technological apparatuses employing Artificial Intelligence (AI) which serve as **"gatekeepers"** in deciding what information to present and how to present it. Along with various AI systems functioning at different levels throughout the larger gatekeeping mechanism, managers, and other professionals responsible for generating, crafting, editing, and presenting information have great power to shape content by deciding how it is laid out, the order in which it is presented to us, and the terms and images used to frame the issues. These gatekeepers include professionals like newspaper and magazine editors, broadcast network executives, writers, producers, and directors, webmasters, public relations practitioners, and other human components of the system. However, with the opening of the Internet to public access at the beginning of the 1990s, and the founding of Google at the end of that decade, we must also include web browsers with proprietary algorithms as 'gatekeepers' that increasingly depend on machine learning for purposes of locating content and presenting search results. Our media system also includes **regulators**, people employed with government bodies such as the Federal Communications

Commission or FCC, the Federal Trade Commission, or FTC, or other regulatory bodies influenced by political processes that form governments. All of this gatekeeping means that by the time most mass communication messages have been received, they may have been reviewed, edited, altered, shortened, expanded, or even intentionally distorted from their original state. But as many traditional mass media (i.e., newspapers, radio, and television), lose audiences to the Internet or other sources, their owners are forced to downsize their staffs, often to the detriment of professional gatekeeping, editing, or fact-checking. In the 21st century, we may be more likely to be influenced by gatekeepers who control the content on YouTube or Facebook, than in the morning paper or the evening news. And as Facebook's founder Mark Zuckerberg finally admitted, shortly after the 2016 presidential election, the corporation he founded is first, a media corporation, and second, a media corporation with a fake news problem. However, Zuckerberg soon qualified his statement, suggesting that Facebook "is not a traditional media company," since it doesn't write the news that appears on the platform. But he admitted that the network "does a lot more than just distribute news, and we're an important part of the public discourse" (2016). Part of the problem, as information scientists and media ecologists would contend, is the proprietary algorithm underlying Facebook. To date, that algorithm systematically facilitates the introduction and sharing of more "fake news" (typically unvetted, unverified and often malicious news items and reports) than

Figure 9.4 Media Use and Consumption Patterns are Changing

"real news" (vetted, peer-reviewed and/or fact-checked news items and reports) throughout its massive information ecology. This is, indeed, a serious problem for a media company (however non-traditional) that services more than a billion users worldwide. More to the point, these media developments have become a serious problem threatening the health and survival of governments, political systems, public institutions, and entire ways of life. Predicting just these sorts of developments, McLuhan suggested that "World War III [will be] a guerrilla information war with no division between military and civilian participation" (1970, 66). The question is, how did we get here?

The Internet as a News-Gathering and Distribution System

In addition to the way technological change has transformed how people communicate interpersonally, technological changes have redefined the traditional roles and characteristics of mass

communication. To reiterate, today we have so many choices – and new challenges—as communicators. To get an initial sense as to how this came to be, and why it is so consequential, consider this brief history of the Internet and World Wide Web.

The Internet as we know it today made its debut in the public domain in 1989 when British-born computer scientist Tim Berners-Lee invented the World Wide Web at the CERN laboratory in Switzerland. The Web was a much more user-friendly overlay of the Internet which was, to that point, a primarily text-based communication system developed out of the ARPANET. Berners-Lee's hypertext transfer protocol (HTTP) went live in 1990 and allowed non-specialist computer users to access a virtually unlimited storehouse of content via uniform resource locators (URLs). This was the practical beginning of what is sometimes referred to as 'Web 1.0' and facilitated both the broadcasting and narrowcasting of media content. While the data transfer rates were very slow compared to today, throughout the 1990s individual users connected to the World

Wide Web interacted through a network of personal computers and could download text, video and audio content at will, and at no or minimal cost. Users could upload content as well, but the process required a bit more effort and so was not nearly as prevalent as downloading. In short, the early days of the Internet was characterized by media consumption, not production.

A decade elapsed before a collection of more efficient and user-friendly applications started to emerge. These included Wikipedia, Myspace, Flickr, Facebook, and YouTube, among others. This fast-growing collection of digital nodes and networks allowed peer-to-peer access to user-generated content and set the stage for what has come to be known as 'Web 2.0.' In addition to downloading and consumption, this much more complex apparatus allowed millions of individual users to produce and share content, as well as comment about and collaborate on that content. To clarify the terminology here, 'Web 1.0' generally describes the older, 'top-down' scenario, when mostly large organizations and companies established web pages that allowed individual users to download content. 'Web 2.0' refers to the new 'bottom-up' scenario, where communities and individuals can also, and very efficiently, upload content and is exemplified by the 'Social Media' genre.

However, these are somewhat idealized descriptions because this distinction is a kind of false dichotomy, here's why. In theory at least the vestiges of Web 1.0 and the new Web 2.0 overlap and exist simultaneously. But in practice, and over time, we are seeing a steady creep toward downloading, streaming, and other modes of media consumption. While today's Internet and the latest connectivity facilitating access supports much more content faster, and high-definition, we seem to be heading back in one key respect, to the early days of the Internet, when content consumption tipped the scale. What's more, an expanding pattern of commercialization and monetization online is significantly qualifying the 'Web 2.0' and 'Social Media' characterizations currently in vogue.

Nonetheless, given these changes in the production and consumption of mediated content (and extending the characterization of audiences as the content of television), it has become a commonplace in industry parlance to say that the source and product of our mass communication media systems is, well, *Us*. Indeed, it is a rather bland statement today to suggest that the ultimate objective of the commercial entities that own the mass media is to make money by attracting more people to their productions. Whether newspapers, magazines, radio, TV, film or Internet content, the products and services advertised in, during, or alongside that content tends to do what it is designed to do: grab and occupy our time and attention. These media processes, and effects, seem more powerful now than ever.

A Matter of Attention

We are learning that changes in our communication systems facilitate changes in our communication habits and practices. The nature of our interactions through different media forms can be highly consequential. At the content-level, multi-mediated entertainment, news, information (and disinformation) certainly grabs our attention. In the process, it alters our perceptions and can be surprisingly effective at helping us 'decide' what to pay attention to the next time we listen to the radio, click through what often seems like an endless number of TV channels, or set off on a cyber-surfing expedition. Some of this media experience, in turn, has been shown to negatively impact how we eat and sleep, and alters the nature and content of our conversations, our teaching and learning, our remembering and, ultimately, our thinking.

Or, as McComb's and Shaw's **Agenda Setting Theory** suggests, the media might not be able to tell us what to think, but they are surprisingly effective at telling us what to think about. And that's important, because it might be enough to sway audiences to pay for all sorts of products and services they did not know they need, or someone to click on a link that activates a malicious string of computer code, or citizens to vote for candidates they barely know anything about. Indeed, especially in this era of alternate facts, fake news, and anonymous hacks, prompting someone to think about something they did not previously think about could be enough to get that proverbial 'butterfly' flapping its wings. That is to say, it might very well have consequences we would not expect. However, while Agenda Setting is a theory that focuses almost entirely media content, it does well to remind us that we do indeed live in an attention economy of the sort computer scientist Herbert

Simon saw emerging in the last quarter of the 20th Century:

In an information-rich world, the wealth of information means a dearth of something else: a scarcity of whatever it is that information consumes. What information consumes is rather obvious: it consumes the attention of its recipients. Hence a wealth of information creates a poverty of attention and a need to allocate that attention efficiently among the overabundance of information sources that might consume it (Simon, 1971; p. 40–41).

Simon lumps together all of the content assaulting our senses in a modern mediated world under the heading of 'information' because he was commenting from the perspective of a computer scientist, not a news/media specialist. Well, if Simon could only see us now. After all, by 2015 according to the Nielson Ratings Company, the average American home was equipped with cable television that offered access to approximately 250 different channels to choose from. An Internet-enabled home allows access to a virtually limitless content repository.

What's more, in addition to the seemingly endless supply of content afforded us through TV and the Internet, hundreds of radio stations, and a staggering array of books, magazines and newspapers still compete for our attention when we walk through any grocery store, mall, airport, train station or tourist hub. But while there is no space in this

chapter to delve into all the details and significance surrounding our changing media consumption behaviors, there are a few other things worth thinking about at this time.

First, the proliferation of media content reported by Nielson and other data-gathering entities are part and parcel to massive increases in multi-media use. No serious observer doubts that small, powerful mobile phones, tablets and computers are a significant and unprecedented development in human communication. Mobile device use, in particular, has resulted in an array of immediate effects that are generally considered to be beneficial. These include unprecedented increases in the speed and 'reach' of personal interactions and (for better or worse), access to a virtually unlimited amount of information.

However, this convergent media use has also resulted in some unintended consequences or 'side-effects' first noticed with the diffusion of television sets throughout American households. According to the Pew Center's 'The Internet and American Life Project (2012), these include sedentary lifestyles, increasing body mass indexes (BMI) and attention anomalies and deficits of various kinds. There is evidence that media convergence via small, mobile communication devices like laptop computers, tablets and smart phones have exacerbated these media maladies, and also contribute to shrinking vocabularies, lack of focus, memory loss, sleep problems, new and less traceable kinds of harassment and exploitation, and all sorts of confusion over the meaning of messages (this last item seems due, at least in part, to a structural deletion

of non-verbal cues). What's more, and for both good and ill, texting, social media, and other mobile and personal media use has, to date, disproportionately impacted the younger generations who are now developing what tend to become life-long media habits. To be sure, the statistics regarding these new media habits and practices are staggering.

For example, concerning the matter of attention and focus, the Pew study reported that teenagers on average "process" (send and receive) more than 3000 text messages a month. In 2013 that number surpassed 4000 texts processed every month and began rising across older age groups as well. Fixing for waking hours (assuming 6-8 hours of sleep every night), 4000 texts averages out to users turning to their screens to process a text message every 300 seconds (or every 5 minutes) day in and day out.

Researchers at Curry College on the outskirts of Boston collected data that showed texting patterns as high as 13,000 texts per month in a college student population during the 2014-2015 academic year. That number averages out to a screen glance with keypad input every 100 seconds or so (less than two minutes). These numbers bring Herbert Simon's concerns over the monopolization of attention to the foreground. Indeed, we may discover that the question of human attention in this age of multi-mediated communication may be one of the most important question informing the future of interpersonal relationships, entertainment, education, democratic societies, even human culture itself.

The Changing Nature of News

With Simon's warning in mind, consider the notions of 'hard' and 'soft' news. These are described, respectively, at Britannica.com in the following ways:

> Traditionally, so-called *hard news* relates the circumstances of a recent event or incident considered to be of general local, regional, national, or international significance. By contrast, *soft news* usually centres on the lives of individuals and has little, if any, perceived urgency. Hard news generally concerns issues, politics, economics, international relations, welfare, and scientific developments, whereas soft news focuses on human-interest stories and celebrity. (2017)

The launch of CNN by Ted Turner and associates in 1980 prompted an expansion in the coverage of events, along with re-definition of news as a commodity with a progressive interlacing of 'hard' and 'soft' content. This blending of content, along with the recent surge in the blurring of 'real news'-qua-information and "fake news"-qua-disinformation, has resulted in substantial confusion in the public regarding what content is legitimate and/or most consequential to our lives and, by extension, worth paying attention to. While the date is somewhat arbitrary, 1980 seems an appropriate year to focus on,

with the founding of CNN, MTV and USA today (a newspaper filled with images and pictures) designed to remind people of TV, their favorite communication technology at the time. For the next twenty years the expansion and interlacing of 'hard' and 'soft' news continued unabated in a generally top-down fashion, from large, mostly for-profit news and media organizations down to individual consumers. During those next two decades, things began to change significantly, as implied in the Nielson reports in general, and in the PEW Internet studies in particular.

Another genre of media theorists and practitioners called media ecologists, who focus less on the specific content of media, are discussed next. Media Ecologists are most concerned with the powerful though often hard to detect role of media format and structure (over media content) in prompting new modes of thought and perception. As we read about the media ecological perspective, keep Simon's observations regarding attention in mind, as they should gain even more relevance.

Understanding Our Media Ecology

To be sure, this blending and blurring of content becomes especially problematic in the 21st Century since a mass medium, by its very nature, is often unable to convey highly complex messages that require in-depth thinking and reflection. While the content of media is significant and consequential, there is another mode of analysis that focuses on the structural aspects

of different media and media systems. Indeed, all media have certain "biases" stemming from their formal properties and underlying structures that can have very real consequences. To help us understand our current mediated world we'll look closely at a number of communication technologies (some new, some old) in terms of their biases, or structural effects, and consider some of their most significant consequences. We begin with brief descriptions of some common mass media through a Media Ecological lens. For example, print-based media have a **linear-sequential bias** that requires readers to use only their eyes in the process of following the rows of text from left to right and down the page. In order to 'get' the information—assuming the author/s adhered to the rules of grammar—readers learn (through more reading!) that certain combinations of words make sentences. In the process readers learn basic logic and analytical skills. This characterization of course applies only to 'Modern/ Western' languages that are visually formatted in this way. Many 'Eastern' languages, including Japanese, Korean and Chinese, are not formatted from left to right, across pages, and since they are based on pictographic and not phonetic alphabets, they have different cognitive and mnemonic (memory) effects. On the other hand, television has an **image bias,** relying primarily on the power of photos, graphics and sound to capture a moment in time, which tends to pressure network executives to hire people based more on physical appearance and vocal appeal than professional preparation, ability, or talent. The Internet is constantly providing messages and ads competing for users' attention, requiring multitasking and multi-layered web pages and images. More recently, rapid technological developments have altered the way media messages are delivered and consumed. Images that look good on a large cinema screen may not look as good on a tiny phone screen, and vice versa. Media Ecologists investigate the intrinsic nature of media in an effort to better understand these structural biases.

So far we have just scratched the surface regarding the biases of several of our most common communication media. Again, Media Ecology is a mode or genre of media studies that focuses, from the inside so to speak, on the How of media. They investigate the formal properties and structural effects of media. In other words, how various media are built. Media Ecologists are keenly interested in, among other things, how various kinds of content (words, images, sounds, etc) are made possible or prohibited, enhanced or constrained, and sharpened or dulled by different media forms like books, radio, telephones, film, TV, blogs, etc. They use the term "bias" specifically to refer to the way different media are predisposed to certain content and are configured toward, or activate, certain sense receptors (written text/eyes, radio/ears, TV/ eyes and ears, etc) and exclude or deactivate others. In so doing, all media encode and alter content in particular ways due to the way we (humans) are built. These media effects, in turn, encourage certain interpretations or 'readings' and discourage others. Taking these claims to their logical conclusion suggests that different media structurally affect and can even direct how media users and audiences think, feel and perceive, regardless of content.

The focus on the How of media highlights the differences and similarities between sending "Message X" through, say, newspaper, radio, TV, blog, or Youtube video. This kind of media bias explains how each medium molds, gives shape to, and embodies different content (words, sounds, images, etc), and subtly urges media users and audiences to notice and pay more attention to some content (or certain aspects of the content), and ignore, or at least consider less significant or meaningful, others. Media Ecologists look for tendencies toward or away from the use of different human senses and capacities (eyes/ seeing, ears/hearing, imagination, emotion, etc). As such, this general perspective conceptualizes media as processes, not things.

When media researchers suggest that media are processes not things, they are pointing to the way media work us over (or 'massage' us, as Marshall McLuhan opined) at the deep level of biological sensory input and 'pre-conscious awareness.' Such claims were a departure from traditional media studies with its focus on the explicit 'surface level' which involves both conscious and pre-conscious attention to and engagement with media content. But while McLuhan sometimes offered vague and confusing suggestions as to how different media systems engage us well below the surface level of media content, many researchers who came after him extended and deepened his analysis of media by offering much more concrete explanations of how these deep-seated communication processes occur.

For example, Gary Gumpert and Robert Cathcart (1985) offer 'four contentions' or claims regarding media that elaborates on McLuhan's suggestion that the 'medium is the message.' According to Gumpert and Cathcart:

1. there are sets of codes and conventions integral to each medium;
2. such codes and conventions constitute part of our media consciousness;
3. the information processing made possible through these various grammars influence our perceptions and values;
4. the order of acquisition of media literacy will produce a particular world perspective which relates and separates persons accordingly (p 24).

The authors illustrate these contentions throughout the remainder of their article, and then further elaborated on them with the help of more than thirty contributors in an edited volume entitled "Inter/Media: Interpersonal Communication in a Media World. Put most simply, these inquiries suggest that the notion of a 'biological generation' should be considered obsolete if we want to better understand the similarities and differences between people today. A biological generation describes human relationships bound primarily by age and is measured by the time it takes, on average, for humans to reproduce (approximately 27 years at the time of this writing).

Gumpert and Cathcart suggest that the biological generation should be replaced with the 'media generation' concept. The latter describes human relationships based primary on media use and the habits of perception fostered by those media. While the biological generation was an appropriate means of understanding human relationships prior to the 20th Century, we are now connected or separated more by media use than age. The reason for this, as Gumpert and Cathcart argue, is because different media constitute unique 'grammars,' or 'logics' that function as modes and codes of thought, perception, and awareness (i.e. ways of knowing). Taking McLuhan's 'medium is the message' idea seriously means rejecting (or at least qualifying) the orthodox view that media content is the most important variable that predicts the identification and grouping of people, different patterns of thought, perception and awareness, and other kinds of 'culture-building.'

In short, different media therefore constitute different 'languages' that require learning specific rules of use (however tacit or unconscious they may be). As is the case with the mostly unconscious learning of any natural language (English, French, Chinese, etc) media grammars and logics are learned through repeated, habitual use. Primary media are our favorite or most-used media forms. They are the new languages. They influence how we think and perceive across the lifespan. For centuries, primary media use changed very slowly, or not at all, during an average human life span. For example, after Gutenberg invented the printing press, for almost 500 years our conventional notion of literacy (reading) progressively became the dominant media used in 'developing' contexts around the world. Some Media Ecologists,

like Elizabeth Eisenstein, have painstakingly researched the cultural and psychic effects of the printing press. In her book *The Printing Press as an Agent of Change* (1979), Eisenstein concludes that this technology played a primary role in ushering in the Renaissance. The printing press facilitated mass-literacy in the traditional sense of the term (i.e. reading words on pages) and helped pull Europeans out of the Dark Ages by fostering linear, logical, critical thinking that made science as we know it today possible for the first time in human history.

Millions of people today still grow up learning that traditional form of literacy (reading books, newspapers and magazines, and such media that require what is termed 'long form' reading). Of course this learning can precede, occur along with, or follow the acquisition and habitual use of a variety of other, newer media forms. And yet, millions of others don't follow that traditional sequence, or any particular sequence at all. Around the start of the 20th Century, with the diffusion of electronic forms of communication (including film, radio and television), widespread (population-level) patterns of media use began to transition more quickly. And here we begin to see the wisdom of the 'media generation' idea.

A growing catalog of new research investigating the causal properties of communication technology bolsters the idea that media are active processes. But again, this is not a new idea, as the general notion was first articulated by Plato, then formally elaborated upon by media scholars like McLuhan, Eisenstein, Postman,

and Gumpert and Cathcart. This accumulated knowledge suggests that different people develop different modes of attention, perception and awareness based primarily upon the media they habitually use, and the order in which they learn to use them.

To review our discussion so far, regular, repetitive media use facillitates access to some content and prohibits other content. Different media therefore promote, through rote use, the acquisition of different media grammars which, in turn, have the tendency to promote particular kinds of consciousness and awareness. These biases, in turn, groups, gathers together (or otherwise connects) and separate (in a sense, disconnect) people accordingly. What's more, with the advent of electronic media forms (from radio to the latest social media systems) physical space no longer determines who connects with or identifies However, this is just a cursory explanation of 'media generations' and 'media gaps' that defy the conventional notion of biological generation as the most accurate way to understand how people relate to one another and how people relate to media. To get a sense how these ecological media processes work, let's consider a mass medium that has been undergoing a significant shift since the advent of electronic media at the beginning of the 20th Century. The book (technically called a 'codex') was a predictable consequence of Gutenberg's movable-type press enjoyed a long reign as the primary mass medium of western civilization. However, books have a hidden nature. As does book reading.

A book (let's say a popular novel) is primarily comprised of fixed words on a page. Assuming, for purposes of illustration, that we are talking about a conventional, type-set manuscript (and barring any congenital or acquired disabilities in the reader), reading that novel requires eyes focused on pages containing words. Since those words are configured in a linear and sequential format, the reader must use their eyes to follow that format in proper sequence in order to 'get' the content. It does not take a media researcher to see how the act of reading supplies a lot of information through single sense. That, in short, is the visual bias of print.

So far, two distinct 'habits of mind' are fostered through this kind of long-form reading: (1) a relatively slow, sequential processing of content, and (2) the development of logical thought patterns through a necessary correspondence between certain structural features of the content being 'consumed' (including subject-verb agreement and other formal aspects of *grammar* as we traditionally think about it). This should add new meaning to the expression '*you are what you eat*.' The reader-qua-consumer of this book should notice that, other than suggesting the book is a novel of some type, there has been no mention of any particular kind of content. And this, in turn, illustrates what McLuhan meant when he said '*The Medium is the Message*.' Finally, when reading (and now the content comes in), our sense of hearing is not activated, however, the imagination is triggered substantially in the process of literally *image-ining* whatever content the book we are reading contains.

On the other hand, watching a film or TV adaptation of that same novel (let's say it is Mary Shelley's Frankenstein) activates some of the same senses, while suppressing or modifying others. We certainly use our sense of sight to consume televised content but we do so through a far less intentional and certainly less linear and sequential process, with our eyes dashing around, scanning the screen in surprisingly haphazard fashion (it is notable that these *saccades* are suppressed to near zero when reading). Of course we also use our ears in the viewing context, however visual media use modifies the sense ratio with a heavy bias toward the eyes.

These processes impact how and to what degree different senses are activated and integrated during different kinds of media use. Media reconfigure perception and awareness, and direct how we attend and what we attend to. All of this results in fundamental changes to the character or underlying nature of consciousness (as imperfectly as we currently describe that). If the last paragraph reads as though ripped from a biology or neuroscience textbook, that is about right, as a 'biological approach' via media ecology, has become a legitimate mode of media research today. And the general idea is easy enough to illustrate.

For example, instead of the imagination being triggered in substantial ways during the reading context, in the filmic and televisual context the content is, in large measure, pre-imagined by the director (or directors), sound designers, set and costume designers, and camera operators, among others. While individual readers and watchers certainly experience and take away their own subjective understandings of the respective content, patterns of perception (and understanding) between the two media contexts tend to manifest in patterned cognitive and emotional responses to the content being relayed through different media. This is why Media Ecologists say that all media are unique meaning-making systems, codes (i.e. 'languages').

Of course, different media also function to include and exclude certain audiences. For example, while most 3 and 4 year olds can certainly watch TV and extract some meaning from the production, the vast majority in that age group cannot read novels. Can you think of some additional examples to illustrate McLuhan's claim that "the medium is the message"? Or, if you want more specific guidance, can you think of any ways Gumpert and Cathcart's four contentions can be illustrated or exemplified in your own life, or the lives of anyone you know?

Next, let's consider some examples illustrating a tightening relationship between the speed and power of digital media and technology and the rate of technological change. These examples also lend further credence to Gumpert and Cathcart's 'media generation' idea. This relationship between media speed and power is simultaneously impacting how much we are required to do, even say, when using various media and technology, as well as how much 'say' we have with respect to where all of this innovation seems to be headed.

Fast Media and the Speed-Up of Media Change

One example from media history concerns a set of transitions in media that store and play audio content. For nearly a century recording disks made of various materials were the go-to technology for sound recording and reproduction. It began with wax and metal cylinders upon which 'sound tracks' were etched during the recording phase. A tiny stylus followed these etched sound tracks during playback. However, fidelity was very low and recording times were short (about 5 minutes). The invention of the record 'album' changed all that. The 'album' originally referred to a collection of themed or otherwise related music or songs and comprised a 'book' of 78rpm, short-playing discs. With the transition to the larger 33 rpm long-playing discs (popularly known as *LPs*) that featured much higher fidelity along with more storage capacity, the listening experience was significantly enhanced.

What's more, an appreciable amount of space opened up on the record cover and sleeve allowing for elaborate cover art, expansive liner notes and drawings and/or photographs that added detail and context to the music. This further bound together artistic themes. For almost half a century the LP, with all of its aesthetic enhancements, survived the introduction, rise and decline of reel-to-reel and tape cassettes without any notable impact.

It was the introduction of the Compact Disk (CD) by Philips in the early 1980s that significantly impacted record album sales by the end of that decade. But while the transition to CDs lengthened storage space for audio content (thereby enhancing the listening experience by doing away with the need to 'flip the record') the reduced physical space of the packaging saw a diminution in cover art, liner notes, etc. That transition from LPs to CDs took just over a decade as the 20th Century was coming to a close.

Next, the CD-to-MP3 transition occurred much more rapidly (in less than a decade) and registered more fundamental changes to music listening. Perhaps the most significant changes stemmed from a separation or unbinding of audio content (music and lyrics) from the wider context, as cover art, liner notes and other thematic threads began to obsolesce with the new efficiencies embodied in the MP3 sound file. The downloading of single songs from iTunes is emblematic of this cultural shift in listening as well as an emerging pattern in technological change. The continuation of that pattern is obvious when we consider recent innovations in 'telephony' (the technical term used to describe telephony technology).

The culture-wide shift in many countries around the world from 'dumb' (generally describing alphanumeric 'brick' or 'flip' phones) to 'smart' phones with multifunction video screen interfaces took just two or three years in most places. While some manufactures have recently reintroduced 'dumb' phones for what is, reportedly, a small population of users who have expressed an interest in 'slowing things down,' the future of the 'smart' phone seems a foregone conclusion.

Given the dizzying power and speed of the latest models, the use of smart phones as mini TVs and movie screens is fast-becoming the global cultural default. What's more, Augmented Reality (AR) and Virtual Reality (VR) features integrated or attached to smart phones serve only to hasten the rate of technological change. An associated media shift from television and movies to online streaming is well underway, and will likely end with a near-total migration to Netflix, Amazon Video, Hulu (among others) facilitated by the 'anywhere, anytime' consumption of multimedia content through the latest phones.

One final example illustrates how increases in both the speed and scale of changes in our media ecology can be highly consequential by prompting some next phase of technological innovation. The ubiquitous use of mice, keyboards and screens that allow people to interface with computers approached its apex at the end of the 20Th Century. Indeed, a consequential shift in human-computer interaction was just getting up to speed during the writing of this chapter. It is the move from keyboard and mouse control to voice and/or gesture control.

What's more, Facebook's Zuckerberg recently announced substantial investment in the research and development of various digital appendages connected to the body, as well as chips implanted in or near the brain to facilitate what is so far being dubbed 'thought control' of computers by humans and, by necessary reciprocation, the 'mind-reading' of humans by computers. Zuckerberg hinted that this innovation will come to pass "within a decade" but who knows. One thing we do know is that inventors and developers of new technologies are notoriously unskilled at estimating 'time to market.' Much of what we do know in this regard we've learned from our media history.

A close reading of that history tells us that the development and diffusion of future technologies, and particularly communication technologies, often occurs in fits and starts. More to the point, however, it tells us that it's much more a matter of 'when' than 'if.' In addition to this 'inevitability thesis,' the diffusion of new technologies tends to be ecological in as much as they affect everything. For now, however, Zuckerberg is promoting his 'thought control' idea as a very practical and therefore logical next step toward enhancing the way amputees can manipulate or otherwise interface with prosthetic limbs. He is talking about a very narrow collection of applications in other words. But again, if the history of technological innovation tells us anything it is that new uses of new technologies find niches elsewhere too. In this case, other innovations like the Internet of Things (IoT) will very likely be among the first to incorporate thought control into its systems and apparatuses (think self-driving cars, 'smart' appliances, robots, homes and office buildings).

This will, in turn, facilitate still more intimate couplings between human beings and their favorite devices and technologies, with artificial intelligences increasingly 'running the show.' With all of this in the offing, another one of McLuhan's quip-like caveats comes to mind: "In this electronic age we see ourselves being translated more and more into forms of information, moving toward

technological extensions of consciousness" (1964, 57). So, we are prompted to ask: What hath God wrought? What changes await? Indeed, the consequences of new media remain, in part, a mystery, but also, in part, predictable. While we might initially have a sense of what the latest media and technology can do for us, we tend to only learn the full story – including what they also do to and with us – much later, after those 'after effects' or side effects' have already done their thing.

Reading, writing, watching, remembering, even thinking (and a host of other long-held human practices and capacities) will not remain untouched as we rush headlong into our new media worlds. That is for certain. The pace of technological change and adaptation has not slowed. To the contrary, most of the media shifts that have occurred in the almost two decades of this century that have so far elapsed (including new mobile technologies, educational technologies and regular 'migrations' away from one social medium to another) spread out into significant portions of human culture in as little as one year – sometimes less.

Content: All types of media must deliver consumers who hear, watch, and read the product known as "content," packaged ideas or information that are expected to provide value of some kind for end users in various contexts. Mass communication in most of the world reflects a basic model of supplier and consumer, and economic gain is its primary purpose. When you are trying to create a message that has meaning for hundreds of thousands, or millions, of people, you need to

find common ground for all of them. What results, often, is content that is "watered down," that sometimes appeals to the lowest common denominator, or is otherwise mainstreamed for broad, popular consumption. Much media content, designed for as many consumers as possible, is targeted at an 8th grade comprehension level. In trying to attract and be meaningful to as many as possible, the result tends to be highly abbreviated and, very often, quality and professional standards are sacrificed in the news organizations' rush to be first, to "get the scoop," or otherwise beat the competition in its desire to earn the highest ratings.. How does consumer feedback (ratings, hits, comments, etc.) impact content? What feedback mechanisms do you feel have the most immediate or most lasting impact? In an era when sensationalism and superficial coverage are the norm for many news outlets, how can we know that what we see or hear is true and accurate (i.e., relatively unbiased and rooted in verifiable facts).

Audience effects: That media content affect audiences are multifaceted, and effects that don't appear immediately can nonetheless have a cumulative and significant impact over time. This concerns both 'real' and 'fake' news. An ice age analogy has been suggested as an appropriate metaphor for audience effects; "just as an average temperature shift of a few degrees can lead to an ice age... so too can a relatively small but pervasive influence make a crucial difference. The 'size' of an 'effect' is far less critical than the direction of its steady contribution" (Gerbner, Gross, Morgan, and Signorielli, 1982, p. 14). For example, media scholar George Gerbner and his team found a "**Mean World Effect**," demonstrating over many years of research that heavy viewers of television news think that the world is "meaner" than it really is, to the point of holding unrealistic views of the actual neighborhoods and communities in which they live (Gerbner, Gross, Morgan, & Signorielli, 1980). Yet, can you think of some ways the impact can go the other way, from audiences to media producers? In what ways can media consumers use their social capital to make ripples in the system and impact what shows up in the media?

Feedback: In most mass communicated messages, feedback is often delayed, diffused, and diverse. For instance, when it comes to a network television news story, we can't give the kind of immediate feedback as we are able to in a person-to-person exchange, nor get an immediate explanation or response to our feedback. Feedback gets to the message creators. —filmmakers, programmers, news editors or reporters, web masters, through a variety of channels: it might be a letter to the editor, a blog post, selecting or not selecting to watch a channel or station; a subscription to hard copy or online newspapers and magazines, or bookmarking a favorite websites. How can one use the social capital of a personal or professional network to amplify the effect of feedback? Have you ever witnessed how petitions, protests, boycott campaigns, etc. can form particularly impactful modes of feedback within the communication industries? Do you ever receive e-mails or posts asking for your support or endorsement of an idea or a campaign?

Media amplification: Because of the driving need to capture attention and deliver consumers to advertisers, media tend to amplify deviant behavior or focus on dramatic or sensationalized events or topics that prompt news consumers to pause and "rubberneck," as if craning our necks to stop and look at the scene of an accident. Violence and deviance of all kinds generate interesting fodder for attention. Then, because of media's **agenda-setting function**, telling us what to think about to the exclusion of other topics, the process tends to result in even more focused attention because of the reduction of coverage of other news items. For example, say there is a dramatic shooting in your town, and because it is a deviant act, all the local news stations, none wanting to be outdone, send news crews to cover it. As the old newsroom adage goes, "If it bleeds, it leads." For the average viewer flipping through channels, seeing a particular item of news flashed on all stations gives a sense of amplification beyond what may really be warranted to guarantee the safety of the community. Is there anything consumers can do to counter this typical amplification effect?

Noise: and other forms of communication, plenty of noise enters the mass communication process. Recall that we should be thinking of noise as anything that interferes with the completeness of the meaning we want to share, from the message itself, to the characteristics of the medium, poor quality images or sounds, misspelled graphics, the inabilities of the senders, differing opinions and biases (cognitive dissonance), or the sheer number of sounds and images we experience at any

given moment, the backdrop of "white noise" that makes individual messages hard to tune into. What do you think works best to ameliorate (reduce) the effects of noise? What strategies do you use to deliver your undivided attention to the multilayered meaning being conveyed through mediated messages? Being "**reflexive**" means to not only absorb meaning from what you view or listen to, but to pay attention to whatever it is about yourself that causes you to react in particular ways. One time-tested way to become a more reflexive (and self-reflective) news consumer is to ask: "In addition to what this information source contains, what kinds of information might be getting systematically omitted in the news report or commentary?" What makes you prefer certain kinds of content, and how do your preferences shape the world?

The Power of Media, Information, and Technological Literacy

The final section of this chapter begins by reminding readers to think about Media Studies in two senses of the term. This dual approach fills out our understanding of mass media and deepens our understanding of mass media. It enriches the conventional notion of *Media Literacy* by incorporating *Information Literacy* and *Technological Literacy* in the mix. To be sure, these three literacies are not the same. Conventional media studies is, put most simply, a blend of 'Media Literacy' and 'Information Literacy.' This approach seeks to understand *The Media* as content-production and distribution entities (public and private news organizations and broadcasting companies, movie studios, book, newspaper and magazine publishing houses, Internet service providers, etc). A combination of Media and Information Literacy helps illuminate the '*What*' and '*For Whom*' of media institutions and organizations.

This combo critically analyzes media source/s and the content they produce and disseminate; the news, information and other programming that we read, hear and watch. 'Source' in this case refers to the entities responsible for creating and initially distributing or sharing media content. Indeed, it is rarely a single source and involves at least two different kinds of 'media convergence' concerning the manner by which different content producers/sources join or come together for common purpose or outcome:

Corporate Media Convergence concerns the ways companies and other commercial entities extend and enhance their ability to produce different media content and operate in different media contexts by acquiring assets and building out their media holdings.

Technological Media Convergence concerns the way single devices progressively incorporate multi-functional capacities to receive, process, produce and relay, and disseminate media content.

These two forms of media convergence operate within an expanding environment of media producers. Along with formally educated and professionally

trained journalists, PR, marketing and other kinds of 'promotion professionals,' we also have third-party endorsers, professional and amateur bloggers and vloggers, hackers, and a host of other known (and sometimes unknown and unidentifiable) sources, distributors, producers and manipulators of media content.

Adding insult to injury much of the content we encounter today increasingly includes both information (verifiable, fact-based content intended to educate or otherwise inform), and disinformation (unverifiable, less-fact-based or entirely false information that is intended to confuse, mislead, or otherwise mis-inform). And to further complicate things, technological media convergence continues to incorporate more artificial intelligence into these content production and dissemination processes.

Historically called 'propaganda,' the term *disinformation* was reserved for activities undertaken by governments, militaries (there often referred to as 'Psy-Ops') and other 'state actors.' Corporations and large organizations also engage in such practices in an effort to discredit or undermine rivals or competitors of various kinds. Today (and especially online) under the heading of 'news' we find both information and disinformation, and everything in between. What's more, in addition to the traditional, large-scale organizations we might recognize (like commercial and public media outlets and governmental actors), the mainstreaming of the Internet opened the door to an unprecedented increase in both information and disinformation that is the product of a broad collection of 'non-state' actors (small and

larger groups, even individuals not affiliated with any particular country or government).

Media and information literacy prompt us to carefully consider the social, political and economic aims of various actors with a focus on content, or what is represented in words, voice and/or image. This content focus helps us detect and understand who has the resources and the power to control what content is represented, to whom, and in what ways. In other words, this combination is a critical approach that investigates what's '*in it*' for the various players involved (media owners, producers, employees, and stockholders, as well as media consumers and audiences). As such, this perspective conceptualizes newspapers, film, radio, TV, the Internet, etc, as more or less 'neutral' **things** through which content creators, producers and distributors accomplish specific tasks.

However, if we constrain our thinking about media and media systems as neutral *things* or *tools* we neglect an important aspect of *Media* (and, by extension, *The Media*) at our own peril. As discussed and illustrated in the previous section on Media Ecology, our efforts at understanding *Media* (without the 'The') as more active technological and perceptual systems and apparatuses can significantly enrich our understanding of *The Media* as well.

To review, analyses of *The Media* have a primary focus on content. By contrast, studies of *Media* investigate communication forms such as printed text, radio, records, tapes, film, TV, telephones, digital and Internet-based applications and systems, etc. Theorists and researchers who seek to understand *Media* often include face-to-face (F2F) interaction as the original communication medium. This focus on the format and structure of media, regardless of the content they carry is the stock and trade of Media Ecology.

In reality these different foci (on media content and media form) largely remain partial pursuits that must be integrated if we hold any hope of navigating and, in part, creating our collective media/ted future. To reiterate, understanding the *what* and *for whom* of *The Media* necessitates a combination of media and information literacy. For example, informed by the technological literacy that is part and parcel to Media Ecology, many contemporary media theorists, researchers, and practitioners suggest that, say, the invention of the printing press prompted the first significant formation of 'news' and the initial *formalization* and eventual *institutionalization* of news as "a broadcast or published report of noteworthy information, especially about recent or important events" (Merriam-Webster, 2016). See the appendix of this textbook for two 'case studies' from media history which clearly illustrate that highly consequential 'side effect' of the printing press called 'Science.'

Changes in media format and structure, along with the continued 'infiltration' of the Internet by various non-corporate entities (including many individual actors with different agendas) suggests that we would do well to hone our media, information and technological literacy skills that include both the latest content-related and form/format-related ideas and insights.

But while there has been a proliferation in the number of books, articles, websites, talks and other works dedicated to media content leveraging various aspects of media and information literacy, there remains a relative lack of work dedicated to the formal properties of media form-centered/technological literacy.

To recap, popular media and information literacy advice today still tends to focus on the content of media, whereas traditional technological literacy tends to focus on a practical understanding of devices, systems, and applications (or, how to use these tools as intended or designed). Two 'tip sheets' related to those more mainstream media and information literacy notions are provided in the supplementary materials for this chapter found in the appendix. The first is a document developed for this textbook entitled: *Website Info Quality— Some General Guidelines*, and lists several of the most frequently encountered Internet domains, including brief descriptions of each, and some things to consider when using the Internet for news, information, research and source material. For these purposes, it should make sense that *.edu* domains appear at the top of the list and *.com*, *.net*, and *.biz* domains at the bottom.

There's no question, reliably assessing an information source's credibility today is no mean feat. No matter the source or domain, however, we should always wonder if the creators of the content are in fact competent, informed professionals in the area or topic they are communicating about. For example, we can ask a number of systematic questions while seeking out legitimate, fact-based

information surrounding particular topics or areas of inquiry, including:

- Does the science reporter have any background in science?
- Are 'political reporters' schooled in politics, government and the basic histories of both?
- Are the journalists people who have formally studied journalism? That is, have they systematically studied television news, or, have they simply watched a lot of news on TV?
- What are the professional qualifications of a web page writer or blogger?

All of these questions should prompt us to remember the acronym WIIFM (What's In It For Me)? For media consumers that question is almost always followed by a unique set of answers. From the commercial media providers' point of view, however, what's in it for them is almost always answered thusly: to make more money—to keep readers reading, listeners listening, watchers watching and, increasingly, to get more screen views and clicks… all to attract more advertising or subscription dollars. All of that can certainly help a media professional earn a promotion, or get a better job. At the very least, for example, more clicks and views translates to more attention taken up. Indeed, as (Herbert) Simon say's, we are deep in an 'attention economy' today.

The other appendix item that fills out our discussion of the various literacies is entitled: General Principles of Media Literacy. These principles continue to be curated and developed online by Patricia Aufderheide, a Professor of Communication Studies in the School of Communication at American University in Washington, D.C. As discussed earlier in this chapter, Aufderheide is actually offering a mix of media and technological literacy. Regardless, as Aufderheide puts it "[w]e know about the world primarily from the media. But the media don't simply give us the world. They interpret reality, tailor it, perform it." Again, Aufderheide's principles contain a mix of media content-centered and media format-centered advice. Consider these two items that illustrate well the bridge she makes between the three kinds of literacy just discussed:

Media have social and political implications. Because media construct reality, under economic terms that shape their messages, and powerfully transmit values, they have important social and political effects on our lives together in society and as members of the public.

Media form and content are closely related in media. Each medium has its own distinctive characteristics. You will get a very different experience of a major event by reading the newspapers, watching TV, listening to the radio, or attending that event in person. A [literate media user] asks: What about the form of this medium influences the content? Is that formal capacity being exploited well, or is it being wasted? What about the form limits the content? Readers should refer to the appendix for the complete list of Aufderheide's "General Principles."

It can certainly be difficult at this point in the 21st Century to know how much of what we are reading, seeing, or hearing is "real." What has been edited out or overlooked because of time, space, financial, or even political considerations? With so much information now literally available at one's fingertips, how can we determine what is reliable? It can sometimes be difficult to detect the difference between traditional/'real,' fact-based information, and 'infotainment' and 'infomercials,' wherein information and marketing strategies are blended almost imperceptibly. To reiterate, there are so many messages vying for our attention, driven by insatiable competition for audience attention (and therefore for money and market share). Media networks are becoming increasingly large conglomerates, with a few large companies owning and cross-advertising increasingly large swaths of the news and entertainment ecosystem. Not only are we discouraged from seeking information from multiple sources—even when we do, the content we get tends to originate at the same conglomerate source.

Thus, a crucial skill in today's communication-saturated world is **media literacy**: knowing how to consider the source of information, how to dig deeper and "read between the lines." Who owns that channel; who sponsors that website? Is it a **.com** (commercial business), **.org** (nonprofit organization), **.gov** (government institution), **.edu** (a college or university), or something else? What are the interests of these different types of institutions? What are the motives of the people involved in distributing that information?

Ask questions of the content you watch and read. Check footnotes. Take a look at the "Web Search Strategy Tip Sheet" in the appendix. These are merely a set of recommendations, or rules of thumb, to keep in mind when thinking about some of the different information sources and portals found online. For example, as you begin to develop a fuller understanding and awareness of any particular news item under scrutiny, ask yourself what sort of information might be missing in that treatment of the news item. Beyond that, try to find another report (or two) on the same news item. Can you locate a report that seems to represent the other end of the political spectrum? How about one that seems to reside in the middle range in terms of political outlook? Make note of any information sources mentioned in the different news items. The aim here, of course, is to move beyond any obvious political ideology and burst the "filter bubbles," break out of the "echo chambers," and get above the top-down "conglomerate clouds" of corporate news.

However, in this age of peer-to-peer/bottom-up content production we can encounter all kinds of content that appears to be a traditional form of 'top-down' news production but is, in fact, new forms of propaganda, fake news, and disinformation. But these distinctions between top-down, bottom-up, and 'real' and 'fake' are fast becoming false dichotomies today as the progressively intertwine, blur, and resist detection. In this age of Social Media, how might you answer these two questions McLuhan posed: Are you moving in ever-diminishing circles? How often do you change your mind, your politics? To reiterate, know your sources, and know how to cite them in both personal and professional communication. Your credibility, and your ability to skillfully engage as an informed participant in today's society, depends on it.

Power is indeed shifting in our modern world, driven largely by developments in our modes of communicating and sharing information. How comfortable are you with a high power distance between you and the sources that produce the mediated content you consume? Are there ways you can use your social capital to become an influential communicator, and not just a consumer? What social paradigm do you subscribe to? As Marshall McLuhan pointed out early on, electronic (and digital) media created a communicative situation (or media ecology) that in many ways resembles the experience of living in a village writ-large—a global village where whispers, gossip and innuendo are easily confused with reality (i.e., 'on-the-ground' physical and social facts). What do you think are the areas of the world to watch as mediated communication brings our world community—our global village—into closer and closer into closer and closer proximity? With all of the information and advice contained in this chapter (and, indeed, in this entire textbook), we should all keep in mind something McLuhan said about this new age of communication: "*There are no passengers on spaceship earth. We are all crew.*"

References

Altkenhead, D. (2012, June 24). Dambisa Moyo: 'The world will be drawn into a war for resources'. The Guardian. Retrieved from http://www.guardian.co.uk/global-development/2012/jun/24/natural-resources-and-development-china

Callick, R. (2012, November 29). International ties no longer a zero-sum game. The Australian. Retrieved from http://www.theaustralian.com.au/national-affairs/in-depth/international-ties-no-longer-a-zero-sum-game/story-fng3y7gt-1226526111321

French, J. P. R. Jr., and Raven, B. (1960). The bases of social power. In D. Cartwright and A. Zander (eds.), Group dynamics (pp. 607–623). New York: Harper and Row.

Gerbner, G., Gross, L., Morgan, M., & Signiorelli, N. (1980). The "mainstreaming" of America: Violence profile no. 11. Journal of Communication, 30(3), 10–29.

Gerbner, G., Gross, L., Morgan, M., & Signiorelli, N. (1982). Charting the mainstream: Television's contributions to political orientations. Journal of Communication, 32(2), 100–127.

Gudykunst, W. B., Matsumoto, Y., Ting-Toomey, S., Nishida, T., Kim, K. and Heyman, S. (1996). The influence of cultural individualism-collectivism, self construals, and individual values on communication styles across cultures. Human Communication Research, 22: 510–543.

Hiebert, R. E., Ungurait, D. F., & Bohn, T. W. (1974). Mass media: An introduction to modern communication. New York: McKay.

Hiebert, R. E., & Gibbons, S. J. (2000). Exploring mass media for a changing world. Mahweh, NJ: Lawrence Erlbaum Associates.

History of the Internet (2014). Retrieved June 21, 2015 from http://www.newmedia.org/history-of-the-internet.html

Hofstede, G. (1984). Culture's consequences: International Differences in work-related values (2nd ed.). Beverly Hills CA: Sage.McCombs, M. E.; & Shaw, D. L. (1972). The agenda-setting function of mass media. Public Opinion Quarterly 36(2): 176.

McLuhan, M. (1964). Understanding media: The extensions of man. New York: Signet.

Miniwatts Marketing Group. (2012, June 30). Internet world stats. Retrieved from http://www.internetworldstats.com/stats.htm

Parsons, P. (2003, March). The evolution of the cables-satellite distribution system. Journal of Broadcasting & Electronic Media 47 (1): 1–16.

Pöllman, A. (April 2013). Intercultural capital: Toward the conceptualization, operationalization, and empirical investigation of a rising marker of sociocultural distinction. SAGE Open 3(2): 2158244013486117, first published on April 23, 2013.

Siebert, F. S., Peterson, T., & Schramm, W. (1956). Four theories of the press. University of Illinois.

Szreter, S. (2000). Social capital, the economy, and education in historical perspective. In T. Schuller (Ed.), Social capital: Critical perspectives (pp. 56–77). Oxford: Oxford University Press.

Chapter Ten
Public Speaking

The thought of giving a speech in public is very exciting to some people. To many others, however, it is a terrifying prospect. Whether you are excited, terrified, or somewhere in between at the idea of giving a speech or presentation to others, you should know that speaking in public is a skill that should be in every communicator's toolkit. You may be called upon to give a speech or presentation in class, as part of your professional work, or in your everyday life. Whether you are addressing your company's board of directors, making a sales pitch, talking to your son's soccer team or to other members of your daughter's PTO, you will use the same basic speaking skills.

Many individuals feel that they are not good speakers, that they are not "natural-born speakers" and therefore cannot give a good speech. One of the first and most important lessons students can learn is that anyone can give a solid, credible, and compelling speech by learning and practicing some important skills. This chapter is designed to give you advice about how to plan, put together, and deliver the best possible speech or presentation.

At the beginning of this textbook you learned about the importance of Aristotle and his principles of **logos** (ideas or argumentation), **pathos** (emotion) and **ethos** (credibility). As you consider, plan, and deliver your speech, keep these three principles always in the forefront of your mind. Make sure that your content and ideas are solid (logos), that you are delivering your speech with passion and appealing to your audience through both your words *and* your feelings (pathos) and that your sources give you credibility (ethos). With these principles guiding your process, you are ready to begin the speechmaking process.

Where to Begin: The Big Picture

You've got to be very careful if you don't know where you are going, because you might not get there.

—Yogi Berra

Sometimes, the most difficult thing about giving a speech is knowing *where to begin*. How will you include everything that you know about your topic? Do

Figure 10.1 Create images in your listeners' minds.

you write out everything that you want to say? Do you jot a few notes? Do you memorize, or just "wing it?" Actually, the best place to begin is to think about the big picture of the speech. The big thinking about a speech begins well before the actual work on the speech itself.

There are four main factors, or questions, you will want to consider as you do the "big thinking" about your speech. You will need to think about *your audience, the occasion, your topic,* and *your purpose.* As you think about each of these areas, the direction of your speech will begin to take shape.

Who is my audience? The answer to this question may seem obvious, but there may be more to this than meets the eye. This thinking involves **audience analysis** and helps you determine both what you will say and how you will say it. Consider audience **demographics**, the characteristics of your audience, including things such as age, gender, ethnic and racial background, religion, education and occupation. Even if the subject matter is the same, you will present your topic differently if you are speaking to a group of

retired college professors or a group of middle school-aged Girl Scouts. You will also want to consider your audience's probable **attitude** toward your topic, as well as their political leanings and emotions and feelings. Is your audience already knowledgeable and interested in your topic, or are you going to need to convince them that they want to hear what you have to say? Keep everything that you know about your audience in mind as you work on your speech.

What is the occasion? In addition to considering what you know about your audience, when and where you deliver your speech will make a difference in what you say and how you say it. Thinking about *why the audience is here* and *why you are here* will help you decide on the **style** of your speech. Will it be formal, perhaps written out carefully and delivered from a **manuscript**? Or is the occasion more informal, requiring an **extemporaneous** speech, spoken in one's own words from brief mental or written notes, or even **impromptu**, presented without time for preparation at all? A classroom informative speech, a college commencement address, a political debate, a sales presentation, or a toast at a friend's wedding will require differing approaches.

What is my topic? On some speech occasions, you will be assigned a topic. This may be the case

if you are delivering an informative speech on a class project, presenting a proposal to a committee, or if you are delivering an award to an honoree. On other occasions, you may be able to choose your topic. Use everything that you know about your audience and about the occasion to inform your choices. Think about not only what interests you, but what interests your audience. Don't choose your topic to please your audience if it doesn't interest you, but do think about your audience as you approach your topic. Think about how to make your topic relevant and interesting to your audience. Remember, the purpose of a speech is to *share your ideas with the audience.* It is intended for them. They need to be interested and they need to care about what you have to say. It is your job to make that topic meaningful for them.

What is my purpose? Finally, think about why you are giving this speech. Do you want simply to entertain the audience? Do you want to inform them or teach them about something? Do you want to persuade them to do something or not to do something? *Why* are you here? *Why* are you talking to them? *What* do you want from them or hope that they will take away from your speech? **Informative** speaking and **persuasive** speaking can look very different. Be sure that you are clear about your purpose in giving this speech.

Gathering and Preparing Your Material

Grasp the subject, the words will follow.

—Cato the Elder

Once you have finished looking at the bigger picture of your speech, it is time to get to work planning the speech. You have considered your audience and the occasion, you have chosen a topic that is of interest to both you and your audience, and you know what you want to accomplish with your speech. What is next?

For most speeches or presentations, you will need to gather content and material for your speech. Most of the time, you will not initially have all the information you need to speak authoritatively on your topic. Even if you are doing something as seemingly simple as introducing another speaker, you will want to find out something about that person. It is time to do some research.

Hopefully, you have chosen a topic about which you already know something. This may help you decide where to go next to look for additional information. Although most of us head initially to the internet, be sure to consider a range of other sources, including books, journals, newspapers and magazines, databases, government publications, media sources, and first-person interviews. Be sure to look for sources that are *credible* and *current*. Look for differing types of materials—facts and statistics, examples, illustrations, stories. These are the pieces that will make your speech come alive.

As you gather your information, be sure to document the source of each piece of information. You will want to cite your sources later, both within the context of your speech and in a list of resources at the end. As an ethical speaker, you will need to give credit for any material that you include. Remember that **plagiarism** includes using any information or ideas that are not your own. If you include a fact or story from a source, you will need to cite it. If you include an idea taken from your research, you will need to cite it. Anything that does not represent your original work or ideas will need to be cited. It is relatively easy to **verbally document** your source within the context of your speech. You will need to say something like, "According to _____ published in the _____ edition of _____, 25 million people will give speeches this year." Giving credit to your sources and citing their information, gives **credibility** and impact to your speech.

Framing Your Speech

Genius is one percent inspiration and ninety-nine percent perspiration.

—Thomas Edison

Thesis Statement

You've done the big thinking about your speech and you've gathered the information that you need; now you need to begin to put the speech together in a way that makes sense to you and in a way that your audience will be able to follow.

A good starting point is to narrow your topic down to one key idea or **thesis statement**. Your thesis statement or key idea is a *one sentence* statement of the main message that you want your audience to take away from your speech. If you imagine that someone listens to your speech and then meets a friend afterward who asks what the speech is about, the thesis would be the one sentence answer that this listener might give. "He said that skateboarding is a misunderstood sport that should get more commercial sponsorships" or "She said that we should all go out and vote during the next election, no matter whom we support."

Note that the thesis statement is more than a simple statement of the **topic**, it is the one *main idea* of the speech. The subject of "the state of Maine" might be an interesting topic for a speech, but it doesn't tell anyone the main idea of where the speech is headed. One possible thesis statement might be, "Maine is a wonderful state in which to take a vacation." Can you see how you have a better idea about what that speech is going to cover? Another possible thesis for the same topic might be, "The state of Maine has earned a reputation as one of the most politically independent states in the United States." These two speeches might be about the same topic of "Maine", but they will be very different speeches. Narrowing your thoughts down to a very clear statement of your main idea is sometimes difficult, but it is worth the effort. Once you do it, the rest of your speech will fall into place much more easily.

Figure 10.2 Putting Lightbulbs in Buckets

Your thesis statement will help you decide both what to include in your speech, and how you will structure it.

Body of the Speech—Your Main Points

Although a speech begins with an introduction, this may not be the first part of your speech that you put together. We will cover the elements of your introduction a bit later. Let's think, first, about how to put together the body of your speech.

If you just string together a lot of ideas or facts, your audience may not be able to remember many of them. It is often helpful to think about 3-5 main points that you would like your audience to remember. You will then explain and elaborate on each of these points and include your details and facts within each main point. Imagine trying to remember twelve items on a grocery list.

Chances are that you may come home from the store with only ten of the twelve! But if you categorize them and remember that there are four dairy items, four vegetables, and four frozen items, you'll do better at re-membering what you need.

So the next step in put-ting this speech together will be to determine the 3-5 main points, within the context of your clear thesis statement, that you want your audience to understand and remem-ber. Let's use the example above about the subject of "the state of Maine" and the thesis of "Maine is a wonderful state in which to take a vacation." You have done some research about Maine and you have a lot of information. Think now about how some of that information fits together. Once again, the choices that you make will change the shape of your speech.

Perhaps you'd like to structure your Maine vacation speech around areas in the state. Your three main points might be "Portland area," "Down East Coast," and "Lakes and Mountains." In this case, you would include informa-tion about each region. But per-haps you'd like to structure your speech around activities. Perhaps your topics might become, "shop-ping," "sailing and water sports," and "hunting and fishing," or even "people," "activities," and "scenery." Once again, these decisions will be based on some of the factors we discussed earlier such as what you know about your audience, what you know about the context, and what your purpose is in giving the speech.

Once you have decided on your main points, you will easily be able to decide which information from your research you want to include in your speech. If you have researched your topic thoroughly, it is likely that you will have more material than you need for your speech. You may not be able to include everything that you know about your subject. Think of your three main points as three buckets or baskets. Every piece of infor-mation that you want to include in your speech must fit into a bucket. If it doesn't fit, it doesn't belong in your speech. For instance, if you've decided to structure your speech about Maine around the three regions mentioned above, but you've found some interest-ing information about Maine's history, or the Maine state flower, it may not belong in your speech. Sometimes, one of the hardest tasks is deciding what to leave out of your speech.

As you fill in each point with your information, remember to give credit to your sources. Be sure to put your information into your own words, but tell the audience where you found your information. Even if you **paraphrase** the author's words, if you use someone else's ideas, you need to give credit. Remember, this verbal documentation gives credibility to your speech. Your audience doesn't need to accept something that is simply your opinion, because you have expert information and facts supporting your ideas.

Beginning—Your Introduction

By now, you should see your speech beginning to come

together. You have a clear central idea, and you are filling out your main points with supporting material. You hope that your audience will remember much of what you have to say, but it is most likely that, even if they do not remember anything else, they will remember the first impression that you make and how you conclude. You want the beginning and ending of your speech to be strong and memorable. You also want to be sure that the whole speech holds together, and this is where transitions between sections will help.

There are three primary things that you want your introduction to do: get your audience interested in your topic and draw them into your speech, explain your main idea, and preview where you will be taking them as they follow you through your speech. Let's look at each of these elements.

Your first job is to get the audience's attention and convince them that they want to hear what you have to say. Remember, the speech is all about them, not about you. If you begin, as many speakers often do, with something like "My speech today is about vacationing in Maine," or "I'm going to talk to you about

taking a vacation in Maine," it really is all about you and what you want to talk about, not about your audience. Think of some ways to present your topic so that your audience wants to hear more about what you have to say. Some common **attention getters** might be a fact or startling statistic, an image, a story, a quote or a rhetorical question. Beginning with a statistic about how many people visit Maine each year, or a story about sailing up the coast on a 19th century windjammer, or asking how many people have ever wished they could get away to someplace to go whitewater rafting have potential to get your audience interested in your topic.

Once you have your audience's attention and interest, you need to make sure they understand exactly what your speech will be about. This is where you will go back to your thesis statement and share this idea with them. Remember how hard you worked to make sure you had a clear sense of purpose? Now you need to share that with the audience. In a few sentences, explain the essence of your speech as clearly as you can. You'll have the rest of your speech to develop your ideas, but providing some 'feedforward' that offers your audience a sense of what to expect will increase and help maintain their interest.

The final section of your introduction will give your audience the **roadmap** of your speech.

You've drawn your audience in, you've explained your main idea, now you need to share with them the direction of your speech. Tell them your three main points. "As we look at the wonderful vacation opportunities in the state of Maine, we're going to look at three popular vacation areas and how they differ. We'll learn about the Portland area, the Down East coastal area, and finally, the Maine lakes and mountains. First, let's look at the Portland area . . ." Your audience will now know what to expect and be able to follow you as you go through your speech.

Transitions—Your Signposts

As you structure your speech, you will want to help your audience stay with you by providing them with some **internal summaries** and **signposts** as you move from point to point. This will help them to bridge the gap between sections of the speech as you move from each main point to the next. So, after you've talked about Portland, you might say something like, "now that we've looked at Maine's largest city, let's move further up the coast and look at the Down East coastal region." You've helped the audience know that you've finished one section and are moving to the next. Hopefully, they will remember the roadmap you provided in your introduction and know where they are in your speech and move along with you. They can see how one main point relates to the next. Then do the same thing after your second main point as you move on to point number three.

Figure 10.3 It's important to use roadmaps and signposts.

Conclusion—Your Ending

Finally, you want the **conclusion** of your speech to be as strong as the beginning. Think of your conclusion as a mirror image of your introduction. Remember the three parts of your introduction: attention getter, explanation of main idea, preview? Now you want to **review** for your audience what they have just heard. Review the three main points. "So we've seen three primary vacation areas in the state of Maine: the Portland area, Down East coastal area, and the lakes and mountains region." Reinforce in the minds of the audience what those important points were. Now give a brief **summary** of the main idea again and then leave your audience with a memorable statement or **clincher** at the end (just as your attention getter worked to get their attention) at the beginning. If your audience remembers nothing else about your speech, they will most likely remember the end. Make sure you finish strong...*with a bang, not a whimper.*

Figure 10.4 Communication apprehension.

Of course, we've chosen a rather simple topic to use as an illustration for this speech, but the basic principles can be applied to any topic or any situation. The same structure can be used for a five-minute classroom speech or an hour-long keynote speech. Your speech may be simple and lean, or lengthy and flowery, but if the structure has good bones, if you have a strong framework and a clear thesis, it will come together well.

Text and Style

Once you have the framework of your speech put together, you will need to consider the style of your speech and what kind of **manuscript** or notes you will use. This will depend on the context or occasion of your speech. For a more formal speech, such as a commencement address or keynote speech, you may prepare a written manuscript in which the speech is written out word for word. For a more informal or **extemporaneous** speech, including a classroom presentation, it is often much better to use a speaking outline or partial notes with bullet points. This will allow you to be much more spontaneous and speak *to* your audience rather than *at* your audience. Although it may seem scary at first to not write everything down, the more you rehearse and practice, the more comfortable you will become. In fact, it is this rehearsal stage that is so often shortchanged. Now that you have the content of your speech prepared, let's talk next about how to prepare *yourself* for this speech.

Preparing Yourself to Give a Speech

Nothing in life is to be feared. It is only to be understood.

—Marie Curie

We mentioned earlier that some people find the prospect of giving a speech or presentation a terrifying idea. If you are one of those people, you are in good company. One survey, in which people were asked what they feared the most, found that more people in the United States are afraid of speaking in public than they are of anything else (Wallechinsky, Wallace, and Wallace, 1977). They feared giving a speech more than they feared death, heights, bugs, snakes, flying, or deep water. Why is it that we are so afraid? Many of us fear public speaking for different reasons. We may think we are not good speakers, we may fall victim to negative thinking, we may expect perfection of ourselves and fear that we will fail, we may be uncomfortable being the center of attention, we may fear the unfamiliar, or we may even have learned from others that we should be fearful (Dwyer, 2005). Whatever the reason that we worry about it, **speaking anxiety** or **speech fright** is not imagined; it is real.

Communication researchers use the term **communication apprehension** to describe "the fear or anxiety associated with real or anticipated communication with others" (McCroskey, 1977). It is the subject of extensive research in the Communication field. For a few speakers, anxiety becomes so debilitating that they cannot overcome it. For most of us, however, although our fear or apprehension is uncomfortable, we can use the nervous energy it produces to our advantage. Instead of allowing the nervousness to get in the way, preventing us from accomplishing our task, we can turn it into useful energy and use the adrenaline much as an athlete might. So the goal is less about *getting rid* of nervousness and more about *using* our nervous energy to help us. This simple mental shift alone can help you channel that energy to work for you.

So what can you do to help you with those butterflies in your stomach? Different techniques will work differently for each individual, but here are a few suggestions that might help:

- Remember that a certain amount of nervousness is a good thing. Your goal is to use it, not to get rid of it.

- Know your topic as thoroughly as possible. Nervousness often arises from not feeling prepared. Know what you are talking about. Make it yours. Own it!

- Use the technique of **visualization** or **mental rehearsal** to imagine a positive image of the speaking occasion. Instead of imagining the worst, think about how well everything could go. Imagine the room, the audience, what you might wear, how you will sound. Take time to sit quietly and picture the perfect speech several times in as much detail as you can manage. You will learn to associate positive images with the upcoming event (Dwyer, 2005).

But remember that mental rehearsal can never substitute for real, on-your-feet rehearsal.

- Practice, practice, practice. Then, when you think you may be ready, practice a few more times. One of the key traps for beginning speakers is that they often don't realize until too late how much rehearsal is necessary to prepare even a very short speech. Give yourself time. Prepare early enough for several days of rehearsal time.

- Be sure that your rehearsals are as close to the speaking situation as you can make them. Get on your feet and say your speech aloud. Use the same notes that you will use. Practice good eye contact, posture, gestures, and facial expressions. If you won't be sitting at your desk or lying on your bed when you give your speech, don't practice it that way!

- Use all of the support that you can get. Rehearse for a friend or family member. Take advantage of other sources, such as a Speaking Center or Communication Lab. Welcome feedback and suggestions from your listeners.

- If you can manage it, try a dress rehearsal in the actual space. Wear what you are planning to wear (something that makes

Figure 10.5 Visualization as "Mental rehearsal"

you feel strong and polished) and practice with the technology you will use. Make sure the computer works. Make sure the sound system works if you will be using one. Know what to expect on speech day.

- Consider what relaxation techniques might help you. Would a run or workout the morning of your speech get the blood flowing and release some energy? Would some slow deep breathing help calm your nerves? Would it be better to eat before your speech or wait until after? Make sure you get enough sleep, give yourself enough time to arrive without creating stress, and physically prepare.

- Remember that your audience really does want you to do well. They are on your side and want you to be successful. Find a familiar face or two in the group and speak to them with sincerity. Make your eye contact real. Latch on to that smile, nodding head, or look of understanding and let it carry you through.

- Finally, remember to be yourself. The audience wants to hear from you and to get to know you. Be yourself. Be sincere. Don't try to be something that you are not.

Presenting the Speech

Avoiding danger is no safer in the long run than outright exposure. Life is either a daring adventure or nothing.

—Helen Keller

The moment has arrived. You've worked hard to think broadly about your speech, to do your research, to structure a framework that supports your topic, to put it all together, to prepare yourself and rehearse your speech, and finally it is time to make the presentation. If you have done a thorough job on all of the preparation, you will not only give a terrific speech, but you may find yourself enjoying the experience. Here are a few last minute things to think about to make sure that your speech is a success.

Physical Considerations

- Remember that your speech begins the moment that it is your turn or that you are called upon. Don't wait until you start to speak to set the tone. Think about your reaction and how you walk to the front of the

room or the podium. Use all of your **nonverbal communication** skills to let everyone know that you are excited to have the opportunity to speak to them.

- Think about your **stance**. You want to appear strong and confident. Make sure your weight is on both of your feet so you won't rock back and forth. Stand tall. If you are not using a podium, move if it feels comfortable, but make sure your movement is purposeful.

- Use your energy to communicate your enthusiasm about your topic. Your audience will never be more interested in your topic than you are. If you sound bored or uninterested, your audience will stop paying attention to you quickly. Remember that nervous energy that you wanted to work *for* you? Now is the time to channel it and use it to capture the audience.

- Use gestures and facial expressions that feel comfortable and convey the meaning that you want to get across to your audience. Don't use artificial gestures just for the sake of gestures, but don't hold back those things that feel natural.

- Make real and meaningful eye contact with your audience. If you've rehearsed enough, you'll only need to glance at your notes occasionally. Find people in the audience that are giving you supportive cues and speak to them. Don't look at the floor, the ceiling, the back wall, or your slides if you have them; look at your audience.

Talk to them and they will respond.

Vocal Considerations

Your voice is a powerful tool in communication. Many of us take our voices for granted, but think about how you can use this tool to help support and convey the meaning of your speech.

- Be sure that you **project** to your audience. Any public speaking situation will probably demand a bit more effort and vocal energy than a one-to-one conversation. Support your voice from your **diaphragm** and speak to the people in the back row. We are almost never bothered by someone who speaks a bit too loudly, but we are often frustrated when we can't hear a speaker well.

- Be sure that you speak clearly. You may need to speak slightly slower than you normally do. Remember to put the ends on words and not let the ends of sentences drop away. Use particular care with any unfamiliar words or terms. Look them up ahead of time and pronounce them carefully.

- Use the full range of expression in your voice. Let your voice rise and fall naturally. Emphasize key words by **verbally underlining** them. Be careful not to let yourself become monotone or flat. This might happen because you are so familiar with what you are saying. You have rehearsed many times. But remember that your audience is hearing your ideas for the very first time. Use your voice to make it meaningful for them.

- Don't be afraid to use **pauses**. There is a difference between a pause and a hesitation. A pause is a *silence that is filled with meaning*. It is the "loud" silence that intensifies what you are saying (Crannell, 2012). Pause after you say something important to let it sink in. Pause before you give a key idea to draw our attention to it. Pause between sections of your speech to let us know that there is a break. A pause can be used in the same way that indentations set paragraphs apart in written work. The proper and liberal use of meaningful pauses can be the difference between an average and an outstanding speaker.

Visual Aids

Depending on your topic and the situation, you may want to use **visual aids** or other supplementary aids to support your speech. Many speakers today use presentation tools such as PowerPoint, Prezi, or Keynote to support their speeches. These can be powerful tools if used correctly—or they can be deadly. If you decide to use one of these tools, there are many books and websites that can help you create your slides and use the tool well. Here are just a few basic principles to keep in mind if you are considering a visual aid.

- Remember that any visual aid is just that: it is an *aid* to you in giving your presentation. It is intended to help the audience understand your message. It is not meant to be decorative or intrusive. The visual aid is not

the star of the show. Keep the focus on you and not on your slides. Use slides only if they will enhance what you have to say, not just for the sake of having slides.

- Do not use your slides as your speaking notes. Slides are intended for your audience and not for you. If you plan to use slides as your notes, you will probably put too much information on the slides. Keep slides simple, with minimal words. Use slides for the powerful visual images that they can provide rather than trying to include many, many words.

- Don't overlook other forms of visual aids. Again, depending on your topic, you may find physical objects, models, maps, videos, audio materials, etc. can enhance what you are saying. If you do use objects, make sure that you practice handling them as you practice your speech. Make sure they will be visible to the entire audience.

Group Presentations

One special situation that you might encounter in your classes is a group presentation. Perhaps you have worked with a group of people and you need to present your project or findings to the class. Your group of 3-to-5 people will need to do one presentation. Although all of the principles discussed earlier will apply, there are some special considerations you will want to keep in mind as you prepare and present a group presentation.

Working on a group presentation will probably require more

time and effort than preparing a presentation on your own. You will need to coordinate the planning, find time to practice together, and think carefully about how your presentation will flow. Plan thoughtfully how you will divide the presentation. Know well ahead of time who will be responsible for each section. Think about the overall introduction and conclusion, as well as the internal summaries and transitions. Who is responsible for beginning and ending? How will you "pass the baton" between speakers? Try to tie each section of the presentation to the other sections as much as possible. Make sure that your entire presentation has continuity of style, detail, and format. You want each section be a part of one whole presentation, not feel as though there are five individual presentations.

Make sure that your group has time to gather and rehearse together several times. It often isn't until you come together that you realize where gaps may be or where there may be difficulties. Think about where and how each member of the group will be arranged as you present your speech. Will you all line up in front of the room? If you have slides, consider who will be responsible for changing the slides? Will each speaker change her own slides or will one person be in charge? Consider having each speaker move to the center of the room as he speaks so he will have the audience's attention and no one is stuck on the side. Finally, remember that each person is part of the entire presentation—even when he is not the person speaking. Be sure that each group member gives full attention to the speaker. With a little bit of extra effort and attention, your group can present a polished overall presentation.

Feedback and Criticism

There is nothing so encouraging as good criticism.

—Samuel Silas Curry

As we conclude our discussion about speaking in public, there is one final topic that we should consider. One of the things that many of us worry about in our speechmaking is the **feedback** that we will receive afterward. Because you may be doing much of your speaking in the classroom, you will probably expect to receive feedback and suggestions from both your professor and your fellow students. It is important that you keep in mind that feedback and **criticism** are necessary for you to get better at what you do, and that receiving and giving feedback and criticism can be very positive experiences. You need to welcome both the opportunity to receive feedback and the responsibility of giving useful feedback to others.

Although we often think of criticism as a negative thing, the definition can actually be quite positive. Criticism has been defined as "being encouraging, affirming, and supportive for the purpose of building confidence" (Petress, 2000). Good constructive criticism simply provides useful comments and suggestions that will help someone improve. Samuel Silas Curry, founder of Curry College and a speech teacher in the late 19th century, defined

criticism as "the comparison of the actual with the ideal" (Curry, 1891). So good criticism, then, is intended to encourage, affirm, support, build confidence, and contribute to a positive outcome.

If you have an opportunity in your class to **critique** each other, take it seriously. You learn both from giving and receiving feedback. Keep an open mind as others tell you how you might improve. Think carefully about the suggestions that you make to others. Just telling them that they were great may make them feel good, but will not help them improve. As members of that *community* created by our *communication*, we have a responsibility to help each other. Here are things that you might consider as you offer suggestions:

- Point out some great qualities first and then follow with some possible ways to improve.

- Be sure to comment on actions and things that can be changed, not personality traits or things which the speaker cannot control. Be as specific as you can.

- Be genuine and show real interest in the speaker.

- Be direct, honest, and respectful.

Conclusion

We are that which we repeatedly do. Excellence, therefore, is not an act but a habit.

—Aristotle

Speaking in public may never become your favorite thing to do, or you may find that you enjoy it and are good at it. The more opportunities that you have to practice your skills in this area, the more comfortable you will become. Good public speaking requires courage, skills, and practice, but it can be one of the most powerful tools for conveying information and your strongly held convictions to others. Give yourself the opportunity to practice your skills in this area and to open yourself up to what can happen when you take the risk and present your ideas. You may be surprised to find how much you will gain from the experience.

References

Crannell, K. (2012). *Voice and Articulation* (5th ed.). New York: Wadsworth

Curry, S.S. (1891). *The Province of Expression*. Boston: The Expression Company

Dwyer, K. (2005). *Conquer Your Speech Anxiety* (2nd ed.). New York: Wadsworth

McCroskey, J.C. (1977). Oral communication apprehension: A review of recent theory and research. *Human Communication Research*, 4, 78–96

Petress, K. (2000). Constructive criticism: a tool for improvement. *College Student Journal*

Wallechinsky, D., Wallace, I., & Wallace, A. (1977). *The book of lists*. New York: Bantam Books.

Appendices

1. Two Epistemological Turning Points

With recent events unfolding around the globe related to education, science, politics, militarism, and immigration, it seems fair to say that we are in the midst of a new **epistemological crisis** (or crisis of knowing). This current crisis of knowing resembles a series of media events that unfolded during the two centuries that led up to the Renaissance. Our current situation, however, seems to far outstrip the depth and reach, as well as the speed and scale, of the historical example detailed below. Before we delve into the details, let's begin with a few pressing questions.

How do emerging media systems, along with the habits and practices of communication that form around them, function to variously constrain and prohibit or, conversely, emancipate and enable the simultaneous dissemination and articulation of facts and grounded evidence on the one hand, along with urban legends, alternative facts, and "fake news" on the other? How, in other words, do some of the latest mass-mediated communication systems, and the contexts for knowing that they create, support different kinds of deliberation, debate, and argumentative tension?

First, we introduce some key terminology; then we outline two illustrative examples—one historical, the other still unfolding—that can help us to understand what's at stake. After all, to understand any current state of affairs, it's always a good idea to have a sense of what has come before. What's more, a clear view of the past can offer valuable insight into where we might be going. First, some key terms.

Heterodoxy refers to the coexistence and promotion of multiple belief systems or explanations regarding some process, scenario, state of affairs, or apparent reality. It is a pluralistic alternative to **orthodoxy**, or the notion that there is only one way (or one best way) to explain or otherwise understand such things. Of course, at first blush, the maintenance of multiple ways of knowing seems like a great idea. Indeed, dissension, deliberation, and debate are time-honored ways whereby human beings have tended eventually to come to a general consensus or collective understanding of our world.

These collective understandings tend to guide us in productive and sometimes even positive ways. For example, over time and through various forms of objective peer review, these well-grounded, evidenced, or "proven" arguments eventually form "communities of agreement," or **intersubjectivities,** around which sound plans, policies, and other courses of action can help us to know what to do or where to go next. However, heterodoxy can sometimes also be a drag, quite literally, on human progress. To understand how and why, we'll next consider two examples (perhaps infamous examples), of significantly opposed outlooks that were treated equally or on a par, such that the popular debate between these two outlooks continued (or, regarding the second example below, appear to be continuing) for too long.

Example 1: Ptolemy's Geocentric vs. Copernicus' Heliocentric Understandings of the Universe

Especially after the invention of the printing press by Johannes Gutenberg in the mid-15 century, sense and nonsense proliferated, running hand in hand for several centuries. This state of affairs was a primary driver of significant confusion; it stalled clarifications and advancements in thinking regarding astronomy and the place of human beings within nature.

Extending both Aristotelian and religious teachings, Ptolemy's explanation emerged, in large measure, from a mix of the Christian orthodoxy of the first and second centuries A.D. and a kind of taken-for-granted intuitive understanding of nature (i.e., that humans are the highest and most perfect creation of God). Ptolemy's theory of the universe was a common intuition based on information gathered primarily through vision, which seemed to indicate that the sun and moon revolve around an epicentered, unmovable earth. Although Ptolemy more or less "nailed it" with the moon, he added so much detail to his "epicyclic model" that it became an overly complex and unwieldly account of the movements of the sun and other heavenly bodies.

Ptolemy's explanation finally collapsed under its own weight, given the accumulation of far more coherent and collective understandings of physics, geometry, gravity, and inertia (among other things) articulated by Copernicus and Galileo during the Renaissance. But for at least a century, these two explanations were disseminated in mass-produced pamphlets and books. The appearance of these directly competing explanations in the mass media of the time in large measure created a situation wherein both explanations were treated as equally valid accounts of the universe to the extent that such phenomena could be detected and measured at that time. Of course, the heliocentric theory eventually became the correct way to understand our solar system. That knowledge then paved the way for our ability to detect and map the existence of other solar systems, star clusters, galaxies, and galactic clusters.

Example 2: Nonanthropogenic vs. Anthropogenic Understandings of the Four Planetary Spheres

This example concerns a continuing debate between proponents of two fundamental outlooks: a nonanthropogenic or "neutral" vs. an anthropogenic or "active" theory with respect to our relationship to the planet. The ongoing nature of this debate is surprising to an increasing number of specialist and nonspecialist observers. Indeed, the vast majority (close to 100% in most fields) of today's accredited geologists, physicists, chemists, biologists, climatologists, oceanographers, and ecologists are aligned with respect to the reality of anthropogenic, or human-induced, processes long under way that affect the planet and can be empirically detected in the geosphere, hydrosphere, biosphere, and atmosphere.

Starting in the 1960s, suggestions regarding a change in terminology began showing up in academic journals, at scientific conventions, and elsewhere to shift the lexicon and thinking describing the natural world; that is, it was proposed that we move from the Holocene to a new geological phase dubbed the *Anthropocene*. The suggestion was based on growing concern regarding a more accurate way of describing the latter part of the quaternary period, the most recent geologic phase. The argument is that with the onset of the Industrial Revolution, anthropogenic processes began tipping the scale in earnest, resulting in a massive spike in the combustion of greenhouse gases. These were detectable in geosediments, including arctic core samples that reveal particulate accumulation and other indicators of unprecedented emissions of carbon dioxide. Along with this, approximately 150 years ago, interested observers began measuring slow increases in the average global temperature, depletion of the arctic ice pack, and rising sea levels.

However, because public awareness depends on the public's habits of selective perception, selective attention, and selective exposure to information, the facts regarding humanity's role in causing these phenomena may not be receiving the attention they deserve. Evidence of the sort already mentioned has reached a sort of "tipping point," whereby the scientific community and many other observers agree that human culture is playing an active role in determining the future of the planet. Geological societies and other accredited scientific bodies and caucuses around the world are now on the verge of formally adopting *Anthropocene* as the official designator of the late-quaternary period. Indeed, according to this broad community of experts, this is the reality underlying systemic processes and effects associated with what has been termed *global warming* and/or *climate change* by various constituencies. But if one reads, listens to, or watches various kinds of deliberations, arguments, or even news reports on the topic, one has to wonder why the resolution of this debate—which is in many ways analogous to that once vibrant controversy regarding helio- and geocentrism—still seems to be an open question to some. These debates seem analogous precisely because the dissemination of these debates is analogous. That is to say, whereas our modern media systems certainly afford us all kinds of conveniences and access to information, we are currently contending with gatekeeping and filtering problems that far outstrip those experienced by media producers and consumers during the early days of the renaissance.

As with the "epistemological lag" induced in that long-running debate between the geo- and heliocentric models, the ongoing nonanthropogenic vs. anthropogenic debate has recently ticked up in both pace and scale. This is problematic in many ways. Meanwhile, the collective human effort to understand data and arguments surrounding geospheric patterns, processes, and effects is complicated by the emerging relationships between humans and communication systems and devices of various kinds. In other words, despite overwhelming scientific support for the anthropogenic argument, the path toward clarity and the path forward with respect to what can and should be done continues to be deliberated as if that argument was no more valid than the non-anthropogenic view—a duality promoted by various media outlets, by various players, and for various reasons. This continuing debate has certainly been encouraged in many ways, including local concerns over the loss of industries such as coal-mining as well as the threat of massive losses in revenue for oil and other petrochemical industries in the face of increasing regulation and other limitations. However, *newer* may not always mean *better* when it comes to how and to what extent our 21st-century means of communication relay, mediate, and morph the incessant exchange and interpretation of symbolic content that is the stuff of human communication. Any number of exercises or assignments can be drawn from this discussion.

Some Examples Worth Considering

- Racial/ethnic/genetic underpinnings vs. sociocultural/environmental underpinnings of crime

- "Free-market" vs. "planned" economies

- "Trickle-down' vs. "distributed" economic theories

- Theistic vs. atheistic explanations/understandings of reality

- Heteronormative/heterosexist vs. nonspecific categorizations of the *human being*

2. General Principles of Media Literacy

by Patricia Aufderheide

Patricia Aufderheid, "General Principles of Media Literacy." Copyright © 2014 by California Newsreel. Reprinted with permission. Concepts drawn from Media Literacy: Resource Guide, Ontario Ministry of Education, 1989, and the work of many teachers.

We know about the world primarily from the media. But the media don't simply give us the world. They interpret reality, tailor it, perform it. In order to be responsible citizens, we need to be media literate. To help you engage in that process, here are eight "key concepts" of media literacy.

1. **All media are constructions.** Media do not simply reflect reality. They present productions, which have specific purposes. The success of these productions lies in their *apparent* naturalness. They don't look like constructions. But they are, and many different constraints and decisions have gone into why they look the way they do.

2. **The media construct reality.** While they themselves are constructions, media productions also construct within each of our heads a notion of the real. We each carry within us a model of reality, based on our observations and experiences. Using that model, we believe that we're capable of distinguishing truth from lies, and are confident that we won't let "them" pull the wool over our eyes. But much of our model of reality comes from the media we've seen, or that other people whom we take as models (our parents, our teachers) have seen. So it's not as easy as it might seem to draw the line between personal lived experience and the world of "the media." In fact, the media are constructing our sense of reality each day.

3. **Audiences negotiate meaning in media.** Even though media carry messages, they aren't received by everybody the same way. When you like a movie your friend hated, that's pretty clear. Each of us 'filters' meaning through our different experiences: our socio-economic status, cultural background, gender, whether we're tired, whether we know somebody involved in the story. But some meanings end up being more widely accepted than others, a fact that reflects the relative clout, or social power, of the filters which affect our different readings.

4. **Media have commercial implications**. Most media production in this country is a business, and must make a profit. Even the so-called "public" media—public television, public radio—have to raise money to survive. When you decode the media, you need to ask yourself: Who paid for this? What's the economic structure underpinning this piece of work? When the producer or writer or director chose the subject and began production, how did financial pressures affect his or her choices?

Mass media do not speak to individuals, but to groups of people—in fact, to demographic markets. You are part of several demographic markets—young people, men or women, people of your region, people with your particular hobby, etc. The more money you have to spend within any particular demographic, the more valuable you are to mass media's marketers.

Mass media's commercial implications also involve ownership in another way. If the same company owns a record company, a movie studio, a cable service, network television, videocassette recording and book and magazine publications (as does Time Warner), it has a powerful ability to control what is produced, distributed and therefore, seen.

5. **Media contain ideological and value messages.** A media literate person is always aware that media texts carry values and have ideological implications. (Ideology in this sense means the set of assumptions for

what we think is normal.) A media literate person does not complain that something is biased; he or she searches out the bias, the assumptions, the values in everything that's made. It's all made by people after all, who interpret the world according to their own values and assumptions. Most often, the media affirm the world as it is, the status quo, the received wisdom, whatever is thought of by the media makers as the consensus. And they become reinforcers of that status quo as a result.

Because media mostly reinforce the status quo, the fact that they carry values may seem almost invisible, orordinary, or not worth noting. It becomes clearer that they carry those values when you disagree with them.

6. **Media have social and political implications.** Because media construct reality, under economic terms that shape their messages, and powerfully transmit values, they have important social and political effects on our lives together in society and as members of the public.

7. **Form and content are closely related in media.** Each medium has its own distinctive characteristics. You will get a very different experience of a major event by reading the newspapers, watching TV, listening to the radio, or attending that event in person. A media literate person asks: What about the form of this medium influences the content? Is that formal capacity being exploited well, or is it being wasted? What about the form limits the content?

8. **Each medium has a unique aesthetic form.** Understanding how to "read" the media also means understanding that they are each art forms as well as information transmitters. We pay attention, in writing, to the well-crafted phrase, the vivid quote, the tightly structured argument. We appreciate editing that sharpens contrasts and makes our heart skip a beat in audio, video and film. We understand the power of a camera to shape our own point of view on entering a scene. When we see how media are constructed, we are able to judge their aesthetic value. We ask two sets of related questions: Did it entertain me, keep my attention, involve me—and how did it do that? Did it tell me more about the world, human affairs, and my part in it—and how did it do that?

(Patricia Aufderheide is a professor in the School of Communication at American University in Washington, D.C.; concepts drawn from **Media Literacy: Resource Guide**, *Ontario Ministry of Education, 1989, and the work of many teachers).*

Additional Resources

Gumpert, G., & Cathcart, R. (1985). "Media grammars, generations, and media gaps." *Critical Studies in Mass Communication 2*(1) 23–35.

McLuhan, M. (1964a). *The Gutenberg galaxy: The making of typographic man.* Toronto, Ontario: University of Toronto Press.

McLuhan, M. (1964b). *Understanding media: The extensions of man.* New York, NY: McGraw-Hill.

McLuhan, M. (1965a). Statement, in reference to *Operating manual for spaceship earth* by Buckminster Fuller (1963).

McLuhan, M. (1965b). *American Scholar 35.*

3. Website Info Quality—Some General Guidelines

The following descriptions constitute a rule of thumb concerning ways to think about Internet-based information. From top to bottom, these move from generally more credible, accurate, and less biased to *potentially* less credible, inaccurate, and more biased.

.edu Educational, not-for-profit institutions. They have a stake in representing information as accurately and are as bias-free as possible. The aim is knowledge advancement and dissemination.

.gov State and federal institutions. They have a "formal duty" to provide accurate and timely information to the public. This credo applies to varying degrees, depending on the relative transparency of the institution.

.org Non-profit organizations. These are generally reliable as public service outlets but may have cloaked or readily apparent political agendas.

.com Wholly commercial entities. They are "generically predisposed" to representing themselves in the best possible light in order to fulfill their primary goal of capital generation and increased stock values for shareholders and other vested interests.

.net Network service hubs (see immediately above and below for similar aims).

.biz Reserved for "business entities." Similar to .com in terms of intrinsic aim, terms, and info reliability.

Below is a nonhierarchical list (without qualification) of all known URL suffix/domains (found at: http://www.learnthenet.com/how-to/understand-domain-names/ as of April 2016)

.com—For businesses and commercial enterprises (most companies use this extension)
.coop—Reserved for cooperatives
.edu—For educational institutions and universities
.gov—Reserved for U.S. government agencies
.info—For informational sites
.int—For organizations established by international treaties
.jobs—For employment-related sites
.mil—For the United States military
.mobi—For sites related to mobile devices
.museum—For use by museums
.name—For use by individuals
.net—For networks; usually reserved for organizations such as Internet service providers
.org—For noncommercial organizations
.pro—For use by licensed professionals, such as attorneys and physicians
.tel—For services connecting phone networks and the Internet
.travel—For travel-related services, like airlines, hotels, and agents

4. Virtual Experience Workshop

Compose a "virtual experience" (in about a page). This is a creative writing assignment that will prepare you for some creative speaking. Attend to your senses. Don't be concerned if you have never done anything like this before. Give it a try— let it flow. A good way to get started is to simply *free associate*. Pick out a memory, a dream, a startling experience, something you noticed on your way to class today. Let your mind wander. Jot down the tidbits of experience (the sights, sounds, smells, tastes, sensations, and feelings, etc.) that come to mind. Then you can begin to piece together a fuller narrative, painting a picture of any particular scene, moment, or event from those various sensations. Be prepared to potentially share your virtual experience with the class.

Some tips to keep in mind during the editing of your virtual experience

- Use the first person. Immediacy is best whenever possible.

  Avoid: *"their slow rhythm makes you feel ... "*

  Instead, say: *"Made me feel... , or l felt..."*

- Be specific: use concrete detail and direct references:

  Avoid: *"kind of," "sort of," "like," "something to that effect,"* etc. Not: *"He was glaring at me, sort of pinning me to the wall."*

  But Instead: *"his glaring eyes pinned me to the wall."*

- Attend to word choice:

  "obnoxious piece of furniture"?! (how about: *Gaudy, kitch,* cheesy, etc). "the *big* palm trees gently swayed"?! (try: *tall, massive, giant,* etc)

- Avoid mixed metaphors:

  From: "herds of human carcasses" to: *"piles,* or *heaps* of human carcasses." From: "determined beam of light" to: "the *intense,* or *focused* beam."

- Avoid passive voice:

  From: *"was being played out"* to: *"played out."*

  From: *"she was walking slowly away from the club"* to: *"she quietly left the club."*

- Extend, describe, elucidate:

  "The fog was terrible and the street lights weren't working well."

(Be specific. Was the fog thick? How thick was it? How badly were the lights working? Were they *sputtering like ancient fluorescent tubes in a filthy highway stop bathroom?*)

"I became very alert" (How alert? Add a couple of adjectives: *"I was hypersensitive... almost supernaturally alert"*)

"I was sore, it was painful" (How sore? How painful? Like what?... try a colorful simile: *"It hurt like a white hot curling iron pressed against the back of my neck!"*

- But avoid gratuitous constructions (more word choice issues):

  "While it takes no great deal of scientific logic to ascertain that the amount of wreckage at the WTC was of monumental proportions... "

  A colloquialism might work here: *"We don't need a rocket scientist to see that..."*

- Other Tips...

  Incorporate dialogue (if possible, as this always enlivens the narrative).

  Weave a theme throughout your narrative (teach a lesson, offer advice, etc.).

  With these tips in mind, you can begin crafting your virtual experience in the space provided.

  like f*ing white hot curling iron on the back of my neck!" *should read:*

  like a white hot curling iron pressed against the back of my neck!"

.5. Three Rhetorical Appeals: Ethos, Pathos, Logos

http://w. faculty.umkc.edu/williamsgh/dialogues/225.rhetorical.appeals.html

"Of the [modes of persuasion] provided through speech there are three species: for some are in the character of the speaker, and some are in disposing the listener in some way, and some in the argument itself, by showing or seeming to show something.

—Aristotle, *On Rhetoric,* 1356b (trans. George A. Kennedy)

When a speaker or writer (referred to from now on as a rhetor) is trying to persuade the audience, the rhetor will make use of various persuasive strategies:

Ethos

"Ethos" is used to describe the audience's perception of the rhetor's credibility or authority. The audience asks themselves: "What does this person know about this topic?" and "Why should I trust this person?" There are two kinds of ethos: *extrinsic* (outside what you have to say) and *instrinsic* (inside what you have to say).

Examples of *extrinsic ethos* would be as follows: If you are a successful professional basketball player talking about basketball to other pro athletes, then your ethos is strong with your audience even before you open your mouth or take pen to paper. Your audience assumes you are knowledgable about your subject because of your experience. If you are a baseball player talking about basketball, instead, then your extrinsic ethos is not as strong because you haven't been playing pro basketball. However, you are still a professional athlete and know something about that kind of life. If you are a college professor of English, then your extrinsic ethos is likely to be pretty weak with your audience given the topic. Change your audience around, however, and the ethos of each hypothetical rhetor might change.

Examples of *instrinsic ethos* would be as follows: Let's say you are that professional basketball player mentioned above, and you start to address your audience and suddenly you stutter and mumble, you get all the rules of basketball wrong ("there's a three-point line?"), and you mispronounce other players' names, and you reveal your ignorance of the history of basketball by mentioning teams that never existed in the NBA. Suddenly your overall ethos takes a nose-dive with your audience, and you become less persuasive. At the other extreme, let us say you are that English professor, and you speak with confidence and reveal that you know a great deal not only about the intricacies of basketball, but also about individual players' records, and the history and origins of the sport. Your overall ethos, which was weak in this context to begin with because the audience was skeptical of what an English professor would know about their sport, suddenly gets stronger. It gets stronger because your intrinsic ethos goes up in the eyes of your; audience.

The use of ethos is a form of "ethical appeal." Note that this is very different from our usual understanding of the word "ethical."

Pathos

"Pathos" is used to describe the rhetor's attempt to appeal to "an audience's sense of identity, their self-interest, and their emotions."

If the rhetor can create a common sense of identity with their audience, then the rhetor is using a pathetic appeal, or a rhetorical appeal using pathos ("pathetic" here means something different than our usual understanding of the word). So if that college English professor mentions having played basketball in high school and convinces the audience that she or he was pretty good, then not only does that fact strengthen the rhetor's ethos, it also makes a pathetic appeal.

"Pathos" most often refers to an attempt to engage an audience's emotions. Think about the different emotions people are capable of feeling: they include love, pity, sorrow, affection, anger, fear, greed, lust, and hatred.

Let's say a rhetor is trying to convince an audience to donate money to a hurricane relief fund. The rhetor can make pathetic appeals to an audience's feelings of love, pity, and fear (the extent to which any of these emotions will be successfully engaged will vary from audience to audience). "Love" will be invoked if the audience can be made to believe in their fundamental connections to other human beings. "Pity" will be felt if the plight of the homeless hurricane victim can be made very vivid to the audience. And "fear" might work if the audience can be made to imagine what they would feel like in that homeless victim's place. If the rhetor works all of these things together properly (and also doesn't misalign ethos and logos), then the audience is more likely to be persuaded.

Logos

"Logos" is the use of logic to persuade your audience. There are various lines of reasoning that we can discuss, but generally, a logical argument usually convinces its audience because of the perceived merit and reasonableness of the claims and proof offered in support of the overall thesis, rather than because of the emotions it produces in the audience (pathos) or because of the status or credentials of the speaker (ethos).

Putting Them Together

Seldom is any one statement an example of only one appeal. For example:

"As your doctor, I have to tell you that if you don't stop smoking, you're going to die."

Don't forget Your Audience!

Always keep your audience in mind. Always, always remember your audience. When thinking about how best to persuade your audience, ask yourself these kinds of questions: What are their values? What do they believe in already? What is their existing opinion of my topic? What are they likely to find persuasive? What works for one audience might not work for another. Finally, while you may not be able to gain a definitive answer to these kinds of questions in the time frame your speech is developed, you can at least get a sense of where they are coming from.

6. Audience Analysis Worksheet

Speech Type: _____

Purpose of Speech: _____

Length of Speech: _____

Speech Topic: _____

Time to be Delivered: _____

Location: _____

Occasion (*Any holidays? Special Events? Notable Visitors coming to town? What sorts of headlines have been in the news over the past couple of weeks? etc*):

_____

_____

_____

_____

_____

_____

NOTE: some of the following details you may already know about the audience involved, some you can discover with a brief survey, others you can only intuit.

Can you associate any of the following with your topic?
Audience Size: _____
Age Range: _____
Gender Ratio: _____
Education: _____
Group Affiliations: _____

_____

Sociocultural Background:

_____

_____

Can you discover any of the following about the audience?
Assumed Knowledge of Topic: _____

Attitude concerning Topic: _____

Values concerning Topic: _____

7. A Listening Self-Assessment

Yes/No

_____   1.   I like to multi-task and think about other things when people are talking.

_____   2.   If people aren't going to take my advice, they shouldn't waste my time telling me their problems.

_____   3.   I'm usually bored when the conversation doesn't center around my interests.

_____   4.   When someone is slow to get a point across, I interrupt to get things moving.

_____   5.   When people speak to me, they most often have to compete with a number of distractions.

_____   6.   I tend to be involved in a lot of misunderstandings.

_____   7.   A person's appearance, grammar, or style of speaking affect how much attention I give them.

_____   8.   I have trouble keeping a confidence.

_____   9.   I usually feel that making my case is more important that someone else's feelings.

_____   10.   When I don't understand something, I will often fake it and smile instead of asking questions.

_____   11.   I'm good at looking like I'm listening when I'm not. Most people don't notice.

_____   12.   I tend to talk when I should be listening.

_____   13.   I trust my intuition and it serves me well.

_____   14.   I can usually tell when people aren't being honest with me.

_____   15.   I am good at soothing conflict situations and finding win-win solutions

Assessing Your Self Assessment

A _perfect score_ would be No to questions 1-12 and _Yes_ to 13-15. If you answered _Yes_ for any number from 1-12, look at these as areas you might want to strengthen. As you place your attention on those areas and make small shifts, notice any subtle changes in your work or home relationships. If you answered _No_ to most of them and _Yes_ to questions 13-15, you have some solid listening foundations. If your answers show areas that you wish to improve, not to worry. You have already begun the process by assessing where you are now and will continue to strengthen these skills as you continue to read and place your attention on listening.

Mini Self Assessment

This mini-assessment is the short version for those who prefer a quicker quiz. It may also be used in addition to the *Self Assessment* and is equally useful for warming up listening and for looking back, over time.

Ask yourself:

1. What are my listening strengths?

2. What are my listening challenges?

3. How will improving my listening skills improve my personal and/or business relationships?

4. Do I listen to my own intuition?
   When I have, has it guided me well?

8. Impromptu Speech Topics

- You should always learn from your mistakes.

- Life is too short to be taken seriously.

- Time is money.

- A friend is like family that you choose for yourself.

- Better safe than sorry.

- Success means many different things to many different people.

- If it ain't broke, don't fix it.

- _____ is a word I've always loved/hated.

- The best (or worst) thing about the news media these days is …

- The best (or worst) thing about television these days is …

- The best (or worst) thing about politics these days is …

- The best (or worst) thing about this College is …

- The one thing every college student needs to know is …

- The most interesting (or useful) thing I've learned at college is …

9. Vocal Variety and Articulation

Vocal Variety Exercises

(1) Read aloud the various iterations of "Oh." Then try "You were wonderful in that scene." The same speaker should run through each list.

"Oh"

1. Mild surprise

2. Great surprise

3. Polite interest

4. Marked indifference

5. Disappointment

6. Pity (the poor thing)

7. Disgust

8. Sarcasm (I told you so)

"You were wonderful in that scene"

1. Warmly

2. (He was good; the others were bad)

3. (He used to be good but isn't anymore)

4. (You were surprised that he wasn't bad)

5. A question

6. He was really bad—forced politeness

7. Sarcasm

8. Exuberant praise

(2) **The "George and Martha" Game:** Two students stand at the front of the room. One is George, the other Martha. Only these two words are spoken during this exercise. Martha, can only repeat "George." George says only "Martha." Try for at least 10 exchanges, doing your best to alter the emotional import and meaning each time.

(3) **Try a few specified vocal variations.** Read each aloud as suggested.

1. **Oh he did?** (Surprise)

2. **Oh he did?** (a threat)

3. **Oh he did?** (fear)

4. **You won't mind will you?** (of course you won't)

5. **You won't mind will you?** (fearful they will)

6. **You aren't going are you?** (*you* really want to know)

7. **You are going aren't you?** (of course she's going)

8. **Why did you do that?** (accusing)

9. **He is a smart boy** (straightforward)

10. **He is a smart boy** (but acts 'stupid')

11. **He is a smart boy** (his brother is not)

12. **He is a smart boy** (despite what you say to the contrary

13. **She wore a blue dress** (after she said she would wear white)

14. **She wore a blue dress** (but everyone else wore white)

15. **He was pretty good** (he was really very good)

16. **He was pretty good** (he was only fair)

Articulation Exercises

Suggested Use: go around the room with each student taking turns. Be sure each iteration has different students trying a new item. Some of these are much easier than others. When two or three students have flawlessly uttered an item, delete it from the list and continue around the room, picking up the pace as you proceed. Pare down the list until the real tongue twisters emerge.

1. Which wily wizard wishes for Willy?

2. The sixth Sheik's sheep is sick.

3. Fetch me the finest French-fried freshest fish that Finney fries.

4. Shy Sarah saw six Swiss wristwatches.

5. One year we had a Christmas brunch with Merry Christmas mush to munch, I don't think you'd care for such. We didn't like to munch mush much.

6. The view from the veranda gave forth a fine vista of waves and leafy foliage.

7. She sells seashells on the seashore.

8. While we waited for the whistle on the wharf, we whittled vigorously on white weatherboards.

9. Grass grew green on the graves in Grace Gray's grandfather's graveyard.

10. Pete Briggs pats pigs, Briggs pats pink pigs, Briggs pats big pigs. Pele Briggs is a pink pig, big pig patter.

11. Amidst the mists and coldest frosts, with the stoutest wrists.and loudest boasts, he thrusts his fists against the posts, and still insists he sees the ghosts.

12. Rubber baby buggy bumpers.

13. Round the rugged rocks the ragged rascals run.

14. Is this the path that passes to the south of the house?

15. I'm not the pheasant plucker, I'm the pheasant pluckers son, I only pluck the pheasant, When the pheasant pluckers done.

16. I slit the sheet, the sheet I slit, and on the slitted sheet I sit.

10. Opinion, Belief, Knowledge, Argument

(some provisional definitions)

OPINION

1.   A belief or conclusion held with confidence but not substantiated by positive knowledge or proof: "The world is not run by thought, nor by imagination, but by opinion."

2.   A judgment based on special knowledge and given by an expert: *a medical opinion.*

3.   A judgment or estimation of the merit of a person or thing: *She has a low opinion of braggarts.*

BELIEF

1.   The mental act, condition, or habit of placing trust or confidence in another: *My belief in you is as strong as ever.*

2.   Mental acceptance of and conviction in the truth, actuality, or validity of something: *His explanation of what happened defies belief.*

3.   Something believed or accepted as true, especially a particular tenet or a body of tenets.

4.   Accepted by a group of persons

KNOWLEDGE

1.   The state or fact of knowing.

2.   Familiarity, awareness, or understanding gained through experience or study.

3.   The sum or range of what has been perceived, discovered, or learned.

4.   Specific information about something.

ARGUMENT

1.   A discussion in which disagreement is expressed; a debate.

2.   A course of reasoning aimed at demonstrating truth or falsehood: *presenting a careful argument for extraterrestrial life.*

3.   A fact or statement put forth as proof or evidence; a reason: *The current low mortgage rates are an argument for buying a house now.*

4.   A set of statements in which one follows logically as a conclusion from the others.

11. Info Speech Outline "Skeleton"

Insert your working title here:_____

Thesis statement: _____

_____

I. Introduction

A.   Attention Statement (startling statistic, fact, quote, story, a rhetorical question, a good joke?)

B.   Statement of Credibility (ethos/why we should listen to you):

C.   Preview statement (what this all about? Where are you taking us?):

Transition: **[transition from Intro to Body (see suggestions in text and on Bb)]**

II. Body

A.   Main Point 1:_____

       1.   Support: [supporting stat, fact, quote, story, example, etc.]

       2.   Support: [supporting stat, fact, quote, story, example, etc.]

Transition: [your transition from MP1to MP2]

B.   Main Point 2: _____

       1.   Support: [supporting stat, fact, quote, story, example, etc.]

       2.   Support: [supporting stat, fact, quote, story, example, etc.]

Transition: [your transition from MP2 to MP3]

C.   Main Point 3: _____

       1.   Support: [supporting stat, fact, quote, story, example, etc.]

       2.   Support: [supporting stat, fact, quote, story, example, etc.]

Transition: [your transition from the body of your speech to your conclusion]

III. Conclusion

A.   Summary Statement: [What was this about? Where have we been?].

B.   Concluding Remark: [your concluding remark should drive your speech home, leave us in awe. End with a bang, not a whimper].

12. Informative Speech Critique Form

SPEAKER: _____ TITLE:_____

PEER/REVIEWER:_____ Time: _____

Ethos: Credibility of <u>Speaker</u>
Pathos: Emotional Connection to <u>Audience</u>
Logos: Sense in/Clarity of <u>Speech</u>

<u>DIRECTIONS</u>: insert specific #s in line provided on left column, circle general # below, add comments as appropriate

| | *Needs Work* | *Fair* | *Good* | *Excellent* |

Effective Introduction   •-1---------2---------3---------4---------5---------6---------7-•
   __Grabs attention
   __Connected topic to audience (Pathos: why should we care?)
   __Established authority (Ethos: why we should listen to you?)
   __Brief preview

   COMMENT/S:_____

Body   •-1---------2---------3---------4---------5---------6---------7-•
   __2 to 4 distinct main points
   __each with 2 or 3 compelling supports (w/some "surface" referencing)
   __Sensible organization/order (logos)
   __Smooth transitions

   COMMENT/S:_____

Effective Conclusion   •-1---------2---------3---------4---------5---------6---------7-•
   __Recap/summary of main points
   __Strong closing (w/a "Bang!"…not a "whimper")

COMMENT/S:_____

Delivery   •-1---------2---------3---------4---------5---------6---------7-•
   __Did the speaker engage with the audience (project energy)?
   __Appropriate rate/tone/pitch/use of pauses?
   __Did the speaker draw you in? (gestures, eye contact?)
   __Was their character/ethos compelling?
   __Effective use of outline (i.e., NOT reading)?

   COMMENT/S:_____

Invention (Topic)   •-1---------2---------3---------4---------5---------6---------7-•
   __Interesting, appropriate topic
   __Annot. Bibliography shows evidence of research and careful thinking
   __Tells us something we don't already know (new facts, specifics, etc.)

OTHER COMMENT/S:

QUESTIONS:

Core Grading Criteria for the Informative Speech

Supporting Material. This is the extent to which you properly support the information you present in the speech, and the degree to which your explanation is coherent, consistent, and relevant to your subject matter. The supporting material should help relay your information. It should not be excessive, as this will tend to confuse your audience.

Organization. This concerns the extent to which your speech flows from one idea to the next. This requires smooth transition that helps the audience makes sense of the information you present.

Style. This includes using language appropriate to the subject matter and audience, and crafting language that makes the key intervals of your speech memorable. Also of concern here is the extent to which you use your body and voice (verbals, *paralanguage and other nonverbals*) to enhance the meaning and attitude of what you are saying (for example: nonverbals that do not dilute or contradict your words, or create problems for the audience understanding or paying attention to you).

Again, the style component involves use of appropriate gestures, eye contact, facial expressions, vocal qualities and personal appearance. Finally, style also involves the extent to which body (through gestures, etc.) and voice (through volume, enunciation, drama, cadence and intonation) are themselves crafted to leave a lasting impression.

Overall Presentation and Delivery. Whether you memorize your speech or use notes is entirely up to you (most students do use note cards). If you present your speech with eyes cast downward, in a monotone reading voice, without any gesturing, you will score low on the delivery component of "style" and possibly hurt your grade in other areas.

A well-marked, easy-to-glance-at key word outline on a small number of note cards works best. Recommend 14 to 16 font (I do not recommend handwritten notes or outlines). Even if you are planning to use a few short direct quotes, a great strategy is to rehearse to the point of barely needing to look at notes. Indeed, this is what you should be striving for.

If you start with this general strategy and continue speaking in "public" settings in college and beyond, you will eventually be able to address an audience with minimal notes or from memory in a spontaneous fashion (i.e., extemporaneously).

Glossary

.com (Chapter 8): a website set up for commercial business purposes, usually for-profit

.edu (Chapter 8): a website set up by an educational institution, such as a school or college

.gov (Chapter 8): a website set up by a governmental institution

.org (Chapter 8): a website set up by an organization, usually a nonprofit

Ableism (Chapter 3): discriminatory language or behavior related to disability

Abstract words (Chapter 3): words (usually not describing tangible objects) that have shades of meaning that convey different impressions to different people under different circumstances

Accommodation: Chapter 8: allowing someone else to have their way at the expense of you having yours, as in the Thomas-Killman conflict resolution model

Accuracy: Chapter 3: using correct terminology

Acronym: Chapter 4: an abbreviation, such as the initials of words in a common phrase

Active-passive listening position: Chapter 5: the spectrum between listening actively, involved in the conversation, or passively, just sitting and receiving

Adjourning stage of group development (Chapter 7): the final stage of group development in which a group finishes its task, celebrates accomplishments, and either disperses or regroups for the next phase

Affective style of communication (Chapter 6): showing connection in a relationship through contact and emotional expressiveness

Affiliation (Chapter 6): a feeling of trust and connection

Affirmations (Chapter 2): targeted positive statements that can, when repeated mentally or orally, help one's mind focus on and create more desired outcomes. For an affirmation to be effective, it needs to be present tense, positive, personal, and specific.

Ageism (Chapter 3): discriminatory language or behavior related to age (young or old)

Agenda-setting function (Chapter 8): the theory that the media may not be successful in telling people what to think, but it is very successful in telling people what to think about.

Alliteration (Chapter 3): the linguistic device of repeating the same initial sound in at least two words

Anomalous (Chapter 3): different from the norm

Artifacts (Chapter 4): objects that convey messages about a person, group, or culture

Assonance (Chapter 3): the linguistic device of repeating the same vowel sound in multiple words

Asynchronous communication (Chapter 1): messages received at a different time from when they were created (such as reading a book)

Attention getter (Chapter 9): a strategy of starting a speech with an interesting fact, story, quote, question, or experience to gain your audience's attention

Attitude (Chapter 9): perspective, viewpoint

Audience analysis (Chapters 5, 9): finding out about the backgrounds and interests of those to whom you will be speaking so you can cater your content and style appropriately

Audience effects (Chapter 8): the ways in which media content impacts audience members, both individually and collectively

Authoritarian leader (Chapter 7): a leader who takes charge and exercises control over a situation

Authoritarian media system (Chapter 8): a media culture in which it is expected that the government or other powerful institutions will act as a gatekeeper, exerting control over broadcast media content

Autocratic (Chapter 86): power rests with one "at the top"

Automatic attention (Chapter 5): paying attention to something without forethought

Avoidance (conflict resolution strategy) (Chapter 8): failing to engage in a conflict situation or to reach a satisfactory outcome for anyone involved, as in the Thomas-Killman conflict resolution model

Avoiding (stage of relationship develoent) (Chapter 6): the stage of relationship dissolution in which partners actively avoid one another

Behavioral-based interview (Chapter 5): interviews that require candidates to demonstrate particular employment-related skills

Bids (Chapter 6): moments of interaction that invite connection

Bonding (Chapter 6): the stage of relationship development in which a partnership becomes publicly recognized

Brainstorming (Chapter 7): coming up with as many options as possible, without deleting any, to stimulate a full slate of ideas before analyzing and selecting an option

Capital (Chapter 89): assets or currency you can use to get what you want

Channels (Chapter 1): means or pathways for conveying messages from one place to another

Chronemics (Chapter 4): the study of how people use time to communicate

Circumscribing (Chapter 6): the stage of relationship dissolution in which participants create boundaries between themselves around certain aspects of their lives

Civic group (Chapter 7): local government or educational groups that operate for the public good

Cliché (Chapter 3): an overused expression

Clincher (Chapter 9): a memorable statement at the end of your speech that leaves your audience with a strong impression

Closed Questions (Chapter 5): questions that offer respondents a particular range of answer choices

Codes (Chapter 8): means of expression particular to media industries; accepted "grammars" fostered by professional training, style guides, community norms, business standards, and technological capabilities

Coercive power (Chapter 8): the use of force, threat, or punishment to cause people to do things

Cognitive linguistics (Chapter 3): the branch of linguistics that interprets language in terms of the concepts, sometimes universal, sometimes specific to a particular tongue, which underlie its forms

Cognitive system (Chapter 2): our internal mental structure through which we take in information, make meaning from it, and integrate it into our overall worldview

Collaboration (Chapter 8): in a conflict situation, working together so that both parties can get a "win-win" of their highest outcome, as in the Thomas-Killman conflict resolution model

Collectivist (Chapter 8): a cultural orientation in which people are encouraged to stay close and act in line with their group

Commercial media paradigm (Chapter 8): a media culture that views and utilizes media as a for-profit business based mainly on advertising revenue

Communication apprehension (Chapter 9): fear of communicating, especially in a public speaking context

Communication (Chapter 1): the dynamic contextual process, conscious or unconscious, or using symbols to share meaning with others

Communicators (Chapter 8): those who communicate. (Under the HUB Model, this term represents professional communicators who create and deliver media content)

Communis: (Chapter 1): a Latin adjective meaning "common or shared;" the root word for the modern English word "communication."

Community group (Chapter 7): groups that draw people together around shared interests; can be either local (face-to-face) or virtual (mediated)

Competition (Chapter 8): seeking to dominate a conflict situation so that one's own needs are met at the expense of someone else's, as in the Thomas-Killman conflict resolution model

Compromise (Chapter 8): in a conflict situation, dividing the desired outcome so that both parties only get part of what they want, as in the Thomas-Killman conflict resolution model

Computer-Mediated Communication (CMC) (Chapter 8): sharing messages through the use of networked computers or other electronic devices

Conclusion (Chapter 9): the ending of a speech, when a speaker reviews and summarizes content and offers a clincher

Concrete words (Chapter 3): words describing tangible or objects or measurable concepts that have a relatively fixed meaning

Connotative meaning (Chapter 3): all of the impressions, emotions, and sensations that go into our personal definition of a word

Consensus (Chapter 7): general agreement on a concept or course of action

Consonance (Chapter 3): the linguistic device of repeating the same consonant sound within multiple words

Consultative style (Chapter 8): a decision-making style in which power and authority are evenly distributed among group members as equals

Content dimension (Chapter 1): the information contained in a message (for example, the utterance, "Come here" typically means that the speaker wants the listener to approach them)

Content (Chapter 8): packaged ideas or information that are distributed in a media market

Contested meaning (Chapter 1): a meaning that is challenged or contested by those seeking to transform it away from the commonly-accepted meaning

Context (Chapters 1, 3): the environment (physical, mental, relational) in which communication takes place

Continuum (Chapter 6): a spectrum from one opposite to another with infinite shades of gradation between them

Cornell Method/outlining/mapping (Chapter 5): systems for taking notes that allow for more careful listening and greater retention of what is heard

Cost/benefit analysis (Chapter 7): deciding an approach based on an analysis of costs (challenges or risks) versus benefits (assets or strengths)

Critical mass (Chapter 1): a size, number, or amount large enough to produce a particular result

Critical-empathetic listening position (Chapter 5): the spectrum between listening critically, clarifying and analyzing the information presented, and listening empathetically, with kindness and without judgment

Cultural formation (Chapter 1): the process by which two or more individuals agree on the "meaning" of a symbol and communicate that meaning to at least one other

Cultural transformation (Chapter 1): the process by which symbolic meanings are contested and changed through social interaction

Culture (Chapter 1): norms, practices, or beliefs that define a grouping of people

Curiosity (Chapter 6): observing how we are feeling and wondering why, without judgment or blame

Democratic culture (Chapter 8): a decision-making style in which decisions are made by voting among members

Democratic leader (Chapter 7): a leader selected through some sort of voting process

Demographics (Chapter 9): information about a population, such as gender, age, income, education, etc.

Denotative meaning (Chapter 3): the publicly agreed dictionary definition of a word

Dialectics: Chapter 6 (66): a way of understanding the world through the interplay of opposing forces

Differentiating (Chapter 6): the stage of relationship dissolution in which partners recognize ways that they are different and make accommodations for their differing needs

Discrimination (Chapter 3): the unjust or prejudicial treatment of different categories of people or things

Discriminatory language (Chapter 3): language that fosters or reinforces attitudes that marginalize or stigmatize people based on social categories

Dyad (Chapters 1, 6): a pairing of two people

Dynamic: (Chapter 1): characterized by constant change, activity, or progress

Emoticon (Chapter 4): images created in a text stream from punctuation marks, intended to resemble a human facial expression to convey emotional meaning

Empathy (Chapter 6): truly feeling and expressing care for the needs and feelings of another

Environment (Chapter 4): physical space, either indoors or outdoors

Ethos (Chapters 1, 9): a communicator's credibility (term from Greek philosopher Aristotle's writings on rhetoric)

Euphemism (Chapter 3): a polite or more socially-acceptable term for something awkward or difficult

Experimenting (Chapter 6): the phase of relationship development in which participants explore possible modes of interaction

Expert power (Chapter 8): power that stems from knowledge or abilities, as in education or training

Expressive language (Chapter 5): using words to convey emotionally evocative meaning

Extemporaneous speech (Chapter 9): spoken or presented in one's own words without a manuscript, perhaps from bullet points or notes, written or mental

External noise (Chapter 1): disturbance or distractions in the environment that impede full communication

Feedback loop (Chapter 1): the cycle created by reactions and responses between receiver and sender in dynamic communication

Feedback (Chapter 8): reactions and responses to communicated messages, which can create a "feedback loop" to impact the next iteration of messages

Figurative language (Chapter 3): rhetorical devices in speech or writing that achieve special impact by using language in particularly descriptive ways

Figure/ground relationship (Chapter 2): the difference in perception between what is noticed (figure) and what is visible but goes unnoticed (ground)

Filters (Chapter 8): the processes (often through human decision-making) by which information is either withheld or provided

Flow (Chapter 5): the term coined by psychologist Mihály Csíkszentmihályi to describe the mental state of operation in which a person performing an activity is fully immersed in a feeling of energized focus, full involvement, and enjoyment in the process of the activity

Focus group (Chapter 7): a group convened by organizations to provide input or opinions, usually on a product, program, or service

Forming phase of group development (Chapter 7): the initial phase of group development, when group members come together and become oriented to one another's personalities and to the task at hand

Frame of reference (Chapter 2): the perspective through which people see the world

Frame (Chapter 1): the packaging or "lens" through which a message comes to us

Friendship/warmth touch (Chapter 4): a touch intended to provide comfort, typically from a familiar individual

Functional leadership (Chapter 7): a horizontal leadership structure in which each group member takes responsibility for a different aspect of the work

Functional/professional touch (Chapter 4): a touch by someone performing a professional task, such as a beautician or a physical therapist

Gatekeeping (Chapters 7, 8): controlling the flow of communication, either in a group, public, or mediated context

Generalizing (Chapter 3): ascribing characteristics of an individual to an entire group

Genuine reciprocity (Chapter 1): full sharing of openness, respect, and commitment to understanding

Gestalt shift (Chapter 2): a fundamental change in perception or awareness, a new way of seeing and thinking about the world

Gestalt (Chapter 1): an organized whole that is perceived as more than the sum of its parts

Green-flag words (Chapter 5): words that induce a favorable reaction

Group cohesion (Chapter 7): a feeling of connectedness among group members

Group synergy (Chapter 7): when working together makes a group's power greater than the sum of the power of the individual group members

Groupthink (Chapter 7): the negative state of collective blindness that occurs when a group's cohesiveness silences individual perspectives to the point that needed information is not considered

Haptics (Chapter 4): the study of touch

Hayakawa's Ladder of Abstraction (Chapter 3): the metaphoric representation of human communication with highest levels of abstraction at the top and highest levels of specificity at the bottom; the schematic reminds communicators to be as specific as possible in communication to truly convey the concrete images in one's mind

Hearing (Chapter 5): the physical process by which sound is perceived

High contact culture (Chapter 4): cultures in which physical contact in public is a norm

Homophobia (Chapter 3): discriminatory language or behavior related to sexual preference or gender presentation

HUB Model of Communication (Chapter 8): the theoretical model of communication proposed in 1974 by Communication scholars Hiebert, Ungurait, and Bohn (hence the "HUB" acronym) describing the interaction of complex forces in-volved in mediated communication among producers and consumers

Hyperbole (Chapter 3): the linguistic device of exaggerating to heighten emphasis or impact

I (Chapter 2): the volitional self that acts as subject, as opposed to the "me," the passive self that serves as the object

Identity negotiation (Chapter 8): the process by which we actively engage in conveying or transforming the ways we show up in the world

Identity (Chapter 1): a person's conception and expression of their individuality or group affiliations

Image bias (Chapter 8): the media's tendency to rely on images, photos, or graphics to convey messages or ramp up their visibility and impact

Impromptu speech (Chapter 9): a speech made at a moment's notice, without a chance for prior preparation

Individual (dysfunctional) roles (Chapter 7): taking a role in a group in which one's individual needs are out of synch with the group process

Individual interview (Chapter 5): a one-on-one interview typically conducted in person at an institution for hiring or admission purposes

Individualist (Chapter 8): a cultural orientation in which people are encouraged to think and act independently of others

Infomercial (Chapter 8): a mediated message in which information and advertising are blended almost imperceptibly

Informational interview (Chapter 5): an interview set up by a prospective candidate to find out about a possible work or educational opportunity

Information literacy (Chapter 1): the ability to identify, locate, evaluate, and effectively use the most useful information for an issue or problem at hand

Informative speaking (Chapter 9): speaking with the intention to inform, or share new information

Initiating (Chapter 6): the stage of relationship development in which parties begin interaction

Instrumental style of relational communication (Chapter 6): demonstrating connection in a relationship through concrete, goal-oriented actions

Integrating (Chapter 6): the stage of relationship development in which partnership is recognized by both partners, who then begin to coordinate their needs

Intensifying (Chapter 6): the stage of relationship development in which participants recognize a degree of connection and prioritize developing their relationship

Interdependence (Chapter 7): a relationship in which each member of a system is mutually dependent on the others

Internal noise (Chapter 1): disturbance or distractions in an individual's mind, body, or emotions that impede full ability to pay attention to communication

Internal summary (Chapter 9): offering a summary of part of one's speech for the purpose of helping an audience stay with the overall structure

Internet (Chapter 8): a mediated electronic communications network that connects computer networks and organizational computer facilities around the world

Intercultural capital (Chapter 8): markers of social capital whose acquisition and/or application transcends, or crosses, cultural boundaries

Interpersonal communication (Chapter 1): engagement between people, with a special focus on dyadic (two-person) relationships

Intersubjective meaning (Chapter 2): a meaning or perception shared by two or more people

Interview (Chapter 5): a conversation with a purpose

Intimacy (Chapter 6): a revealed state of emotional transparency ("into-me-see")

Intimate space (Chapter 4): the area within approximately 18 inches of one's body where intimate touch (holding, snuggling, nursing, etc.) takes place

Intrapersonal communication (Chapters 1, 2): communication within oneself

Jargon (Chapter 3): specialized language related to a certain occupation or field of study

Johari Window (Chapter 6): a schematic diagram developed by Joseph Luft and Harry Ingham that represents how information is known or hidden in evolving relationships

Kinesics (Chapter 4): the study of movement, including body language and facial expressions

Laissez-faire leader (Chapter 7): from the French term for "allow to do" or "let it be;" a leader that lets a group function with little or no direction

Learning group (Chapter 7): groups that come together for a fixed duration to learn a topic or skill

Legitimate power (Chapter 8): power stemming from one's role, title, or position, whether elected or appointed

Libertarian media system (Chapter 8): a media culture in which individual rights are considered most important, and it is assumed that truth is mostly likely to emerge from a free and open discussion

Linguistic relativity (Chapter 3): the idea that our thoughts and actions are influenced by the language we speak

Listening (Chapter 5): the process of receiving, constructing meaning from, and responding to messages from others

Logos (Chapters 1, 9): a communicator's use of argumentation to persuade (term from Greek philosopher Aristotle's writings on rhetoric)

Long-term memory (Chapter 5): the capacity of the human mind to store information and experiences, whether consciously or unconsciously, for an extended period, perhaps forever

Looking-glass self (Chapter 2): the vision of "me" that we think we see reflected in the gaze of others

Love/Intimacy touch (Chapter 4): a touch that conveys intimacy as part of a loving, personal, or familial relationship

Low contact culture (Chapter 4): cultures in which it is considered invasive or appropriate to share physical contact in public

Maintenance roles (Chapter 7): roles that support group communication by making the group climate feel positive for everyone involved

Mandate (Chapter 7): reason for existing; job to do

Manuscript (Chapter 9): a speech written out word-for-word

Marginalize (Chapter 3): confining certain categories of people to the lower or outer edges of society

Maslows's Hierarchy of Needs (Chapter 6): a theory of human development published by psychologist Abraham Maslow in 1943 that organizes developmental stages in a hierarchical manner, beginning with an individual's most basic physiological needs to their ultimate self-actualization

Mass communication (Chapter 8): transmitting messages rapidly and simultaneously to large numbers of people

Medium (Chapters 1, 8): a means of conveying something (plural = "media")

Mass media: Chapter 8 (91): media such as newspapers, television, radio, magazines, and films, that are intended for consumption by a broad audience

Me (Chapter 2): the passive self that serves as object, as opposed to the "I," the volitional self that acts as subject

Media amplification (Chapter 8): the tendency by media industries to focus on deviant behavior or happenings to the exclusion of normal occurrences

Media ecology (Chapter 1): the interdisciplinary field of media theory that investigates the nature of media themselves as complex dynamic systems influencing human thought and society

Media literacy (Chapter 8): the skill of knowing how to analyze the source of information and to competently utilize, evaluate, and produce messages in our mediated world

Mediated communication (Chapters 1, 8): transferring messages via electronic device instead of face-to-face

Mediation (Chapter 7): means for resolving conflict in an open, productive manner, considering the needs of all sides

Metacognitive awareness (Chapter 5): a person's view of him- or herself as a thinker and/or learner

Metaphors (Chapter 3): the linguistic device of likening one thing to another through actual description, e.g., "he is a rock."

Microcosm (Chapter 6): a world in miniature, with aspects that represent the whole

Model (Chapter 1): a symbolic representation of an entity or system that invites analysis or comparison

Motivated listening (Chapter 5): listening actively in an interested, focused way

Multitasking (Chapter 5): paying attention to multiple things at once; research has shown this is accomplished by circuit-switching rather than being actually simultaneous

Mutuality of concern (Chapter 7): the degree to which members of a group share the same level of commitment to the group experience

Neuro-Linguistic Programming (NLP) (Chapter 2): a psycho-communicative framework that explores the relationships between how we think (neuro), how we communicate (linguistic), and our patterns of behavior and emotion (programmes)

Noise (Chapters 1, 8): anything that stands in the way of full, effective sharing of meaning

Noise-Induced Hearing Loss (NIHL) (Chapter 5): hearing loss that takes place due to exposure to loud sounds

Nonverbal communication (Chapters 4, 9): communication other than written or spoken language that shares meaning

Normative meaning (Chapter 1): a standard meaning that many people generally agree upon

Norming phase of group development (Chapter 7): the stage of group development in which norms, roles, and guidelines for acceptable and unacceptable behavior are established

Norms (Chapter 7): recurring patterns of behavior or thinking that come to be accepted in a group as the "normal" or usual way of doing things

Objective meaning (Chapter 2): knowing something by using an external, agreed-upon way of perceiving or measuring it

Olfactics (Chapter 4): the study of the role of scent and smell in communication

Onomatopoeia (Chapter 3): the linguistic device of using a word that sounds like what it means (as in "boom," "squish," or "buzz.")

Open Questions (Chapter 5): questions that give respondents room to answer in many different ways

Oxymoron (Chapter 3): a particularly compressed paradox that juxtaposes seemingly opposite things, as in "definite maybe."

Paradigm shift (Chapter 8): experiencing a fundamental shift in our understanding of how the world works

Paradigm (Chapter 8): our understanding of how the world works

Paradox (Chapter 3): a statement or proposition that seems self-contradictory or absurd but in reality expresses a possible truth

Paralanguage (Chapter 4): using vocal characteristics to add emphasis or meaning to language

Paraphrase (Chapter 9): to express in one's own words

Paternalistic culture (Chapter 8): from the Latin "pater" (father); a culture in which it is expected for leaders to act in a parental style, both providing for and also controlling or intruding on the affairs of those under them

Pathos (Chapters 1, 9): a communicator's ability to use emotion to persuade (term from Greek philosopher Aristotle's writings on rhetoric)

Perception (Chapter 2): the ability to see, hear, or become aware of something through the senses

Perceptual filters (Chapter 2): ways we look at things based on expectations, assumptions, and experiences

we've learned through life, which cause us not to take in certain information from our environment that may be challenging to our existing understandings

Perceptual role (Chapter 2): ways of seeing something or someone based on the role we hold with them (e.g., a parent and a spouse may see us in very different ways)

Performing phase of group development (Chapter 7): the stage of group development in which a group is focused on actively accomplishing the goal for which it was convened

Personae (Chapter 2): outward appearances and behaviors that we show the world around us in various roles

Personal space (Chapter 4): the area between 18 inches and four feet (approximately an arm's length) around a person

Personification (Chapter 3): the linguistic device of applying human attributes or thoughts to animals, plants, or inanimate objects

Persuasive speaking (Chapter 9): speaking with the intent to persuade others of our point of view

Plagiarism (Chapter 9): using any information or ideas that are not our own

Politically Correct (PC) (Chapter 3): consciously avoiding forms of expression or action that exclude, marginalize, or insult certain groups of people

Power distance (Chapter 8): cultural orientation that addresses the most "natural" ways of holding and exercising power

Power (Chapter 8): the ability to enact one's will and get things done

Precision (Chapter 3): being specific, exact, and accurate

Primary group (Chapter 7): a grouping that satisfies one's basic human needs, such as a family or tribe

Primary question (Chapter 5): a question opening a new subject

Prime (Chapters 2, 3): to prepare the mind to see or interpret information in a particular way

Private dimension (Chapter 6): the quality of a relationship that is experienced privately by the participants

Problem-solving group (Chapter 7): groups, either temporary or longstanding, that are brought together to solve a problem through coordinating action and pooling resources toward a desired goal

Process leadership (Chapter 7): a group role that addresses the group's well-being and works to make the group process comfortable so that members can contribute freely and fully

Projecting (Chapter 6): ascribing one's own thoughts, attitudes, or traits to others

Proxemics (Chapter 4): the study of how we use space to communicate, both in terms of personal proximity, as well as through architectural and interior space design

Public communication (Chapter 1): transferring information to large numbers of people through speech-making or presentation through public media

Public dimension (Chapter 6): the image of a partnership that is presented publicly

Public group (Chapter 7): a group that is convened to interact for the benefit of an audience

Public space (Chapter 4): the area in which public communication takes place, generally more than 12 feet away from a person

Public voice (Chapter 4): the stronger voice used to project speech to a number of people, or in a large space

Pygmalion Effect (Chapter 2): a self-fulfilling prophecy in which expectations create our actual lived reality; based on the Greek myth of Pygmalion, a sculptor that fell in love with a sculpture he had created

Racism (Chapter 3): discriminatory language or behavior related to race or ethnicity

Receptive language (Chapter 5): using words or sounds to show that a message has been received

Red-flag words (Chapters 5, 6): words that induce a negative reaction, such as anger or fear

Reductive-expansive listening position (Chapter 5): the spectrum between listening reductively, delving into details, or expansively, widening one's view to the entire context

Referent power (Chapter 8): power that stems from personal likeability or charisma

Reflected appraisals (Chapter 2): comments made by other people about our worth

Reflexive (Chapter 8): paying attention to your own reactions to things

Regulators (Chapter 8): government institutions charged with overseeing media content

Relational dialectics (Chapter 6): contradictory feelings or needs that co-exist together in a relationship, such as the need for both connection and independence

Relational energy (Chapter 6): various feelings that flow between people in a fluid, complex, and ever-changing way

Relationship dimension: Chapter 1 (7): how our messages, both verbal and nonverbal, communicate relational information (in contrast to the content dimension of the message)

Relationship (Chapter 6): a connection with meaning between two or more parties

Repetition (Chapter 3): the linguistic device of repeating words or phrases multiple times to add emphasis

Responsive self-concept (Chapter 2): how we think of ourselves in response to how we are received by others

Review (Chapter 9): going back over material in your speech to emphasize it and aid the audience's retention of points made

Reward power (Chapter 8): power through offering rewards or incentives to encourage desired behaviors

Rhetoric (Chapters 1, 9): the art of effective or persuasive speaking or writing

Salient (Chapter 2): that which is made noticeable or important to us

Sapir-Whorf Hypothesis (Chapter 3): the idea proposed by Edward Sapir and Benjamin Lee Whorf that the structure of a language affects the perceptions of reality of its speakers and thus influences their thought patterns and worldviews

Schema (Chapter 5): interrelated thoughts, experiences, or concepts that are linked in the mind and foster particular ways of thinking about things

Screening/telephone interview (Chapter 5): typically an initial contact made by telephone to identify candidates that can be ruled out of an interview process

Second/on-site interview (Chapter 5): an interview in which candidates who have already been screened are brought to a site for both sides to learn more about each other

Secondary questions (Chapter 5): follow-up questions to gain more information

Selective attention (Chapter 2): the perceptual filter that causes us to only pay attention to certain messages

Selective exposure (Chapter 2): the perceptual filter that causes us to only expose ourselves to certain messages

Selective perception (Chapter 2): the perceptual filter that causes us to perceive certain messages in certain ways

Selective retention (Chapter 2): the perceptual filter that causes us to only retain or remember certain messages

Self as Object (Chapter 2): the concept put forward by philosopher George Herbert Mead that humans are able to perceive themselves from an external lens as an object, a "me," in contrast to the "I" that is active and internal to oneself

Self-concept (Chapter 2): the mental image or perception that one has of oneself

Self-disclosure (Chapter 6): the act of sharing important personal information about one's inner world to others

Self-fulfilling prophecy (Chapter 2): the phenomenon whereby our expectations create our reality

Semantic noise (Chapter 1): an impediment to understanding that is built into the language of the message itself

Semantic reactions (Chapter 5): strong emotional responses to words, either positive or negative

Sender-receiver (Chapter 1): all communicators, as we are constantly sending and receiving messages simultaneously in all we do

Service group (Chapter 7): a group of people who come together, usually as volunteers, to contribute a service to the world

Sexism (Chapter 3): discriminatory language or behavior related to biological sex

Sexual arousal (Chapter 4): intimate touch intended for sexual stimulation

Shared leadership (Chapter 7): the model of leadership in which all members of a group hold a degree of accountability for the outcome of the group's work

Shared meaning (Chapter 1): when two or more parties agree on what something "means"

Short-term memory (Chapter 5): the capacity for holding a small amount of information in the mind in an active, readily available state for a short period of time

Signpost (Chapter 9): a stated marker in a speech indicating that one is moving from one point to the next or providing information as to where the structure of the speech is going

Simile (Chapter 3): the linguistic device of likening one thing to another as a comparison, e.g., "She moves like a gazelle."

Situational leadership (Chapter 7): the leadership model that shows how different types of leadership (delegating, participating, telling, or selling) can all be appropriate for various situations

Small group communication (Chapters 1, 7): organized communication between 3 to 13 (or so) people

Small group/committee interview (Chapter 5): an interview held by a team or committee representing the institution

Social capital (Chapters 1, 8): the social currency held by people that enables desired outcomes

Social comparisons (Chapter 2): how we see ourselves in comparison with others, particularly in terms of socially desirable attributes

Social construction (Chapter 1): the process by which people determine through social interaction what things "mean"

Social Exchange Theory (Chapter 6): a theory put forward in the 1960s by sociologist George Homans that people choose to make, maintain, or end relationships based on the relative "costs" and "rewards" offered within the relationship

Social group (Chapter 7): a group that comes together for the sake of socializing

Social loafing: Chapter 7 (76): the phenomenon by which people tend to decrease their individual effort when working in groups as compared to working alone

Social organizing principles (Chapter 3): rules, spoken or unspoken, that we use to determine which characteristics are relevant in fitting people into groupings

Social Penetration Theory (Chapter 6): a theory of human interaction proposed by Irwin Altman and Dalmas Taylor in 1973 that views human's self-concept comprised of layers, through which self-disclosure allows deeper engagement

Social responsibility media paradigm (Chapter 8): a media culture best typified by public broadcasting, which views media as a public service, and is therefore paid for by some combination of Public (tax) money and donations from supporters

Social space (Chapter 4): the area approximately 4-12 feet around a person, in which social interaction with acquaintances generally takes place

Social/Polite Touch (Chapter 4): brief exchanges of physical contact that convey affiliation, such as a handshake

Socialization (Chapters 2, 8): the process by which people become trained to think and behave "appropriately" within their social environment

Specificity (Chapter 3): the quality of being concrete and specific in describing things

Speech rate (Chapter 4): how fast or slow a message is uttered

Speed bias (Chapter 8): the tendency of the media to reduce phenomena into short bites and to prioritize speed over depth

Spiral of Silence (Chapter 1): the communication theory proposed by German political scientist Elizabeth Noelle-Neumann that describes the process by which one opinion becomes dominant as those who perceive their opinion to be in the minority do not speak up because society threatens individuals with fear of isolation

Spotlighting (Chapter 3): calling attention to a particular attribute of someone in a way that makes it seem relevant, although it may not be

Stagnating (Chapter 6): the stage of relationship dissolution in which there is no new energy in the relationship and it becomes stale

Stigmatize (Chapter 3): making something seem bad or disgraceful

Storming phase of group development (Chapter 7): the stage of group development in which conflict may arise as members try to establish where they fit in (or not), discover the roles they play, and argue their positions

Strategic flexibility (Chapters 1, 3): possessing a broad repertoire of skills from which to draw, and to know which skill is most suitable for a situation

Strategic silence (Chapter 4): deliberate pauses that enhance the impact of an uttered message

Stress interview (Chapter 5): an interview in which a candidate is deliberately subjected to stressors in order to demonstrate their ability to cope effectively with stress

Study group (Chapter 7): a group formed among students to learn course material, work on projects, or prepare for exams

Subjective meaning (Chapter 2): knowing something internally through one's own perception or lived experience

Summary (Chapter 9): a concise statement reviewing main points covered

Supportive behavior (Chapter 7): engaging in behaviors that communicate support to others, such as active listening and expressing empathy for feelings

Symbolic interaction (Chapter 1): the notion put forward by sociologist Herbert Blumer, a student of George Herbert Mead, that people act toward things based on the meaning those things have for them, and these meanings are derived from social interaction and modified through interpretation

Symbol (Chapter 1): a thing, such as an object, a word, a color, a behavior, etc., that represents or stands for something else

Synchronous communication (Chapter 1): messages received at the same time they are created (such as talking on the telephone)

Target audience (Chapter 3): the people with whom you seek to communicate

Task group (Chapter 7): a group convened to complete a task, usually of finite duration

Task leadership (Chapter 7): taking leadership over an area of completing a group task

Task roles (Chapter 7): a group role that directly contributes to completion of the group's main task or goal

Task/testing interview (Chapter 5): an interview in which candidates must demonstrate particular knowledge or skills relevant to a particular role

Team (Chapter 7): a small number of people with complementary skills who are committed to a common purpose for which they hold themselves mutually accountable

Terminating (Chapter 6): the stage of relationship dissolution in which a partnership is publicly severed

"The map is not the territory" (Chapter 2): the adage put forward by philosopher Alford Korzybski suggesting that there is a fundamental separation between perception and reality; our mental representations of the world are completely inadequate to represent the fullness of reality itself

Therapy/help group (Chapter 7): a group in which individuals meet to share their challenges and receive mutual support or therapy

Thesaurus (Chapter 5): a book that lists words in groups of synonyms (words that mean the same thing) and related concepts

Thesis statement (Chapter 9): a one-sentence statement of the main message you want your audience to receive from your speech or writing

Thomas-Kilmann Conflict Resolution Model (Chapter 8): the model proposed by Kenneth Thomas and Ralph Kilmann in 1974 demonstrating five different conflict resolution styles that vary based on differing levels of assertiveness (for one's own needs) and cooperativeness (with the needs of another)

Tinnitus (Chapter 5): constant ringing of the ears caused by exposure to loud sounds

Topic (Chapter 9): a matter dealt with in a text, discourse, or conversation; a subject

Traditional leadership (Chapter 7): a style of leadership that typically involves one central individual, who holds the main responsibility for the group's functioning

Transactional Model of Communication (Chapter 1): the modern model of communication that assumes people are connected through communication by engaging in transactions, recognizing that each of us is a sender-receiver, not merely a sender or a receiver, and that communication affects all parties involved, so communication is fluid/ simultaneous

Trigger (Chapter 6): a past emotional wound that causes a disproportionate negative reaction when similar experiences are encountered

Understatement (Chapter 3): the linguistic device of deliberately downplaying something for humorous or dramatic effect

Verbal interjections (Chapter 4): words used to create interest or impact, such as "wow" or "boom"

Verbally document (Chapter 9): to orally disclose the source of one's information related within the context of a speech, presentation, or conversation

Virtual group (Chapter 7): a group that interacts through mediated communication to work, play, or socialize together from different locations

Visualization/mental rehearsal (Chapter 9): imagining one's performance mentally before carrying it out physically

Vocal expression (Chapter 4): how words are emphasized to give emotional impact in oral speech

Vocal fillers (Chapter 4): vocalized sounds such as "um" and "ah" that fill gaps in speech

Vocalics (Chapter 4): the many ways we use our voice to convey meaning

Volume (Chapter 4): the loudness or softness of a person's voice

Win-Win (Chapter 8): a paradigm for living in which all participants' needs are valued and strategies are developed to allow everyone to get what they want

Withhold (Chapter 6): information relevant to a relationship that is held back and not shared

Word choice (Chapter 3): strategic selection of words to accomplish a purpose

Word (Chapter 3): a sound or a combination of sounds, or its representation in writing or printing, that symbolizes and communicates a meaning

Work group (Chapter 7): a group convened within an organizational context, typically in an enduring way, to coordinate efforts around some aspect of the organization's work

Working memory (Chapter 5): the system that actively holds multiple pieces of transitory information in the mind, where they can be manipulated

World view (Chapter 2): the mental "lens" through which we view the world

Zero-sum Game (Chapter 8): a paradigm for living in which beings are considered to be inherently in competition, thus success for one must come at cost to another

Author Biographies

John Barrett has been teaching at Curry College since 1997. In addition to teaching courses in writing, literature, and in the theatre concentration, he serves as the technical director for all Curry Theatre productions. Professor Barrett is also co-founder of the Communication Scholars Program at Curry. He holds a B.A. from Boston College, and an M.A. from The Catholic University of America.

Brecken Chinn teaches communication and writes extensively on the topic for professional publications. A multiple award winner for Excellence in Programming from the Voice of America, she was also named an Exceptional Women award winner by Boston's radio broadcasting community. Her interests include women's and gender studies and intercultural communication. She holds a Ph.D. in international communication from the University of Maryland, and a master's degree in human development and psychology from the Harvard Graduate School of Education.

Dorria L. DiManno has taught communication for more than 20 years, following a career in broadcast television and independent media production. She is professor of communication at Curry College, where she also heads the film studies concentration. Her special interests include media literacy and the roles of women in the media. She holds an M.S. in mass communication/public relations from Boston University, and an Ed.D. from Johnson & Wales University.

Marcy Holbrook began her career in public relations and later founded and worked as artistic director for a children's theatre, before becoming executive director of Melrose Mass Television. She has taught communication for 15 years, and is a senior lecturer in the Curry College Communication Department. She is also certified in Mediation. She holds an M.A. and a B.A. from Murray State University.

Robert MacDougall, authorship team leader, has been teaching communication for 20 years. He is professor of communication at Curry College and coordinator of the video game studies concentration. He also served as coordinator of the Faculty Center for Professional Development & Curriculum Innovation. His teaching and research center on the cognitive, social, and epistemological roles played by communication media and technology today and throughout history. He holds an M.A. and a D.A. from the University at Albany.

Anjana Mudambi has been teaching communication for more than 10 years, including courses in intercultural communication, cultural studies, conflict management, and research methods. She is currently an assistant professor of communication at Curry College. Her interests revolve around social justice and include various aspects of identity, discourse, and immigration. She holds a Ph.D. from the University of New Mexico and an M.A. from Ohio University, both in intercultural communication.

Vicki H. Nelson is the founder and director of the Curry College Speaking Center and a senior lecturer in the Curry College Communication Department. She has been teaching communication for 35 years, including courses in career Speech, public speaking, and oral interpretation. She holds an M.A. from Emerson College and a B.A. from Juniata College.

Sharon Sinnott is an accomplished entrepreneur, administrator, educator, and speech consultant. She founded two successful businesses and continues her extensive college teaching and business consulting experience in the Boston area. She is also a former principal of a local elementary school. She has an M.A. from Emerson College in organizational communication and a B.A. from Bryant University in business education.

Ruth Spillberg is a long-time member of the International Listening Association, and has taught courses in effective listening and interviewing to over 1,500 college students of all ages and backgrounds. She approaches effective listening as a communication skill you can use throughout your lifetime. She holds a B.A. and an M.A. from Syracuse University, and an M.Ed. from Curry College.

9 781516 505043